Java 2 Enterprise Edition (J2EE) Web Component Developer Exam

Alain Trottier

Java 2 Enterprise Edition (J2EE) Web Component Developer Exam Cram2 (Exam 310-080)

International Standard Book Number: 0-7897-2862-1

Library of Congress Catalog Card Number: 2002113788

Printed in the United States of America

First Printing: December 2002

05 04 03 02 4 3 2 1

Trademarks

All terms mentioned in this book that are known to be trademarks or service marks have been appropriately capitalized. Que Certification cannot attest to the accuracy of this information. Use of a term in this book should not be regarded as affecting the validity of any trademark or service mark.

Warning and Disclaimer

Every effort has been made to make this book as complete and as accurate as possible, but no warranty or fitness is implied. The information provided is on an "as is" basis. The author and the publisher shall have neither liability nor responsibility to any person or entity with respect to any loss or damages arising from the information contained in this book or from the use of the CD or programs accompanying it.

Publisher
Paul Boger

Executive Editor
Jeff Riley

Development Editor
Susan Brown Zahn

Managing Editor
Thomas F. Hayes

Project Editor
Carol Bowers

Copy Editor
Krista Hansing

Indexer
Heather McNeill

Proofreader
Juli Cook

Technical Editor
Steve Heckler

Team Coordinator
Rosemary Lewis

Multimedia Developer
Michael Hunter

Page Layout
Michelle Mitchell

Que Certification • 201 West 103rd Street • Indianapolis, Indiana 46290

A Note from Series Editor Ed Tittel

You know better than to trust your certification preparation to just anybody. That's why you, and more than two million others, have purchased an Exam Cram book. As Series Editor for the new and improved Exam Cram2 series, I have worked with the staff at Que Certification to ensure you won't be disappointed. That's why we've taken the world's best-selling certification product—a finalist for "Best Study Guide" in a CertCities reader poll in 2002—and made it even better.

As a "Favorite Study Guide Author" finalist in a 2002 poll of CertCities readers, I know the value of good books. You'll be impressed with Que Certification's stringent review process, which ensures the books are high-quality, relevant, and technically accurate. Rest assured that at least a dozen industry experts—including the panel of certification experts at CramSession—have reviewed this material, helping us deliver an excellent solution to your exam preparation needs.

We've also added a preview edition of PrepLogic's powerful, full-featured test engine, which is trusted by certification students throughout the world.

As a 20-year-plus veteran of the computing industry and the original creator and editor of the Exam Cram series, I've brought my IT experience to bear on these books. During my tenure at Novell from 1989 to 1994, I worked with and around its excellent education and certification department. This experience helped push my writing and teaching activities heavily in the certification direction. Since then, I've worked on more than 70 certification-related books, and I write about certification topics for numerous Web sites and for *Certification* magazine.

In 1996, while studying for various MCP exams, I became frustrated with the huge, unwieldy study guides that were the only preparation tools available. As an experienced IT professional and former instructor, I wanted "nothing but the facts" necessary to prepare for the exams. From this impetus, Exam Cram emerged in 1997. It quickly became the best-selling computer book series since "*...For Dummies*," and the best-selling certification book series ever. By maintaining an intense focus on subject matter, tracking errata and updates quickly, and following the certification market closely, Exam Cram was able to establish the dominant position in cert prep books.

You will not be disappointed in your decision to purchase this book. If you are, please contact me at etittel@jump.net. All suggestions, ideas, input, or constructive criticism are welcome!

Ed Tittel

Contents at a Glance

Table of Contents

About the Author

Alain Trottier observes the .com warfare of Southern California as a technology management consultant (Strategic Business Resources) and an adjunct professor at Vanguard University. He has been in the tech sector for two decades. On the electronics side, he has worked with RF gear, nuclear power plants, and electromechanical devices. On the IT side, he has held roles as a technologist, a developer support specialist, a programmer, an architect, and a manager. Alain got a kick out of being in the U.S. Submarine Navy (nuclear power division), and he was impressed with his bosses at Chevron's world-class research center. He was astonished by the .com bubble while at Adforce and then Winfire, where he experienced a meteoric IPO and then a subsequent flameout. He has been through a get-it-right-at-all-cost experience in a Fortune 30 company, and he also has witnessed the other extreme, in which one bets it all on a get-it-out-there-at-no-cost venture.

Alain enjoys a difficult technological challenge and likes the people even better. He believes that his degrees in religion (Bachelor of Arts, Master of Arts with a specialization in the linguistics of ancient religious texts) is a terrific way to broaden one's abilities. He has certifications from both Microsoft and Sun, so his bias is simply what works best for a given situation. If you have a question, comment, or even a challenge, the author would be delighted to hear from you. Please contact him (think Chief Technology Ambassador) from the book's Web site, at `www.inforobo.com/scwcd/examcram`.

About the Technical Reviewer

Steve Heckler is a freelance programmer and IT trainer specializing in .NET, Java, ColdFusion, Flash ActionScript, and XML. Based in Atlanta, Georgia, he works with clients nationwide. In addition, he is the author of the *Sun Certification Instructor Resource Kit (310-025, 310-027): Java 2 Programmer and Developer Exams* and *Sun Certification Instructor Resource Kit (310-080): Java 2 Web Component Developer Exam.* He is currently writing an ASP.NET-related book for Addison-Wesley.

Before being self-employed, Steve served nearly seven years as vice president and president of a leading East Coast IT training firm. He holds bachelors and masters degrees from Stanford University.

Dedication

This book is dedicated to my wife, Patricia, the love of my life, and to my son, Devyn, who brings us tremendous joy and is already my hero.

Acknowledgments

I would like to thank Jeff Riley (the acquisitions editor) and Margot Malley (my agent), who made this book possible. Thank you Susan Brown Zahn (development editor) for your valuable guidance and encouragement. It was a terrific experience working with Que's team; their contributions added much to the book. I admit having fun talking about and even sparring over the details. Every book purchase is a nod to Que's preeminent team.

We Want to Hear from You!

As the reader of this book, *you* are our most important critic and commentator. We value your opinion and want to know what we're doing right, what we could do better, what areas you'd like to see us publish in, and any other words of wisdom you're willing to pass our way.

As an executive editor for Que Certification, I welcome your comments. You can email or write me directly to let me know what you did or didn't like about this book—as well as what we can do to make our books better.

Please note that I cannot help you with technical problems related to the *topic* of this book. We do have a User Services group, however, where I will forward specific technical questions related to the book.

When you write, please be sure to include this book's title and author as well as your name, email address, and phone number. I will carefully review your comments and share them with the author and editors who worked on the book.

Email: `feedback@quepublishing.com`

Mail: Jeff Riley
Executive Editor
Que Certification
201 West 103rd Street
Indianapolis, IN 46290 USA

For more information about this book or another Que title, visit our Web site at `www.quepublishing.com`. Type the ISBN (excluding hyphens) or the title of a book in the Search field to find the page you're looking for.

Introduction

Welcome to the Sun Certification Exam Cram2! This book aims to help you get ready to take—and pass—the Sun Certified Web Component Developer for J2EE Platform (310-080) exam. This introduction explains Sun's certification programs in general and talks about how the Exam Cram2 series can help you prepare for Sun's certification exams.

Exam Cram2 books help you understand and appreciate the subjects and materials you need to know to pass Sun certification exams. Each Exam Cram2 book is strictly focused on exam preparation and review. Exam Cram2 books are not intended to teach you everything you need to know about a technology. Instead, they cover the topics that you are likely to encounter on the certification exam. The books are built around the vendor's objectives and the author's experience with the exams.

Despite the intense focus on the exam that Exam Cram2 offers, I recommend that you begin your exam preparation by taking the self-assessment included in this book. This tool will help you evaluate your own knowledge and experience base in terms of the requirements for a Sun Certified Web Component Developer for J2EE Platform.

I strongly encourage you to install and configure the software and tools that you'll be tested on. Nothing beats hands-on experience and familiarity with the technology when it comes to answering the questions you're likely to encounter on a certification exam. Book learning is essential and unavoidable, but hands-on experience will reinforce that knowledge and allow it to really sink in.

The Sun Java Technology Professional Program

How do you compress XML? How do you facilitate distance learning, that method by which the student is not physically present in the same location as the instructor? How do you expose some accounting data to the internal auditors, but provide access to other data from the same repository only to the board of directors and still other data to the public? How do you build an exchange in which your client can interface with its partner's back end without a lot of manual intervention? In just a few years, Java has become one of the most effective technologies used to address these and even more difficult challenges. Java's power, simplicity, and rich APIs enable you to meet the challenges of back-end systems. Java's popularity has been steadily increasing, so it no longer fights for legitimacy. Now the issues are those faced only by mature technologies, such as speed, build-or-buy third-party components, and versioning.

One of the results of Java's popularity is the high demand for skilled Java programmers and developers. However, because of Java's brief existence, experienced Java programmers are hard to find. Few in the field have more than five years of experience in developing Java applications. This is a problem for both employers and programmers. Employers cannot rely on the traditional number of years of experience in selecting senior-level Java programmers and software engineers. Star Java programmers have a hard time differentiating themselves from entry-level Java programmers.

The Java certification exams provide a solution for both employers and programmers. Employers can identify skilled Java programmers by their certification level. Programmers and software engineers can attest to their knowledge of Java by citing their certification credentials.

The Java certification program consists of four certification exams:

- **Programmer exam**—The Programmer exam tests the candidate's knowledge of the Java language and basic API packages. The exam consists of 59 multiple-choice questions.

- **Developer exam**—The Developer exam tests the candidate's ability to complete an extended programming assignment and answer questions concerning the issues and trade-offs involved in the assignment's completion. Programmer certification is a prerequisite to Developer certification.

- **Web Component Developer exam**—The Web Component Developer exam tests the candidate's knowledge of developing Java Web applications using Java servlets and Java Server Pages (JSP). The exam consists of 60 multiple-choice questions. Programmer certification is a prerequisite to Web Component Developer certification. This book prepares you for this exam.

- **Architect exam**—The Architect exam tests a candidate's familiarity with the technologies used to build Java-based enterprise applications and the candidate's ability to resolve issues in Java application design. This exam focuses on much higher-level software- and system-engineering skills than the other exams. It consists of a 48-question multiple-choice exam, an architecture and design project, and a 4-question essay exam.

I've spent a good amount of time with Microsoft products and languages (I'm also a Microsoft Certified Solution Developer). I was intrigued to see how the Redmond giant would respond to Sun's foray into programming languages. I think Gates's team was taken by surprise at how quickly Sun convinced IT masses to use Java.

Typical of Microsoft, the marketing team downplayed the significance of Java but internally jumped on the Java bandwagon. In fact, it was Microsoft that produced the best Integrated Development Environment (Visual J++). I think Microsoft did an excellent job with this product overall. It is the top Java tool in terms of ease of use and effectiveness of the GUI. However, the marketing team in Washington got carried away and made this tool a little too Windows friendly. In fact, it was easy to write Java programs with Visual J++ that worked only on Windows. Of course, this infuriated Scott McNealy. The situation was the classic case of the leader making better use of an invention but then trying to bully the inventor out of business.

I still am a Microsoft fan. The company has a lot of smart people working there who are doing their best. Alas, I don't use Visual J++ because it doesn't make a clear distinction about what is Windows only and what is portable as defined by Sun. If given a chance, I would yell at the people who advised Mr. Gates to do it that way. I would then turn around and ask him to add one little button to Visual J++ that would let me toggle between Windows only (I agree that this need is important) and Sun-compliant portable (a must-have) modes. Microsoft is important to the future of Java, so let's hope its people have the courage to listen to better advice than they have been getting.

I am still impressed with Java's hybrid nature (best parts of several languages) and how the designers rethought the principles at the heart of designing a language. Although many areas will continue to be implemented better (faster, more efficient, and so on), I like the structure of Java. It feels good to use, and Sun is open about the broken parts.

Java is moved along by the Java Community Process, which holds the responsibility for the development of Java technology. It is an open, inclusive organization of active member and nonmember public input. If you point your browser to `www.jcp.org/introduction/overview/index.en.jsp`, you can pitch in or just watch. Warts and wins are published for all the world to see. This is a gutsy move by Mr. McNealy. Few companies are confident and shrewd enough to hang their favorite underwear out to dry in public like that. This is paying off handsomely where Java has been marketing gold; Sun deserves its just reward. Now a word to Mr. McNealy: Please, I realize Bill has more toys, but could you put that aside for a moment and invite his top guns over for a bash on your yacht, where they might slip out a few tricks about their awesome development tools (such as the Java compiler) and Web services expertise?

The portability of Java should be credited to world-class design and effective marketing. The computer language industry is fractured, so it is impressive that Sun could convince so many to build Java Virtual Machines for all the operating systems. Without this cooperation, Java would be dead.

Having taken many Microsoft exams, I looked forward to experiencing Sun's concept of an academic grilling. The quality of Sun's exams is comparable to that of MS exams. However, the technology being tested is cleanly and openly defined, so I think that Sun's certifications represent a closer correspondence to the skills being tested. To that end, I hope deeply that this book will help you pass the Sun Certification Web Component Developer (SCWCD) exam.

Attaining Java certification is not easy. As you saw with the basic certification exam, the Programmer exam, it is difficult. Besides, I wouldn't want to bother with something if it was pedestrian and wasn't worth much. The SCWCD exam covers every major aspect of the Java language associated with Web site building. Fortunately, trivial things such as retrieving the servlet-specification version are ignored in this book because they are not on the exam. Being told what to skip helps bring the significant matters into sharper focus.

The most important content to study is that of the core classes and interfaces of the servlet API packages. To pass this exam, you must acquire both breadth and depth of experience with servlets and JSP.

About This Book

Each topical Exam Cram chapter follows a regular structure, along with graphical cues about important or useful information. Here's the structure of a typical chapter:

- **Opening hotlists**—Each chapter begins with a list of the terms, tools, and techniques that you must learn and understand before you can be completely comfortable with that chapter's subject matter. We follow the hotlists with one or two introductory paragraphs to set the stage for the rest of the chapter.

- **Topical coverage**—After the opening hotlists, each chapter covers a series of at least four topics related to the chapter's title. Throughout these sections we highlight topics or concepts likely to appear on a test using a special Exam Alert layout, such as this:

This is what an Exam Alert looks like. Normally an Exam Alert stresses concepts, terms, software, or activities that are likely to relate to one or more certification test questions. For that reason, any information offset in an Exam Alert is worthy of considerable attention on your part. Indeed, most of the information that appears on the Cram Sheet appears as Exam Alerts within the text.

Pay close attention to material flagged as an Exam Alert; although all the information in this book pertains to what you need to know to pass the exam, I highlight certain items that are really important. You'll find what appears in the rest of the chapter to be worth knowing as well. Because this book's material is very condensed, I recommend that you use this book along with other resources to achieve the maximum benefits.

In addition to the Exam Alerts, I have provided tips that will help build a better foundation for J2EE knowledge. Although the information might not be on the exam, it is certainly related and will help you become a better developer.

This is how tips are formatted. Keep your eyes open for these, and you'll become a J2EE Web Component Developer guru in no time!

- **Practice questions**—Although we talk about test questions and topics throughout the chapter, this section presents a series of test questions and explanations of both correct and incorrect answers. We also try to point out especially tricky questions.
- **Details and resources**—Every chapter ends with a section titled "Need to Know More?", which provides direct pointers to Sun and third-party resources offering more details on the chapter's subject.

Chapter 12, "Sample Test," includes a sample written test. This provides a good review of the written material presented throughout the book and will ensure that you're ready for the exam.

Chapter 13, "Answer Key," is an answer key for the sample test. Each answer option is discussed. The discussion provides insight into why the correct answer is the best choice and why the other answers are incorrect.

I've included several appendixes that look "under the hood" a bit. These appendixes are resources on the Java servlet, API, and JSP syntax. You'll also find a glossary that explains terms and an index that you can use to track down terms as they appear in the text.

Finally, the tear-out Cram Sheet in the front of this book represents a condensed and compiled collection of facts, figures, and tips that I think you should *memorize* before taking the exam. Look at the Cram Sheet one last time just before entering the testing center. When the exam begins, you can simply dump this information out of your head and onto the notepaper or whatever is provided to you by the testing center.

Getting Started

To use this book, you will need a computer and operating system that support the Java 2 Platform. Many operating systems, including Windows, Linux, and Solaris, support the Java 2 Platform. Ports of the Java 2 Platform to many other operating systems are in the works. The examples used in this book were developed under Tomcat running on Windows 2000. However, they will run under all servlet containers that are implemented according to specification on the Java 2 Platform.

How to Use This Book

Start with Chapter 1, "Servlet Methods and Life Cycle," and proceed through each chapter of the book in order, working through all review and exam questions. As noted previously, passing the Programmer exam is a prerequisite to taking the Developer exam, so that level of familiarity is assumed.

Given all the book's elements and its specialized focus, I've tried to create a tool that will help you prepare for—and pass—Sun's Web Component Developer for J2EE Platform exam. Please share your feedback with me through Que Publishing.

The Book's Web Site

To help you with your certification studies, a Java certification Web site has been put together to supplement the information presented in this book. The Web site provides a forum for feedback on the certification exams and contains any corrections for errors that are discovered after the book's printing. The URL for this Web site is `www.inforobo.com/scwcd/examcram`. If you have any questions, comments, or suggestions concerning the book, its Web site, or the certification exams, please direct them to `atrottier@hotmail.com`.

Que Publishing

The staff of Que Certification is committed to bringing you the very best in computer reference material. Each Que Certification book is the result of months of work by authors and staff who research and refine the information contained within its covers.

As part of this commitment to you, the reader, Que invites your input. Please let us know if you enjoy this book, if you have trouble with the information or examples presented, or if you have a suggestion for the next edition.

Please note, however, that Que staff cannot serve as a technical resource during your preparation for the Sun certification exams or for questions about software- or hardware-related problems. Please refer instead to the support options and information available at `www.sun.com`.

If you have a question or comment about any Que book, there are several ways to contact Que Publishing. We will respond to as many readers as we can. Your name, address, or phone number will never become part of a mailing list or be used for any purpose other than to help us continue to bring you the best books possible. You can write to us at the following address:

Que Certification
Attn: Jeff Riley
201 W. 103rd Street
Indianapolis, IN 46290

If you prefer, you can fax Que at 317-581-4666.

You also can send email to Que at the following Internet address:

`feedback@quepublishing.com`

Que is an imprint of Pearson Technology Group. To purchase a Que book, call 800-428-5331.

Self-Assessment

Sun's Java technology's primary claim is "Write once, run anywhere." Many people and companies agree. Because most Java programmers are self-taught, the skill levels out there vary wildly. It is not easy to figure out whom you would really want on your team to be responsible for a key piece of development. Although it is not a guarantee, a certification exam does two things. First, it weeds out the lightweights. Second, it encourages programmers to study the more useful aspects of the language. Some people publicly deride certifications of any kind—and Sun's in particular. However, if they had to choose between two people to join them on a project that is behind schedule, knowing little else about the individuals, they would choose the certified person.

The same issue faces hiring managers. They are under immense pressure. How can they adequately interview, test, and get to know someone well enough to invite him or her into a multiyear relationship? Regardless of how much chit-chatting they do with potential candidates, a certification substantiates the claims made throughout the resume. Like it or not, certifications are having a significant impact on the hiring and review cycles in companies, both large and small. I like them because they clarify one's position: "Yes, I know my stuff and, yes, I'm willing to follow process."

One of the biggest fears among hiring managers is that they hire a guru who turns out to be a cowboy coding things in a unique way or in a way that doesn't help the team. How could you know? The guy or gal might have been scintillating during the interviews and the experience.... Face it, the boss will need you to play the game according to the rules, especially on large and complex projects. A certification is a credible statement that you are willing to rigorously throw all that synaptic firepower at building great stuff, but within project boundaries. If this is your attitude, then I want to work with you. Let's share Java secrets and kick Internet butt together.

Java Web Applications in the Real World

Java has grown up quickly. Like a child actor who never gets a chance to be a kid, Java started experiencing big-people issues during youth. Allowing Java to play just wasn't in the plans. Now, in less than a decade, Java spans from back-end servers, to the traditional desktop, to diverse hand-held and embedded devices. What is impressive about this is that although we all know Sun is pushing hard, the market is pulling Java equally hard. Currently, the loudest vacuum noise can be heard coming from the Web services sector. Your timing is outstanding because this certification covers the most salient aspects of Java that Web services are begging for.

This exam includes what I call two of the three legs of J2EE. The three legs are JSP, servlets, and Enterprise JavaBeans. There is a definite jump in complexity when a project goes from standalone Java applications to JSP and servlets. There is an equal jump again when you start dealing with EJB. If you look at the job boards, the majority of the postings ask for Java, JSP, servlets, and JavaBeans. A minority of them also ask for Enterprise JavaBeans, but they pay more for this, so that will be the next step after you obtain your Web Component Developer certification.

The Ideal Web Component Developer Certification Candidate

Ask yourself the hard questions. Don't go through the motions of preparing for this exam unless you are committed. Most likely you are serious, so now you have to decide what is the best way to prepare for the exam. The following list outlines the tasks and topics you will be tested on. Use them to diagnose the level of familiarity you have with the topics covered by the Sun Certified Web Component Developer exam. Even if you score high, I recommend that you review all chapters of the book because they point out the actual material on the exam, the specifics that will be asked. At least answer the questions. Your weak areas will require carefully reading the appropriate chapters, practicing with code, and taking the chapter quizzes. The amount of work ahead of you depends on how much of the material you already know. With each item here, ask yourself, "Can I comfortably do this?" In the end, you will need to be able to do the following:

- Retrieve HTML form parameters from the request.
- Retrieve a servlet-initialization parameter.
- Retrieve HTTP request header information.
- Set an HTTP response header. Set the content type of the response.
- Acquire a text or binary stream for the response.
- Redirect an HTTP request to another URL.
- Identify triggers and benefits that cause a browser to use HTTP methods `GET`, `POST`, and `HEAD`.
- Access values and resources within request, session, and context scopes.
- Know the purpose and sequence of the servlet life-cycle methods init, service, and destroy.
- Use a RequestDispatcher to include or forward to a Web resource.
- Identify the structure of a Web application and Web archive file.
- Name the WebApp deployment descriptor.
- Name the directories where you place Web resources.
- Name and describe deployment descriptor elements.
- Configure the deployment descriptor to handle exceptions and errors.
- Configure Web applications for security.
- Configure servlets and listeners through the deployment descriptor.
- Retrieve servlet context-initialization parameters.
- Use a servlet context listener.
- Use a servlet context attribute listener.
- Use a session attribute listener.
- Distinguish the behavior of servlets in a distributable Web application.
- Identify correctly constructed code for handling business logic exceptions.
- Match that code with correct statements about the code's exception handling.
- Be able to return an HTTP error using the `sendError` response method.
- Return an HTTP error using the `setStatus` method.

- Identify the configuration that the deployment descriptor uses to handle each exception.
- Understand how to use a RequestDispatcher to forward the request to an error page.
- Specify error handling declaratively in the deployment descriptor.
- Identify the method used to write a message to the WebApp log.
- Be able to write a message and an exception to the WebApp log.
- Retrieve a session object across multiple requests to the same or different servlets within the same WebApp.
- Store objects into a session object.
- Retrieve objects from a session object.
- Respond to the event when a particular object is added to a session.
- Respond to the event when a session is created and destroyed.
- Expunge a session object.
- Know when a session object will be invalidated.
- Understand URL rewriting.
- Define authentication.
- Identify `BASIC`, `DIGEST`, `FORM`, and `CLIENT-CERT` authentication types.
- Define data integrity.
- Define auditing.
- Describe malicious code and Web site attacks.
- Identify the deployment descriptor element names (and their structure) that declare a security constraint, a Web resource, the login configuration, and a security role.
- Identify which attribute scopes are thread safe.
- Understand the differences between the multithreaded and single-threaded servlet models.
- Identify the interface used to declare that a servlet must use the single-thread model.
- Write and use JSP tags.
- Given a JSP tag type, use the equivalent XML-based tags.

- Use the `page` directive.
- Import a Java class into the JSP page.
- Use a session in a JSP page.
- Declare that a JSP page is or uses an error page.
- Understand the JSP page life cycle.
- Use JSP's implicit objects: `request`, `response`, `out`, `session`, `config`, `application`, `page`, `pageContext`, and `exception`.
- Write scriptlet code.
- Declare the use of a JavaBean component within the page.
- Specify, for `jsp:useBean` or `jsp:getProperty` tags, the name of an attribute.
- Specify, for a `jsp:useBean` tag, the class of the attribute.
- Specify, for a `jsp:useBean` tag, the scope of the attribute.
- Access or mutate a property from a declared JavaBean.
- Specify, for a `jsp:getProperty` tag, the property of the attribute.
- Specify, for a `jsp:setProperty` tag, the property of the attribute to mutate and the new value.
- Code JSP page attributes, including their scopes.
- Identify techniques that access a declared JavaBean component.
- Know the tag library descriptor elements for tag libraries.
- Be able to write a tag library descriptor in XML notation.
- Understand the tag life cycle.
- Identify triggers for event methods (`doStartTag`, `doAfterBody`, and `doEndTag`).
- Identify valid return values for the event methods.
- Understand how to use `BODY` or `PAGE` constants in event methods.
- In the custom tag handler, know how to access a given JSP page's implicit variable and the page's attributes.
- Identify methods that return an outer tag handler from within an inner tag handler.

- Given a scenario description with a list of issues, select the design pattern that would best solve those issues.
- Match a design pattern with its benefits.
- Know how to use these patterns: Value Objects, MVC, Data Access Object, and Business Delegate.

I Think I'm Ready, So What's Next?

If you can't do any of the previously listed tasks, stop. You'll need to do some fundamental studying before tackling this book and exam. You know Java and you know how to take a certification exam—after all, you can't take the Web Component Developer for J2EE Platform exam without first holding the Programmer for Java 2 Platform certification. So buckle down and work your way through all the chapters. If you can do all the tasks listed, just take the chapter quizzes, this book's practice exam, and free mock exams on the Internet. Then you should take the real exam. If you are between these extremes, take your time and thoroughly read the chapters that you need most.

Be careful about mock exams. You can retake them until you get 100% correct, but that is testing only your ability to recognize correct answers for questions you have already seen. If you don't really understand the material, your grade will plummet with new questions on the same topics. On the other hand, there are many ways to ask a question; the more of them you master, the fewer that will stump you on the exam.

Servlet Methods and Life Cycle

Terms you'll need to understand:

- ✔ Redirection
- ✔ Servlet life cycle
- ✔ Servlet forwarding and includes
- ✔ Servlet attribute
- ✔ Context parameters
- ✔ Application session
- ✔ **GET**, **POST**, **PUT**
- ✔ Session
- ✔ Scope
- ✔ Listeners

Techniques you'll need to master:

- ✔ Retrieve HTML form parameters from the request.
- ✔ Retrieve a servlet initialization parameter.
- ✔ Retrieve HTTP request header information.
- ✔ Set an HTTP response header. Set the content type of the response.
- ✔ Acquire a text or binary stream for the response.
- ✔ Redirect an HTTP request to another URL.
- ✔ Identify triggers and benefits that cause a browser to use HTTP methods **GET**, **POST**, and **HEAD**.

- ✔ Access values and resources within request, session, and context scopes.
- ✔ Know the purpose and sequence of the servlet life cycle methods **init**, **service**, and **destroy**.
- ✔ Use a RequestDispatcher to include or forward to a Web resource.

JSP and Servlet Overview

Servlets are Java's answer to CGI, server-side Web request processors. JSP pages are easy to code so that nonprogrammers can help. The idea behind having both is to provide a way for nonprogrammers (think lower cost) to contribute functionality through JSP. Most of the code in a Web application will go into servlets. JSP enables the separation of presentation and business layers; this is its key architectural benefit.

Two key objects in the servlet process are the request and response objects. The request object is a wrapper for the information sent by the client. The container parses the request and puts the information in an `HttpServletRequest` object that is passed to the servlet. Going the other way, the container wraps the response parameters with the `HttpServletResponse` object, which is passed back to the container.

The container manages the servlet life cycle. It does so by initializing a servlet with a call to the `init` method, a call to the `service` method upon every request, and a call to a servlet's `destroy` method just before removing it from memory. The container also enables you to monitor context and session events with listeners that are event-driven triggers. When an attribute changes, special targeted methods are called, in a typical event programming model.

Servlets are invoked within a container, or a special-purpose Java environment for handling HTTP requests. As with all areas of Java, servlet objects also have scope. When something has context scope, it is application-wide and all users can share data. Session scope means that for a given user, data is shared across page views. Each user has his or her own session scope. Request scope restricts data to only that page. You write a servlet by subclassing `HttpServlet`, an abstract class. You subclass it to create a servlet that overrides at least one of the following methods: `doGet`, `doPost`, or `doPut`. Rarely will you need to override the class's `service` method because it already forwards HTTP requests to the appropriate servlet method.

The client sends HTTP methods `GET`, `POST`, and `PUT` to Web servers. Depending on the request type, the client sends a query string or the form data are collected into the request parameter set, with the query string first. The `GET` request has a limit on the amount of information it can send, but a `POST` can send an unlimited amount of information with its request. A `PUT` is for uploading a file. These three servlet methods are what finally do something with a request: `doGet` handles `GET`, `doPost` handles `POST`, and `doPut` handles `PUT`.

In a typical JSP/servlet request, the sequence of events starts with a browser sending a request to a Web server. The server hands the request to a servlet container. The container loads the servlet class (if it isn't already loaded), instantiates the servlet with request and response objects, calls the servlet's `init` method, then calls its `service` method, and lastly calls the `destroy` method. The `service` method, in turn, calls `doGet`, or one of the `doXXX` methods. Notice that the `destroy` method is called later, when the application or container is shut down.

Figure 1.1 illustrates a high-level diagram of how a container processes an HTTP request, including the JSP and servlet relationship.

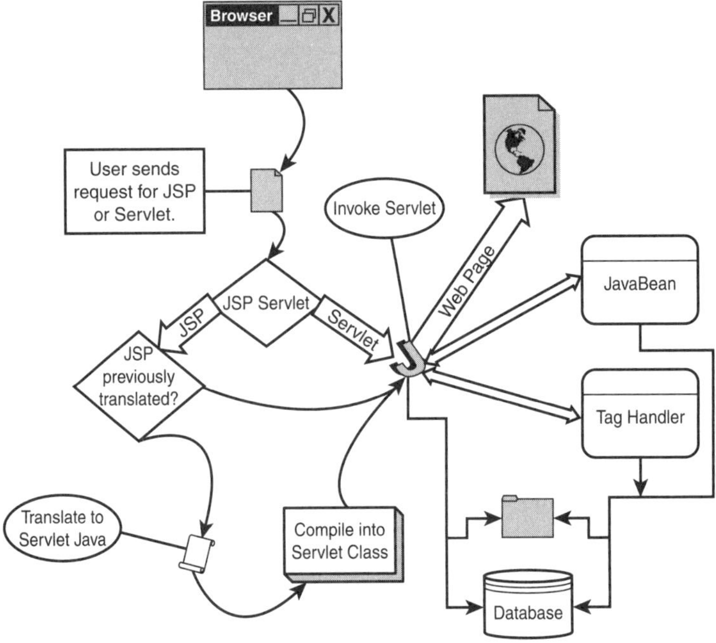

Figure 1.1 How a container handles an HTTP request.

Listing 1.1 is a complete, but admittedly simple, servlet example.

Listing 1.1 A Small Servlet

```
import java.io.*;
import javax.servlet.*;
import javax.servlet.http.*;

public class SimpleServletExample extends HttpServlet
{
    // doGet() - SCWCD Exam Objective 1.1
```

(continued)

Listing 1.1 A Small Servlet *(continued)*

```
    public void doGet(HttpServletRequest request,
                      HttpServletResponse response)
        throws IOException, ServletException
    {
        // set the MIME type
        response.setContentType("text/html");

        // use this to print to browser
        PrintWriter out = response.getWriter();

        out.println("<html>");
        out.println("<head>");
        out.println("<title> A simple servlet. </title>");
        out.println("</head>");
        out.println("<body>");
        out.println("<h1>ExamCram Examplle</h1>");
        out.println("<p>A simple servlet.</p>");
        out.println("</body>");
        out.println("</html>");
    }
}
```

When you write a servlet, you must compile it and then place it in the appropriate directory. The container manages the servlet life cycle. When the servlet container starts, it preloads your servlet in memory if that option is specified in the web.xml configuration file. If your servlet is not already loaded (not listed in the web.xml configuration file), its instance is created as soon as a request for it is received by the servlet container.

Sometimes a servlet is loaded when the container starts (the Web deployment descriptor lists this servlet), and sometimes it is upon the first request for a servlet. Either way, the container loads the class and instantiates an instance of it. When an HTTP request for it arrives, the container calls your servlet's `init` method, if there is one. This method is invoked only once in the servlet's lifetime. You should place one-off functionality in this method (such as establishing a database connection or initializing session-wide variables). Going forward, the container calls the `service` method each time a request is received for your servlet. You write a servlet by extending the `HttpServlet` class. The `service` method (already part of `HttpServlet`) then passes the request to the appropriate method, such as the `doGet` method if it is a `GET` request, or the `doPost` method if it is a `POST` request. The `doXXX` methods are the ones you need to override and the ones on which you will spend most of your effort. The servlet processes the request (code you write in `doGet` and `doPost` does the actual work on the request), returning a response to the container. The container sends the text of the response back to the browser.

Web Applications

A Web application is a collection of servlets, JSP pages, HTML documents, and other Web resources (such as image files, compressed archives, and other data). This collection might be packaged into an archive or exist as separate files in an open directory structure. Because you have many servlet classes, JSP pages, HTML pages, and other supporting libraries and files for a given Web application, there are many complicated dependencies. Using standard JAR tools, you can package the collection into a Web application archive, a single file with the .war extension that contains all the components of a Web application.

Normally, Web applications run on only one Java Virtual Machine (JVM) at any one time. When we talk about deploying a Web application, we mean that the collection of files comprising a Web application is placed into a Web server's runtime engine. In some cases, you'll want to deploy your Web application in a Web farm for the jump in speed you get when a Web application runs on several VMs simultaneously. This is called a distributable Web application, and it involves a file called the deployment descriptor that configures the container (see Chapter 2, "Deploying Web Applications," for more about web.xml).

A distributable Web application is written so that it can be deployed in a Web container and distributed across multiple Java virtual machines running on the same host or different hosts. The two keys to making this possible are how you thread the servlets and what you tell the deployment descriptor. With the right combination of these, your Web application will run on several VMs simultaneously. The servlet declaration, which is part of the deployment descriptor, controls how the servlet container provides instances of the servlet. Normally, the servlet container uses only one instance per servlet declaration. However, for a servlet implementing the `SingleThreadModel` interface, the servlet container may instantiate multiple instances to handle a heavy request load and serialize requests to a particular instance.

If a servlet is marked in the deployment descriptor (more on this follows) as distributable and the application implements the `SingleThreadModel` interface, the container may instantiate multiple instances of that servlet in each JVM of the container or across many machines (clustering servlets usually through serialization). The container has a complicated task in managing requests, sessions, and contexts across JVMs. How each vendor accomplishes this is beyond the scope of this book. You do need to know that to convert your Web application into a distributable one, you must implement the SingleThreadModel interface and mark the servlet as distributable in the deployment descriptor.

Handling HTTP GET, POST, and PUT Requests

The service method calls the doXXX methods. This method is where your servlet does most of its labor. From this method your code handles HTML responses. The vast majority of requests will be GET and POST. At first it is easy to confuse the two, so look at Table 4.1, which provides a list of differences between GET and POST requests.

Table 1.1 GET vs. POST Request

GET	**POST**
Query string or form data is simply appended to the URL as name-value pairs.	Form name-value pairs are sent in the body of the request, not in the URL itself.
Query length is limited (about 1KB).	Query length is unlimited.
Users can see data in the address bar.	Data is hidden from users.
http://mycompany.com/support?Name=John+Smith&Product=go+kart&Complaint=the+engine+is+sputtering+oil	**http://mycompany.com/support <values of Name, Product, and Complaint are in request body>**
doGet	**doPost**
For getting (retrieving) data only.	For causing a change on the server (store data in a database).
ASCII.	ASCII + binary.
Easy to bookmark.	Hard to bookmark.

GET

GET is by far the champion request type on the Internet. It is normally used for simple HTML page requests. Your servlet handles it with this syntax:

```
public void doGet(HttpServletRequest request,
                  HttpServletResponse response)
    throws IOException, ServletException
   { //your code here}
```

If this method is all you had in your servlet, it would handle the majority of your Web server's needs regarding this servlet. Notice that the init and service methods involved in a request are already provided by the

HttpServlet class, so they don't need to be overridden (although you can do so).

GET requests can be bookmarked in most browsers. However, **POST** requests usually cannot because they are typically targeting a dynamic resource. The browser often can't cache a resource expecting a **POST** type of request.

The types of events that generate a GET request are clicking on a hyperlink, changing the address directly by typing in the address textbox on a browser or application that has HTML functionality, and submitting an HTML form in which the method header is set to get, as in method=get. Also, a GET request is triggered when selecting a favorite from the Favorites list and using JavaScript to change location.href. Usually the browser is configured to send a GET request even if no method is set explicitly by the HTML.

The benefits of the GET method are as follows:

- It retrieves information such as a simple HTML page or the results of a database query.
- It supports query strings (name-value pairs appended to URL). Servers usually limit query strings to about 1,000 characters.
- It allows bookmarks.

POST

The POST type of request is most often used by HTML forms. It has this syntax:

```
public void doPost(HttpServletRequest request,
                   HttpServletResponse response)
    throws IOException, ServletException
   { //your code here}
```

The HTML form has fields whose names and values are sent to the server in key-value pairs. The POST is designed for posting long messages (for example, to a bulletin board, newsgroup, or mailing list); providing a block of data, such as the result of submitting a form; and submitting long data fields to a database (such as a SQL insert of lengthy string). Sometimes the action performed by the POST method doesn't return a standard HTML page. Also, it's the preferred format for data that needs to be submitted securely.

Normally, this method is used to process a form submitted by a browser. You will very likely be looking for form field names and values. This occurs when a browser or application submits an HTML form with the `method` attribute set to `post`, as in `method=post`.

The benefits of the `POST` method are listed here:

- It sends information to the server such as form fields, large text bodies, and key-value pairs.
- It hides form data from the browser's address bar. The form data isn't passed as a query string, but rather in the message body.
- It sends unlimited-length data as part of its HTTP request body.
- While the URL is retained, the data submitted via `POST` is not included in a bookmark.

PUT

The `PUT` type of request is a means of uploading files to the server. Although uploading is its original intent, I have not seen it used much. Instead, `POST` is generally used to upload files, but you need to associate `PUT` with uploading files for the exam.

The `doPut` method is called by the server (via the `service` method) to handle a `PUT` request. Uploading files from a browser has always been difficult. The idea behind the `PUT` operation is to make uploading straightforward. It is supposed to allow a client to place a file on the server, just like sending a file by FTP. The javadoc for this method warns that when overriding this method, you should leave intact any content headers sent with the request.

HEAD

A browser or application sometimes pings a server (for example, for the last-modified date). The `service` method calls `doGet` with a response object that has only headers (no body).

The `HEAD` method returns the same header lines that a `GET` method would return; however, no body or content is returned. This is often accomplished by calling `doGet`, setting the headers, and then returning the response (without any body) to the requester.

The primary benefit of this method is message size. The `HEAD` method receives and returns very small messages. Therefore, it is fast and lightweight on both ends.

Form Parameters

The interface that defines the form parameter methods is `ServletRequest`. This interface is implemented by the Web container to get the parameters from a request. Parameters are sent in the query string or posted form data. The following four methods retrieve parameters:

- `getParameter(String)`—You use this method if you know the particular parameter name. It returns the value of a request parameter as a string, or `null` if the parameter does not exist. Use this method when you are sure the parameter has only one value; otherwise use `getParameterValues()`. Be careful: If you use this method with a multivalued parameter, you won't get an error. You will get the first value in the array returned by `getParameterValues()`.
- `getParameterMap()`—You use this method to create a map of the form parameters supplied with this request.
- `getParameterNames()`—This one returns an `Enumeration` of string objects containing the names of the parameters contained in this request, or an empty `Enumeration` if the request has no parameters.
- `getParameterValues(String)`—This method returns an array of values as strings, or `null` if the parameter does not exist. If the parameter has a single value, the array has a length of `1`. One of the common uses of `getParameterValues()` is to process `<select>` lists that have their `multiple` attribute set.

The following code snippet demonstrates how you would retrieve the parameters from a request. This is how you could walk the request object's parameter list.

```
Enumeration parameterNames =
            request.getParameterNames();

// acquire text stream for response
PrintWriter out = res.getWriter ();

while (parameterNames.hasMoreElements()) {
    String name =
        (String)parameterNames.nextElement();
    String value = request.getParameter(name);
    out.println(name + " = " + value + "<br/>");
}
```

Retrieving a Servlet Initialization Parameter

A Web application includes many parts; it rarely is just one class or file. It can be a combination of JSP pages, servlets, tag libraries, JavaBeans, and other class files. The Java Virtual Machine keeps track of them all with a `ServletContext` object that maintains information (context) about your Web application. You access the `ServletContext` for information about the application state. The `ServletContext` enables you to get application-level initialization parameters. Although there are several trivial methods (for example, methods for getting the major and minor version of the Servlet API), the exam expects you to be very familiar with initialization parameters. You can also set and get application attributes. One very interesting capability is to create a `RequestDispatcher` object to forward to or include other application components. The `ServletContext` object is how you can set, get, and change application-level (not session-level) attributes and talk to the servlet container.

When you see *context*, think application scope. The `getInitParameter` and `getInitParameterNames` methods retrieve context-wide, application-wide, or "Web application" parameters. The `getInitParameter` method returns a string containing the value of the parameter (you provide the name), or `null` if the parameter does not exist.

The following code snippet shows an example of retrieving servlet initialization parameters.

```
Enumeration params =
        getServletConfig().getInitParameterNames();
while (params.hasMoreElements())
{
    String param = (String) params.nextElement();
    String value =
        getServletConfig().getInitParameter(param);
    writer.println("<li><b>" + param +
                   "</b> = " + value);
}
```

Retrieving HTTP Request Header Information

The request header specifies the file wanted, the date, image file support, and more. The following code snippet shows a typical way to display the header parameters by walking through an `Enumeration` of them.

```
Enumeration e = request.getHeaderNames();
while (e.hasMoreElements())
{
    String headerName = (String)e.nextElement();
    String headerValue =
                   request.getHeader(headerName);
    out.println("<tr><td bgcolor=\"#CCCCCC\">" +
                headerName);
    out.println("</td><td>" + headerValue +
               "</td></tr>");
}
```

Acquiring a Text and Binary Stream for the Response

The `ServletResponse` interface has the method `getWriter`, which returns a `PrintWriter` object that can send strings to the client. Calling `flush` on the `PrintWriter` commits the response. The other thing you can do is use the method `getOutputStream` to send binary data.

You can also send a binary file to a browser from a servlet. Because it isn't text, you have to write the file to the servlet's output stream starting with the following snippet:

```
ServletOutputStream out = res.getOutputStream();
```

Actually, you can use `PrinterWriter` or `ServletOutputStream` for text, like so:

```
ServletOutputStream out = response.getOutputStream();
out.println("<html>");
out.println("<head>");
out.println("<title>Get Certified</title>");
out.println("</head>");
out.println("<body>");
```

and:

```
response.setContentType("text/plain");
PrintWriter writer = response.getWriter();
writer.println("some HTML");
```

Next, you set the file type in the response object using one of the standard Multipurpose Internet Mail Extension (MIME) protocols. Then you use an HTTP response header named `content-disposition`. This header allows the servlet to specify information about the file's presentation. Using that header, you can indicate that the content should be opened separately (not actually in the browser) and that it should not be displayed automatically, but rather upon some further action taken by the user. Returning binary files to clients is a challenge in practice but is easy to understand for the exam.

Redirecting an HTTP Request to Another URL

Web pages have a tendency to move around, breaking their old URLs. Instead of returning a useless 404 error page, you can use the `sendRedirect` method, which sends a temporary redirect response to the client and sends with the client a new location URL. You can use relative or absolute URLs because the servlet container translates a relative URL to an absolute URL before sending the response to the client.

sendRedirect() sets the response status to **SC_MOVED_TEMPORARILY** and sets the Location header. It also resets the response buffer before generating the redirect page. However, the previous headers are not altered. You must call **sendRedirect()** before the response body is committed. You can use a relative or absolute path. Lastly, it handles clients without redirect capability by returning a response page with a hyperlink to the new location.

When redirecting, avoid sending a bad URL to the client or attempting to redirect after the response has already been committed. The bad URL will not produce an error from the server (the container doesn't validate the URL), but the client won't be happy about getting an incorrect URL. After using this method, the response is committed and can't be written to, or you'll get an error. One nice feature is that this method writes a short response body that includes a hyperlink to the new location. This way, if the browser doesn't support redirects, it still gets the new link. Use the following syntax for this method:

```
// Suppose this portion of the server is down.
// Redirect the user to an explanation page.
redirectPath = "./error/notAvailable.html";
response.sendRedirect(redirectPath);
```

Servlet Objects and Scope

You should know about four scopes: page, request, session, and context. Page scope can see all three, but none of the others can see objectives or variables declared at the page level. Accessibility goes up as you go left to right in this list. Context objects can be accessed by the other three even though context scope can't see the other three.

This objective requires you to understand how to set and get name-value attributes at three different levels. The breadth of scope increases from request to session to context, the widest scope. Table 1.2 provides a definition of the three object scopes of concern under this objective: request, session, and application.

Table 1.2 Request, Session, and Application Scope

Name	Accessibility	Lifetime
Request	Current, included, or forwarded pages	Until the response is returned to the user
Session	All requests from the same browser within the session timeout	Until session timeout or the session ID is invalidated (such as when the user quits the browser)
Application	All requests to the same Web application	Life of container or when explicitly killed (such as through container administration action)

When can you access an attribute? The answer depends on which object was used to set the attribute. If you set an attribute with the request object, the scope of that specific attribute is only request. You can't access it once the request is complete. You can't see this attribute in another request even if it is in the same session. Conversely, any attribute set with the `ServletContext` object can be seen in all sessions and all requests.

Request

When a user hits a URL with a servlet at the other end, the servlet container creates an `HttpServletRequest` object. It passes this object as an argument to the servlet's service methods (`doPut`, `doGet`, and `doPost`). There is a lot of information in this object, including the login of the user making this request (`getRemoteUser`) and the name of the HTTP method with which this request was made (`getMethod`). However, this exam objective is restricted to header information.

The following list of methods summarizes the request (interfaces: `ServletRequest` and `HttpServletRequest`) methods you need to be familiar with. Although all are fair game, I list here only those that might be on the exam:

- `getAttribute(`*`String name`*`)`—Returns the value of the named attribute as an object, or `null` if no attribute of the given name exists

- `getAttributeNames()`—Returns an `Enumeration` containing the names of the attributes available to this request
- `getCookies()`—Returns an array containing all of the cookie objects the client sent with this request
- `getHeader(java.lang.String name)`—Returns the value of the specified request header as a String
- `getHeaderNames()`—Returns an enumeration of all the header names this request contains
- `getHeaders(java.lang.String name)`—Returns all the values of the specified request header as an `Enumeration` of String objects
- `getIntHeader(java.lang.String name)`—Returns the value of the specified request header as an integer
- `getMethod()`—Returns the name of the HTTP method with which this request was made—for example, `GET`, `POST`, or `PUT`
- `getParameter(java.lang.String name)`—Returns the value of a request parameter as a string, or `null` if the parameter does not exist
- `getParameterNames()`—Returns an `Enumeration` of string objects containing the names of the parameters in this request
- `getParameterValues(java.lang.String name)`—Returns an array of string objects containing all the values that the given request parameter has, or `null` if the parameter does not exist
- `getRequestDispatcher(java.lang.String path)`—Returns a `RequestDispatcher` object that acts as a wrapper for the resource located at the given path
- `getSession()`—Returns the current session (`HttpSession`) associated with this request, or creates one if the request does not have a session
- `getSession(boolean create)`—Returns the current `HttpSession` associated with this request, or returns a new session if there is no current session and `create` is `true`
- `removeAttribute(java.lang.String name)`—Removes an attribute from this request
- `setAttribute(java.lang.String name, java.lang.Object o)`—Stores an attribute in this request

Several `HttpServletRequest` methods are not mentioned specifically in the objectives, so focus on those listed.

Session

A session is made up of multiple hits from the same browser across some period of time. The session scope includes all hits from a single machine (multiple browser windows, if they share cookies). Servlets maintain state with sessions. The following code snippet demonstrates how you can use session attributes.

```
HttpSession session = request.getSession();

//get these from the HTML form or query string
String dataName = request.getParameter("dataname");
String dataValue =request.getParameter("datavalue");
if (dataName != null && dataValue != null)
{
    session.setAttribute(dataName, dataValue);
}

//session data
Enumeration names = session.getAttributeNames();
while (names.hasMoreElements())
{
    String name = (String) names.nextElement();
    String value =
            session.getAttribute(name).toString();
    out.println(name + " = " + value + "<br/>");
}
```

To summarize, you can use sessions to track a single user over a short time. You get the session object (`HttpSession`) from the request object. To track multiple users over time, you must jump to context, covered next.

Context

A Web application includes many parts; it rarely is just one class or one JSP. To help manage an application, you will sometimes need to set and get information that all of the servlets share together, which we say is context-wide. An example is using a login servlet to create an application-level attribute such as application name, like so:

```
ServletContext context = config.getServletContext();
context.setAttribute(
       "productColor", "blue");
```

Besides setting and retrieving your custom attributes, you can get additional information from the servlet container, such as its major and minor version, the path to a given servlet, and more. The following summarizes the additional methods you might use:

- `getAttributeNames()`—Returns an `Enumeration` object containing the attribute names available within this servlet context

- `getContext(String uripath)`—Returns a `ServletContext` object that corresponds to a specified URL on the server
- `getInitParameter(String name)`—Returns a string containing the value of the named context-wide initialization parameter, or `null` if the parameter does not exist
- `getInitParameterNames()`—Returns the names of the context's initialization parameters as an `Enumeration` of string objects, or an empty `Enumeration` if the context has no initialization parameters
- `getNamedDispatcher(String name)`—Returns a `RequestDispatcher` object that acts as a wrapper for the named servlet
- `getRequestDispatcher(String path)`—Returns a `RequestDispatcher` object that acts as a wrapper for the resource located at the given path

Servlet Life Cycle

A few guaranteed exam questions will be on the life-cycle methods `init`, `service`, and `destroy`. You have to know each one's purpose and when it is invoked. Be careful to practice with these methods because the servlet life cycle is not obvious. The container calls these three methods in this order. Ordinarily, that is how the container talks to your servlet. With some containers, you can modify this behavior, but the exam will assume this order.

The `init` method is called the first time the servlet is invoked. This happens one time. However, the `service` method is called every time a servlet is requested. Lastly, the `destroy` method is called once upon the removal of the servlet from memory because of explicit removal or lack of use (for example, the session expires). You can configure the container to load certain servlets upon startup (`<load-on-startup/>` in web.xml, the deployment descriptor), but most of them will be loaded upon first request. Either way, the `init` method is called first. Place in this method things you will use across requests, such as database connections, and class member values such as finalized constants.

When is **init** called? The **init** method may be called when the server starts (web.xml configuration), when first requested, and sometimes when the container-management console is used, if the container's vendor provides this functionality as part of the server administration. Remember, it is called only *once* in a servlet's lifetime, it is not used to send information back to the browser (**HttpServletResponse** is not a parameter), and it throws a **ServletException** to the container.

The `destroy` method, like `init`, is called only once. It is called when the servlet is taken out of service and all pending requests to that servlet are completed or have timed out. This method is called by the container to give you a chance to release resources such as database connections and threads. You can always call `super.destroy` (`GenericServlet.destroy`) to add a note to the log about what is going on. You might want to do this even if only to place a timestamp there.

Servlets are loaded in one of three ways. The first is when the Web server starts. You can set this in the configuration file. Reload can happen automatically after the container detects that its class file (under the servlet subdirectory, for example, WEB-INF/classes) has changes. The third way, with some containers, is through an administrator interface.

Servlets are run each in their own thread. When the **synchronized** keyword is used with a servlet's service method, requests to that servlet are handled one at a time in a serialized manner. This means that multiple requests won't interfere with each other when accessing variables and references within one servlet. It also means that the processing capabilities of the servlet container are reduced because the more efficient multithreaded mode has been disallowed for a given servlet that has been declared with the **synchronized** keyword.

Using a RequestDispatcher

The RequestDispatcher is used to include or forward to a Web resource. It is a powerful tool that you can use to perform programmatic server-side includes or route the whole request to another servlet or JSP with a forward. You can get the RequestDispatcher in three ways. The first two are through the application context with `ServletContext.getRequestDispatcher` (absolute paths) or with `ServletContext.getNamedDispatcher` (relative and absolute paths). Either returns a RequestDispatcher object that acts as a wrapper for the named servlet (in web.xml, the Web application deployment descriptor). The final way is with `ServletRequest.getRequestDispatcher` (relative and absolute paths). Be careful: If the path begins with a `/`, it is interpreted as relative to the current context root. You will get a `null` if the servlet container cannot return a RequestDispatcher.

Notice that forwarding is different from redirection (it returns a new URL to the browser). The RequestDispatcher doesn't redirect; instead, it "dispatches" or performs forwarding. It can also include output from the resource in a response. The specification allows the resource to be dynamic or static. If it is dynamic, such as a servlet, the container invokes that servlet and then includes the output. If it is static, such as a text file, the container will include the text as is. The following code snippet demonstrates how one servlet can transfer the request to another servlet.

```
getServletConfig()
     .getServletContext()
     .getRequestDispatcher("/HelloWorldExample")
     .forward(request, response);
```

You can also include content from a static page or another servlet. You would use a snippet such as the following:

```
RequestDispatcher dispatcher =
     getServletContext().getRequestDispatcher(path);
   dispatcher.include(request, response);
```

Notice that the included servlet cannot set headers. The servlet cannot change the response status code, either (if you try, it will be ignored). The best way to send along information from the calling servlet to the called servlet is to use a query string or, even better, to use the `setAttribute` method to set request object attributes where they are easy to access.

There is a matter of timing to consider as well. You can call an include anytime, but the forward must be called before the response is committed. Otherwise, you'll throw an `IllegalStateException` exception.

To summarize:

- `ServletContext.getRequestDispatcher()`—This method uses absolute paths.
- `ServletRequest.getRequestDispatcher()`—The path may be relative but cannot extend outside current servlet context.
- `ServletRequest.getNamedDispatcher()`—This is the name of the servlet for which a dispatcher is requested, and it is in the web.xml file (see Chapter 2 for more about web.xml).

Event Listeners

Listeners enable you to respond to events such as when an attribute value changes or when one is removed. These objects have methods that the container invokes when life-cycle events occur. To make this happen, you define a listener class by implementing a listener interface like so:

```
public final class ContextListener
   implements ServletContextListener
```

The container invokes the listener method and passes it information (methods in the `HttpSessionListener` interface are passed an `HttpSessionEvent`) about that event.

Suppose that you had the following snippet that removes an attribute:

```
ServletContext context = event.getServletContext();
//Date startDate = context.getAttribute("StartDate");
context.removeAttribute("StartDate");
```

When this executes, it triggers the attribute listener. The container calls listener methods in your servlets in which you have extended as in the following (edited from Tomcat's `ApplicationContext` class):

```
// Notify interested application event listeners
Object listeners[] = context.getApplicationListeners();
ServletContextAttributeEvent event =
  new ServletContextAttributeEvent(context.getServletContext(),
                                   name, value);
for (int i = 0; i < listeners.length; i++)
{
    ServletContextAttributeListener listener =
        (ServletContextAttributeListener) listeners[i];
    context.fireContainerEvent("beforeContextAttributeRemoved",
                               listener);
    listener.attributeRemoved(event);
    context.fireContainerEvent("afterContextAttributeRemoved",
                               listener);
}
```

The following listener interfaces and methods are covered by the exam:

- When a servlet is initialized or destroyed:
    - `javax.servlet.ServletContextListener`.
    - `contextDestroyed(ServletContextEvent sce)`. Notification that the servlet context is about to be shut down.
    - `contextInitialized(ServletContextEvent sce)`. Notification that the Web application is ready to process requests.
- When a context attribute is added, removed, or replaced:
    - `javax.servlet.ServletContextAttributeListener`.
    - `attributeAdded(ServletContextAttributeEvent scab)`. Notification that a new attribute was added to the servlet context.
    - `attributeRemoved(ServletContextAttributeEvent scab)`. Notification that an existing attribute has been removed from the servlet context.

    - `attributeReplaced(ServletContextAttributeEvent scab)`. Notification that an attribute on the servlet context has been replaced.
- When a session is initialized or destroyed:
    - `javax.servlet.http.HttpSessionListener`.
    - `sessionCreated(HttpSessionEvent se)`. Notification that a session was created.
    - `sessionDestroyed(HttpSessionEvent se)`. Notification that a session became invalid or timed out.
- When a session attribute is added, removed, or replaced:
    - `HttpSessionAttributeListener`.
    - `attributeAdded(HttpSessionBindingEvent se)`. Notification that an attribute has been added to a session.
    - `attributeRemoved(HttpSessionBindingEvent se)`. Notification that an attribute has been removed from a session.
    - `attributeReplaced(HttpSessionBindingEvent se)`. Notification that an attribute has been replaced in a session.

The behavior of these listeners in a distributable is exactly the same as those discussed in the previous section, with one notable exception: Be careful about how your vendor handles event notification of addition, removal, or replacement because it might affect the listener for only that context. No other context, such as other JVMs on the same or other machine, will know about the listener events.

Practice Questions

Question 1

Read the following code snippet:

```
public void doGet(HttpServletRequest request,
                  HttpServletResponse response)
    throws IOException, ServletException
{
    //;
}

// doPost() - SCWCD Exam Objective 1.1
public void doPost(HttpServletRequest request,
                   HttpServletResponse response)
    throws IOException, ServletException
{
    doGet(request, response);
}
```

What two statements are true regarding this snippet when the servlet received an HTTP **POST** request? (Choose two.)

- ❑ A. An exception is thrown because you can't call **doGet** from **doPost**.
- ❑ B. It compiles, but no HTML is generated by either of these methods.
- ❑ C. **doPost** calls **doGet**, sending along the request and response objects.
- ❑ D. **destroy** is automatically called immediately after successful completion of the **doPost**.

Answers B and C are correct. The `doPost` method does call `doGet`, sending along the request and response objects. However, `doGet` doesn't add any text to the output stream. The `destroy` method is called when the session is invalidated, not immediately after a request.

Question 2

Which two of the following methods are defined in the **Servlet** interface? (Choose two.)

- ❑ A. **getServlet**
- ❑ B. **service**
- ❑ C. **finalize**
- ❑ D. **destroy**

Answers B and D are correct. The `getServlet` and `finalize` methods are not defined by the `Servlet` interface.

Question 3

Which two of the following objects are passed to a servlet's service method in a servlet that extends **HttpServlet**? (Choose two.)

- ❑ A. **HttpRequest**
- ❑ B. **HttpServletRequest**
- ❑ C. **HttpServletResponse**
- ❑ D. **HttpResponse**

Answers B and C are correct. `HttpServletRequest` and `HttpServletResponse` methods are passed to the `service` method, which passes them to the appropriate `doGet`, `doPost` or `doPut` method in a servlet that extends `HttpServlet`.

Question 4

How does the URL-rewriting mechanism keep track of a given session ID?

- ❍ A. It uses cookies to contain the session ID.
- ❍ B. It adds a **jsessionid** to the end of the URL.
- ❍ C. It uses form fields.
- ❍ D. The URL-rewriting mechanism doesn't track the session ID.

Answer B is correct. The URL-rewriting mechanism keeps track of a given session ID with the `jsessionid` parameter added to the query string, as in `www.mycompany.com/jsessionid=87`. The session ID is never kept in a form field. Servlets do use cookies, but don't do so when you use URL rewriting.

Question 5

What will be the result of trying to compile and request the following servlet? (Assume that it is in the correct directory and that the request correctly refers to it.)

```
import java.io.*;
import java.util.*;
import javax.servlet.*;
import javax.servlet.http.*;

public class GetParameters extends ServletContext
{
    public void doGet(HttpServletRequest request,
                      HttpServletResponse response)
    throws IOException, ServletException
    {
        Enumeration parameterNames =
                    request.getParameterNames();

        // acquire text stream for response
        PrintWriter out = request.getWriter ();

        while (parameterNames.hasMoreElements()) {
            String name =
                (String)parameterNames.nextElement();
            String value = request.getParameter(name);
            out.println(name + " = " + value + "<br/>");
        }
    }
}
```

- ❍ A. The class will compile and return the list of parameter names.
- ❍ B. The class will compile but will return an error.
- ❍ C. The class will not compile.
- ❍ D. The class will compile and return the form field names.

Answer C is correct. A servlet extends `HttpServlet`, not `ServletContext`. Also, the `PrintWriter` is retrieved from the response object not the request object, as shown in the question code snippet. Otherwise, it would have compiled and returned the list of parameter names. Notice that the content type is not set, which is bad form, but still works.

Question 6

Which method takes a relative path?

- ❍ A. **ServletContext.getRequestDispatcher()**
- ❍ B. **ServletRequest.getRequestDispatcher()**
- ❍ C. **ServletRequest.getNamedDispatcher()**
- ❍ D. **ServletResponse.getRequestDispatcher()**

Answer B is correct. The `ServletRequest.getRequestDispatcher` method takes a relative path.

Question 7

What is wrong with the following code snippet?

```
String[] params =
        getServletConfig().getInitParameterNames();
```

- ❍ A. The method should be **getInitParameterNames()**.
- ❍ B. There is nothing wrong with this code.
- ❍ C. It should be **ServletConfig().getInitParameterNames()**.
- ❍ D. The method returns an **Enumeration**, not a **String** array.

Answer D is correct. The method returns an `Enumeration`, not a `String` array. It should have been this:

```
Enumeration params =
        getServletConfig().getInitParameterNames();
```

Need to Know More?

Sun's excellent J2EE Tutorial—java.sun.com/j2ee/tutorial/1_3-fcs/doc/J2eeTutorialTOC.html

The Java Language Specification—java.sun.com/docs/books/jls/second_edition/html/j.title.doc.html

Exam objectives for the Sun Certified Web Component Developer For J2EE Platform—http://suned.sun.com/US/certification/java/exam_objectives.html

The Java Servlet 2.3 Specification—http://jcp.org/aboutJava/communityprocess/first/jsr053/index.html

Sun's official Servlet page—http://java.sun.com/products/servlet/

Java Software FAQ Index—http://java.sun.com/docs/faqindex.html

Tomcat—An implementation of the Java Servlet 2.2 and JavaServer Pages 1.1 Specifications, http://jakarta.apache.org/tomcat/index.html

Java Training by the MageLang Institute—www.magelang.com/

Servlets.com, Web site companion to *Java Servlet Programming* by O'Reilly—www.servlets.com/

Glossary of Java Technology-Related Terms—http://java.sun.com/docs/glossary.html

Deploying Web Applications

Terms you'll need to understand:

✓ Web application
✓ Web archive file
✓ Web app deployment descriptor
✓ Initialization parameters
✓ Authentication, authorization
✓ Security constraints
✓ Web resource
✓ Deployment

Techniques you'll need to master:

✓ Identify the structure of a Web application and Web archive file.
✓ Name the Web app deployment descriptor.
✓ Name the directories where you place Web resources.
✓ Name and describe deployment descriptor elements.
✓ Configure the deployment descriptor to handle exceptions and errors.
✓ Configure Web applications for security.
✓ Configure servlets and listeners through the deployment descriptor.

Web Application Overview

A Web application is a collection of server-side resources, including servlets, JSP pages, HTML documents, and other files (configuration files, image files, and compressed archives). This collection can be packaged into an archive or can exist as separate files in an open directory structure. Because you have many servlet classes, JSP pages, HTML pages, and other supporting libraries and files for a given Web application, many dependencies exist. Using standard JAR tools, you can package the collection into a Web application archive, a single file with the .war extension that contains all the components of a Web application.

Web applications typically run on only one JVM. To deploy it, you place the collection of files into a Web server's runtime. A distributable Web application is written so that it can be deployed in a Web container, distributed across multiple Java Virtual Machines running on the same host or different hosts. The two keys to making this possible are how you thread the servlets and how you declare certain elements in the deployment descriptor. For example, the `servlet` element in the deployment descriptor can define a security role for a given servlet. However, the deployment descriptor doesn't handle everything. Notice that the deployment descriptor doesn't handle threading—I wish it did. If you wanted to guarantee that no two threads will execute concurrently in the servlet's `service` method, you would implement the `SingleThreadModel` interface.

When a servlet is marked in the deployment descriptor (more on this later) as distributable and the application implements the `SingleThreadModel` interface, the container may instantiate multiple instances of that servlet in each VM of the container or across many machines (clustering servlets usually through serialization). The container has a complicated task in managing requests, sessions, and contexts across JVMs. How each vendor accomplishes this is beyond the scope of this book. You do need to know that to convert your Web application into a distributable one, you must implement the `SingleThreadModel` interface and mark the servlet as distributable in the deployment descriptor.

All enterprise applications start by reading initialization or configuration information, usually in an initialization file. This is how they configure themselves initially. Web applications likewise use configuration files, but with a significant improvement over most applications. Servlet containers' configuration files are written in standard XML. This is so much better than the ad hoc formats most of us have had to toil with.

How vendors implement their containers varies. For example, Tomcat uses several configuration files (such as CATALINA_HOME\conf\server.xml). In addition, each Web application has a configuration file called a deployment descriptor (such as CATALINA_HOME\APPLICATION_HOME\WEB-INF\web.xml). For a given Web application, the container parses this deployment descriptor for initialization instructions.

Figure 2.1 illustrates a high-level diagram of how a container processes an HTTP request and shows the roles of all the pieces that affect a Web application.

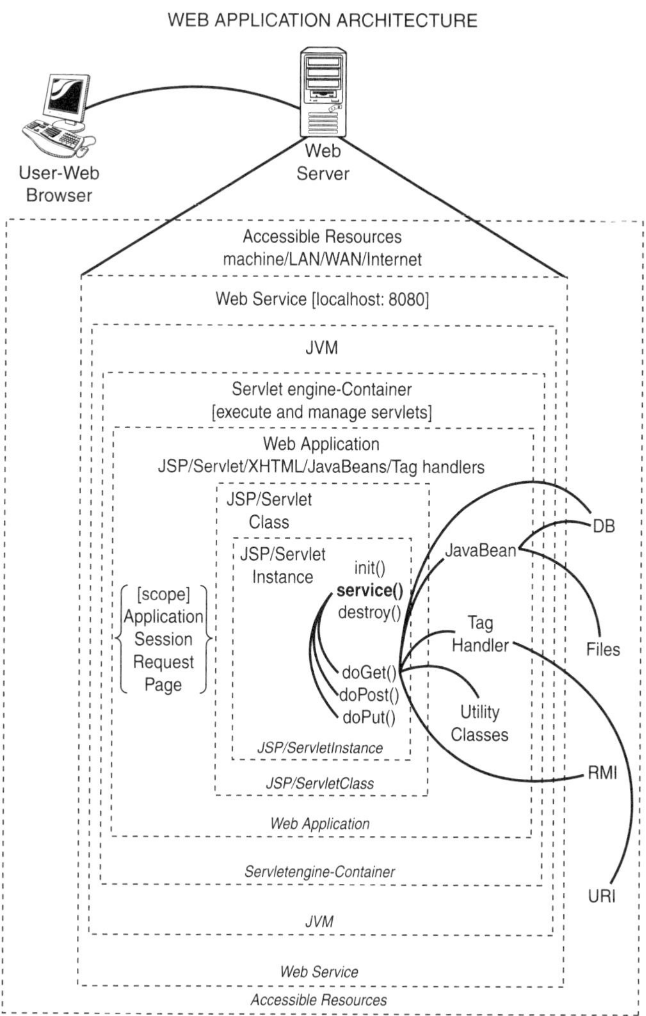

Figure 2.1 How the Web application architecture handles an HTTP request.

The structure of a Web application is on the exam. You need to know where a few things go, including the deployment descriptor, the class files, the JAR files, and all the HTML and JSP pages. The location of these is included in Table 2.1.

Table 2.1 Web Application Structure

Name	Files	Directory
Deployment Descriptor	web.xml	/WEB-INF/web.xml
Class files	MyServlet.class	/WEB-INF/classes/ MyServlet.class
JAR files (servlets, beans, utility classes)	myApp.jar	/WEB-INF/lib/myApp.jar
Other files (HTML, JSP)	index.html	/

The following is the Web application structure for a sample Web application:

```
/index.html
/copywrite.jsp
/contact.jsp
/images/background.gif
/images/logo.gif
/WEB-INF/web.xml
/WEB-INF/taglib.tld
/WEB-INF/lib/shoppingBean.jar
/WEB-INF/classes/com/myCompany/servlets/Shopping.class
/WEB-INF/classes/com/myCompany/util/CurrencyFormat.class
```

Using one of the Web applications that comes bundled with Tomcat, you can dissect the structure into actual paths. The root directory is TOMCAT_HOME\webapps\examples. If you had the file TOMCAT_HOME\webapps\examples\hello.jsp, you would call this file with `http://localhost:8080/examples/hello.jsp` (just change the port to whatever one you have your server listening to). Notice how Tomcat converts the URL into a path; see Table 2.2.

Table 2.2 Web Application Path

Description	URL	Directory
Installation root		C:\dev\java\jakarta-tomcat-4.0.1
Server root	**http://localhost**	TOMCAT_HOME\webapps
Web application	**http://localhost:8080/examples**	TOMCAT_HOME\webapps\ examples
Static resource	**http://localhost:8080/ examples /index.html**	TOMCAT_HOME\webapps\ examples\index.html

(continued)

Table 2.2 Web Application Path *(continued)*

Description	URL	Directory
JSP	**http://localhost:8080/ examples/hello.jsp**	TOMCAT_HOME\webapps\ examples\hello.jsp
JSP	**http://localhost:8080/ examples/jsp/dates/date.jsp**	TOMCAT_HOME\webapps\ examples\jsp\dates\date.jsp
Servlet	**http://localhost:8080/ examples/servlet/ HelloWorldExample**	TOMCAT_HOME\webapps\ examples\WEB-INF\classes\ HelloWorldExample.class

Now that you have seen the overall structure of one Web application, the next section explains in detail how the container uses the deployment descriptor.

Although servlets have a predefined class directory, JSP pages go in the application root. In Tomcat and containers from other vendors, the example application JSP files are placed in an example application with a JSP director. However, the exam expects you to know that HTML and JSP files go in the root directory, described by the forward slash alone (/).

Deployment Descriptor

The deployment descriptor (web.xml) is your Web application's initialization file. When the application is first started, the container reads this file. This XML document's definition isn't long; the following is the DTD for web.xml, where the `web-app` element is the root of the deployment descriptor for a Web application. (See `www.w3.org/TR/REC-xml#dt-element` for an element definition.)

```
<!ELEMENT web-app (icon?, display-name?, description?, distributable?,
context-param*, filter*, filter-mapping*, listener*, servlet*,
servlet-mapping*, session-config?, mime-mapping*, welcome-file-list?,
error-page*, taglib*, resource-env-ref*, resource-ref*, security-
➥constraint*,
login-config?, security-role*, env-entry*, ejb-ref*,  ejb-local-ref*)>
```

Remember that the star (*) means zero or more occurrences of the same element, and the question mark (?) means zero or one occurrence of the same element. A name with neither a star nor a question mark is required. As an example, `web-app` has no required elements, so your Web application will start without a deployment descriptor.

You don't have to know all 77 elements. The elements that you must be familiar with for the exam—and their subelements—are `context-param`, `listener`, `servlet`, `servlet-mapping`, `session-config`, `error-page`, `taglib`, `security-constraint`, `login-config`, and `security-role`. The main elements are defined in Table 2.3.

Table 2.3 Web–App Elements

Element	DTD
context-param	<!ELEMENT context-param (param-name, param-value, description?)>
listener	<!ELEMENT listener (listener-class)> <!ELEMENT listener-class (#PCDATA)>
servlet	<!ELEMENT servlet (icon?, servlet-name, display-name?, description?, (servlet-class|jsp-file), init-param*, load-on-startup?, run-as?, security-role-ref*)> <!ELEMENT servlet-name (#PCDATA)> <!ELEMENT servlet-class (#PCDATA)> <!ELEMENT load-on-startup (#PCDATA)> <!ELEMENT run-as (description?, role-name)> <!ELEMENT security-role-ref (description?, role-name, role-link?)>
servlet-mapping	<!ELEMENT servlet-mapping (servlet-name, url-pattern)>
session-config	<!ELEMENT session-config (session-timeout?)> <!ELEMENT session-timeout (#PCDATA)>
error-page	<!ELEMENT error-page ((error-code | exception-type), location)> <!ELEMENT error-code (#PCDATA)> <!ELEMENT exception-type (#PCDATA)>
taglib	<!ELEMENT taglib (taglib-uri, taglib-location)> <!ELEMENT taglib-location (#PCDATA)> <!ELEMENT taglib-uri (#PCDATA)>
security-constraint	<!ELEMENT security-constraint (display-name?, web-resource-collection+, auth-constraint?, user-data-constraint?)> <!ELEMENT auth-constraint (description?, role-name*)> <!ELEMENT web-resource-collection (web-resource-name, description?, url-pattern*, http-method*)> <!ELEMENT user-data-constraint (description?, transport-guarantee)>
login-config	<!ELEMENT login-config (auth-method?, realm-name?, form-login-config?)>
security-role	<!ELEMENT security-role (description?, role-name)>

The order of elements is important. If you place these elements in the wrong order, the container will choke. More to the point, the exam expects you to know the order.

Listing 2.1 is a deployment descriptor example.

Listing 2.1 A Deployment Descriptor

```
<?xml version="1.0" encoding="ISO-8859-1"?>

<!DOCTYPE web-app
    PUBLIC "-//Sun Microsystems, Inc.//DTD Web Application 2.3//EN"
    "http://java.sun.com/j2ee/dtds/web-app_2_3.dtd">

<!-- Deployment Descriptor for a Web Application -->

<web-app>
    <servlet>
        <servlet-name>Authentication03</servlet-name>
        <servlet-class>org.apache.tester.Authentication03</servlet-class>
        <init-param>
              <param-name>debug</param-name>
              <param-value>0</param-value>
        </init-param>
        <load-on-startup>1</load-on-startup>
        <security-role-ref>
            <role-name>alias</role-name>
            <role-link>tomcat</role-link>
        </security-role-ref>
    </servlet>

    <servlet-mapping>
        <servlet-name>Authentication03</servlet-name>
        <url-pattern>/protected/Authentication03</url-pattern>
    </servlet-mapping>

    <error-page>
        <error-code>412</error-code>  <!-- SC_PRECONDITION_FAILED -->
        <location>/ErrorPage02</location>
    </error-page>

    <error-page>
        <exception-type>org.apache.tester.TesterException</exception-type>
        <location>/ErrorPage04</location>
    </error-page>

    <login-config>
        <auth-method>BASIC</auth-method>
        <realm-name>Authentication Servlet</realm-name>
    </login-config>

    <security-role>
        <description>Security role we are testing for</description>
        <role-name>tomcat</role-name>
    </security-role>
```

(continued)

Listing 2.1 A Deployment Descriptor *(continued)*

```
    <security-constraint>
        <web-resource-collection>
            <web-resource-name>General Protected Area</web-resource-name>
            <url-pattern>/protected/*</url-pattern>
        </web-resource-collection>
        <auth-constraint>
            <role-name>tomcat</role-name>
        </auth-constraint>
    </security-constraint>

    <taglib>
        <taglib-uri>
                http://www.yourcompany.com/yourTagLibrary
        </taglib-uri>
        <taglib-location>
           /WEB-INF/yourTagLibrary.tld
        </taglib-location>
    </taglib>

</web-app>
```

Notice that the `web-app` element is the root of the deployment descriptor for a Web application. At least a few of these elements shown are guaranteed to be on the exam. I strongly recommend that you scan the actual DTD, even though the exam covers only the elements in this chapter.

The following is a heavy edit of the XML DTD for the Servlet 2.3 deployment descriptor. The sections describe the key elements, all of which are either mentioned directly in the objectives or alluded to. I skipped several elements, such as the `description` element (`<!ELEMENT description (#PCDATA)>`), because they don't require explaining. This is a subelement included in many others, but it isn't explained here and won't be asked about on the exam. Other elements, such as `ejb-link` (`<!ELEMENT ejb-link (#PCDATA)>`), are not self-describing but aren't in this chapter because they are not on the exam.

context-param

The following is the DTD for the `context-param` element of the deployment descriptor:

```
<!ELEMENT context-param (param-name, param-value, description?)>
<!ELEMENT param-name (#PCDATA)>
<!ELEMENT param-value (#PCDATA)>
```

The `context-param` element contains the declaration of a Web application's servlet context-initialization parameters. In other words, these are the initialization parameters for the application. You can access these parameters in your code using the `javax.servlet.ServletContext.getInitParameter()` and `javax.servlet.ServletContext.getInitParameterNames()` methods. The `param-name` element contains the name (unique in the Web application) of a parameter. The `param-value` element contains the value of a parameter.

Example

The following is an example of the `context-param` element of the deployment descriptor:

```
<web-app>
    ...
    <context-param>
        <param-name>test</param-name>
        <param-value>SCWCD</param-value>
    </context-param>
    <context-param>
        <param-name>difficulty</param-name>
        <param-value>medium</param-value>
    </context-param>
    ...
</web-app>
```

The two types of initialization information retrievable from within a servlet are application and servlet-initialization parameters. The **context-param** element defines the application parameters retrieved with the following:

```
ServletContext context = getServletContext();
enum = context.getInitParameterNames();
while (enum.hasMoreElements()) {
    String key = (String)enum.nextElement();
    Object val = context.getInitParameter(key);
}
```

The **init-param** element within the **servlet** element defines servlet parameters retrieved with the following:

```
Enumeration enum = getInitParameterNames();
while (enum.hasMoreElements()) {
    String key = (String)enum.nextElement();
    String val = getInitParameter(key);
}
```

Notice that, in the case of **servlet/init-param**, the **getInitParameterNames** and **getInitParameter** methods are defined by the **ServletConfig** interface, which is implemented by **GenericServlet**, which is inherited by **HttpServlet**, which is then inherited by your servlet.

listener

The following is the DTD for the `listener` element of the deployment descriptor:

```
<!ELEMENT listener (listener-class)>
<!ELEMENT listener-class (#PCDATA)>
```

The `listener` element indicates the deployment properties for a Web application listener bean. The `listener-class` element declares that a class in the application must be registered as a Web application listener bean. The value is the fully qualified class name of the listener class.

Example

The following is an example for the `listener` element of the deployment descriptor:

```
<web-app>
    ...
<listener>
   <listener-class>listeners.MyListener</listener-class>
</listener>    ...
</web-app>
```

servlet

The following is the DTD for the `servlet` element of the deployment descriptor:

```
<!ELEMENT servlet (icon?, servlet-name, display-name?, description?,
➥(servlet-class¦jsp-file), init-param*, load-on-startup?, run-as?,
➥security-role-ref*)>
<!ELEMENT servlet-name (#PCDATA)>
<!ELEMENT servlet-class (#PCDATA)>
<!ELEMENT init-param (param-name, param-value, description?)>
<!ELEMENT load-on-startup (#PCDATA)>
<!ELEMENT run-as (description?, role-name)>
<!ELEMENT security-role-ref (description?, role-name, role-link?)>
<!ELEMENT role-link (#PCDATA)>
<!ELEMENT role-name (#PCDATA)>
```

The `servlet` element declares a servlet. This element most likely will be on the exam. A `servlet-name` element contains the canonical name of the servlet that is unique within the Web application. It is used to reference the servlet definition elsewhere in the deployment descriptor. Use either the `servlet-class` tags or the `jsp-file` tags in your servlet body, but not both. If it's `jsp-file`, use the full path to the JSP file within the Web application. This path is relative to the Web application root directory. The `servlet-class` element contains the fully qualified class name of the servlet. The `init-param` element contains a name/value pair as an initialization param of the servlet. You retrieve these as follows:

```
PrintWriter writer = response.getWriter();
Enumeration params =
        getServletConfig().getInitParameterNames();
```

```
while (params.hasMoreElements())
{
    String param = (String) params.nextElement();
    String value =
        getServletConfig().getInitParameter(param);
    writer.println(param + " = " + value);
}
```

The `load-on-startup` element indicates that this servlet should be loaded (should be instantiated and have its `init()` called) upon startup of the Web application. The optional contents of these elements must be an integer indicating the order in which the servlet should be loaded. If the value is a negative integer, or if the element is not present, the container is free to load the servlet whenever it chooses. If the value is a positive integer or `0`, the container must load and initialize the servlet as the application is deployed. The container must guarantee that servlets marked with lower integers are loaded before servlets marked with higher integers. The container may choose the order of loading of servlets with the same `load-on-start-up` value. The `run-as` element specifies the identity to be used for the execution of the Web application.

The `security-role-ref` element contains the declaration of a security role reference in the Web application's code. You use this to link a security role name defined by `security-role` to a role name that is hard-coded in the servlet. The declaration consists of an optional description, the security role name used in the code, and an optional link to a security role. If the security role is not specified, the deployer must choose an appropriate security role. The value of the `role-name` element must be the string used as the parameter to the `HttpServletRequest.isUserInRole(String role)` method. The `role-link` element is a reference to a defined security role and must contain the name of one of the security roles defined in the `security-role` elements.

Example

The following is an example of the `servlet` element of the deployment descriptor:

```
<web-app>
    ...
    <servlet>
        <servlet-name>
            shoppingCart
        </servlet-name>
        <servlet-class>
            ShoppingCartServlet
        </servlet-class>
        <init-param>
            <param-name>customerCount</param-name>
            <param-value>0</param-value>
        </init-param>
```

```
        <run-as>
            <description>Security role for customer</description>
            <role-name>customer</role-name>
        </run-as>
    </servlet>
    ...
</web-app>
```

servlet-mapping

The following is the DTD for the servlet-mapping element of the deployment descriptor:

```
<!ELEMENT servlet-mapping (servlet-name, url-pattern)>
<!ELEMENT servlet-name (#PCDATA)>
<!ELEMENT url-pattern (#PCDATA)>
```

The `servlet-mapping` element defines a mapping between a servlet and a URL pattern. The `servlet-name` element contains the canonical name of the servlet that is unique within the Web application. The `url-pattern` element contains the URL pattern of the mapping and must follow the rules specified in Section 11.2 of the Servlet API Specification.

Example

The following is an example of the `servlet-mapping` element of the deployment descriptor:

```
<web-app>
    ...
    <servlet-mapping>
        <servlet-name>
            shoppingCart
        </servlet-name>
        <url-pattern>
            /commerce/shoppingCartServlet
        </url-pattern>
    </servlet-mapping>
    ...
</web-app>
```

login-config

The following is the DTD for the `login-config` element of the deployment descriptor:

```
<!ELEMENT login-config (auth-method?, realm-name?, form-login-config?)>
<!ELEMENT auth-method (#PCDATA)>
<!ELEMENT realm-name (#PCDATA)>
<!ELEMENT form-login-config (form-login-page, form-error-page)>
<!ELEMENT form-login-page (#PCDATA)>
<!ELEMENT form-error-page (#PCDATA)>
```

The `login-config` element is used to configure the authentication method that should be used, the realm name that should be used for this application, and the attributes that are needed by the form-login mechanism. The `auth-method` element is used to configure the authentication mechanism for the Web application. As a prerequisite to gaining access to any Web resources that are protected by an authorization constraint, a user must be authenticated using the configured mechanism. Legal values for this element are `BASIC`, `DIGEST`, `FORM`, and `CLIENT-CERT`. The `realm-name` element specifies the realm name to use in HTTP BASIC authorization. The `form-login-config` element specifies the login and error pages that should be used in form-based login. If form-based authentication is not used, these elements are ignored. The `form-login-page` element defines the location in the Web app where the page that can be used for login is found. The path begins with a leading `/` and is interpreted relative to the root of the WAR. The `form-error-page` element defines the location in the Web app where the error page that is displayed when login is not successful is found. The path begins with a leading `/` and is interpreted relative to the root of the WAR.

Example

The following is an example of the `login-config` element of the deployment descriptor:

```
<web-app>
    ...
    <login-config>
      <auth-method>DIGEST</auth-method>
      <realm-name>DIGEST-Based Authentication</realm-name>
      <form-login-config>
        <form-login-page>/security/login.jsp</form-login-page>
        <form-error-page>/security/errors/error.html</form-error-page>
      </form-login-config>
    </login-config>
    ...
</web-app>
```

error-page

The following is the DTD for the `error-page` element of the deployment descriptor:

```
<!ELEMENT error-page ((error-code | exception-type), location)>
<!ELEMENT error-code (#PCDATA)>
<!ELEMENT exception-type (#PCDATA)>
<!ELEMENT location (#PCDATA)>
```

The `error-page` element contains a mapping between an error code or exception type and the path of a resource in the Web application. The `error-code` element contains an HTTP error code, `ex: 404`. The `exception-type` element contains a fully qualified class name of a Java exception type. The `location` element contains the location of the resource in the Web application, relative to the root of the Web application. The value of the location must have a leading `/`.

Example

The following is an example of the `error-page` element of the deployment descriptor:

```
<web-app>
    ...
    <error-page>
        <error-code>404</error-code>
        <location>/errors/NotFoundErrorPage</location>
    </error-page>

    <error-page>
        <exception-type>com.yourCompany.YourCustomException</exception-type>
        <location>/errors/CustomExceptionErrorPage</location>
    </error-page>
    ...
</web-app>
```

The **error-page** element is used to define both the **error-code** (for example, what page to return for a 404 error) and the **exception-type** (for example, what page to return for an exception such as the **ArithmeticException**).

security-role

The following is the DTD for the `security-role` element of the deployment descriptor:

```
<!ELEMENT security-role (description?, role-name)>
```

The `security-role` element contains the definition of a security role. The definition consists of an optional description of the security role and the security role name.

Example

The following is an example of the `security-role` element of the deployment descriptor:

```
<security-role>
<description>
    This role includes all customers who have been
    approved to access the partner Web site.
</description>
<role-name>partner</role-name>
</security-role>
```

security-constraint

The following is the DTD for the security-constraint element of the deployment descriptor:

```
<!ELEMENT security-constraint (display-name?, web-resource-collection+,
auth-constraint?, user-data-constraint?)>
<!ELEMENT web-resource-collection (web-resource-name, description?,
url-pattern*, http-method*)>
<!ELEMENT web-resource-name (#PCDATA)>
<!ELEMENT url-pattern (#PCDATA)>
<!ELEMENT http-method (#PCDATA)>
<!ELEMENT auth-constraint (description?, role-name*)>
```

The security-constraint element is used to associate security constraints with one or more Web resource collections. The web-resource-collection element is used to identify a subset of the resources and HTTP methods on the resources within a Web application to which a security constraint applies. If no HTTP methods are specified, the security constraint applies to all HTTP methods. The web-resource-name element contains the name of this Web resource collection. The auth-constraint element indicates the user roles that should be permitted access to this resource collection. The role name used here either must correspond to the role name of one of the security-role elements defined for this Web application or must be the specially reserved role name *, which is a compact syntax for indicating all roles in the Web application. If both * and role names appear, the container interprets this as all roles. If no roles are defined, no user is allowed access to the portion of the Web application described by the containing security-constraint element. The container matches role names based on case when determining access.

Example

The following is an example of the security-constraint element of the deployment descriptor:

```
<web-app>
    ...
    <security-constraint>
        <web-resource-collection>
            <web-resource-name>TrustedCustomerArea</web-resource-name>
            <url-pattern>/protected/customer/*</url-pattern>
        </web-resource-collection>
        <auth-constraint>
            <role-name>trustedCustomer</role-name>
        </auth-constraint>
    </security-constraint>
    ...
</web-app>
```

session-config

The following is the DTD for the `session-config` element of the deployment descriptor:

```
<!ELEMENT session-config (session-timeout?)>
<!ELEMENT session-timeout (#PCDATA)>
```

The `session-config` element defines the session parameters for this Web application. The `session-timeout` element defines the default session-timeout interval for all sessions created in this Web application. The specified timeout must be expressed in a whole number of minutes. If the timeout is `0` or less, the container ensures that the default behavior of sessions is never to time out.

Example

The following is an example of the `session-config` element of the deployment descriptor:

```
<web-app>
    ...
  <session-config>
    <session-timeout>30</session-timeout>
  </session-config>
    ...
</web-app>
```

taglib

The following is the DTD for the `taglib` element of the deployment descriptor:

```
<!ELEMENT taglib (taglib-uri, taglib-location)>
<!ELEMENT taglib-location (#PCDATA)>
<!ELEMENT taglib-uri (#PCDATA)>
```

The `taglib` element is used to describe a JSP tag library. The `taglib-location` element contains the location (as a resource relative to the root of the Web application) of the tag library description file for the tag library. The `taglib-uri` element describes a URI, relative to the location of the web.xml document, identifying a tag library used in the Web application. See Chapter 10, "Custom Tag Libraries," for more on tag libraries.

Example

The following is an example of the `taglib` element of the deployment descriptor:

```
<web-app>
    ...
<web-app>
    ...
    <taglib>
        <taglib-uri>
                http://www.yourcompany.com/yourTagLibrary
        </taglib-uri>
        <taglib-location>
           /WEB-INF/yourTagLibrary.tld
        </taglib-location>
    </taglib>
    ...
</web-app>
    ...
</web-app>
```

Practice Questions

Question 1

Consider the following code snippet:

```
    <taglib>
        <taglib-uri>
                http://www.yourcompany.com/
yourTagLibrary
        </taglib-uri>
        <taglib-location>
           /WEB-INF/yourTagLibrary.tld
        </taglib-location>
    </taglib>
```

Which two statements are true regarding this snippet? (Choose two.)

- ❑ A. You can instantiate the library class by pointing the browser to **www.yourcompany.com/yourTagLibrary**.
- ❑ B. The Web server instantiates the **yourTagLibrary** library upon starting.
- ❑ C. The **taglib-location** element contains the location of the tag library description file, not the tag-handler class.
- ❑ D. The URI must be unique.

Answers C and D are correct. Option A is wrong because the URI is simply a unique way to refer to the library; it is not an actual resource to get with a browser. The `taglib` element doesn't address when the container instantiates a library class.

Question 2

What is the correct declaration of a **security-role**?

❍ A.

```
<security-role>
        <description>Security role we are testing for
➥</description>
        <role-name>tomcat</role-name>
    </security-role>
```

❍ B.

```
<security-role>
        <description>Security role we are testing for
➥</description>
        <name>tomcat</name>
    </security-role>
```

❍ C.

```
<security>
        <description>Security role we are testing for
➥</description>
        <role-name>tomcat</role-name>
</security>
```

❍ D.

```
<security-role>
        <description>Security role we are testing for
➥</description>
        <role>tomcat</name>
</security-role>
```

Answer A is correct. This is the correct DTD for a `security-role`. All the other options have incorrect elements.

Question 3

Which directory is the location for myApp.jar?

❍ A. /WEB-INF/

❍ B. /WEB-INF/classes/

❍ C. /WEB-INF/lib/

❍ D. /

Answer C is correct. The JAR files go in the /WEB-INF/lib/ directory.

Question 4

Regarding the Web application directory structure, what two statements are true about the WEB-INF directory? (Choose two.)

- ❑ A. This is the root directory of the Web application.
- ❑ B. The WEB-INF directory is not part of the public document, so no files contained in this directory can be served directly to a client.
- ❑ C. All JSP and XHTML files are stored here.
- ❑ D. This directory contains all resources related to the application that are not in the document root of the application, including the Web application deployment descriptor.

Answers B and D are correct. Option A is wrong because the WEB-INF directory itself is placed in the application root directory. Option C is wrong because these JSP and XHTML files go in the root directory, not the WEB-INF directory. If you have a servlet in the classes directory, you can enter `http://hostname:port/servlet/ServletName` to serve that servlet, but if you place a servlet or any resource in the WEB-INF directory, there is no way to reach it from a browser.

Question 5

Which two of the following are elements of the Web application descriptor? (Choose two.)

- ❑ A. **servlet-type**
- ❑ B. **init-param**
- ❑ C. **listener-param**
- ❑ D. **error-type**

Answers B and D are correct. There is neither a `servlet-type` nor a `listener-param` element.

Question 6

Which two of the following are elements in the deployment descriptor that declare how to handle exceptions? (Choose two.)

- ❑ A. **error-page**
- ❑ B. **exception**
- ❑ C. **error-type**
- ❑ D. **exception-page**

Answers A and C are correct. The `error-page` element defines what resource the container should use for a given error, such as the 404 error condition. `error-type` handles Java exceptions such as `ArithmeticException`.

Question 7

How do you declare BASIC authentication for a given servlet?

❍ A.

```
<login>
    <auth-method>BASIC</auth-method>
    <realm-name>Authentication Servlet</realm-name>
</login>
```

❍ B.

```
<login-config>
    <method>BASIC</method>
        </login-config>
```

❍ C.

```
<security-config>
    <auth-method>BASIC</auth-method>
    <realm-name>Authentication Servlet</realm-name>
</security-config>
```

❍ D.

```
<login-config>
    <auth-method>BASIC</auth-method>
    <realm-name>Authentication Servlet</realm-name>
</login-config>
```

Answer D is correct. This option is the only correct syntax shown. The `login-config` element is used to configure the authentication method that should be used, the realm name that should be used for this application, and the attributes that are needed by the form-login mechanism.

Question 8

Which directory is the location for a Web application's class files?

❍ A. /WEB-INF/

❍ B. /WEB-INF/classes/

❍ C. /WEB-INF/lib/

❍ D. /

Answer B is correct. You place your servlets and utility classes in /WEB-INF/classes/.

Question 9

How do you declare initialization parameters for a servlet?

❍ A.

```
    <servlet>
        <servlet-name>Authentication03</servlet-name>
        <servlet-class>org.apache.tester.Authentication03
</servlet-class>
        <init-param>
              <param-name>debug</param-name>
              <param-value>0</param-value>
        </init-param>
    </servlet>
```

❍ B.

```
    <servlet>
        <servlet-name>Authentication03</servlet-name>
        <servlet-class>org.apache.tester.Authentication03
</servlet-class>
        <servlet-init-param>
              <param-name>debug</param-name>
              <param-value>0</param-value>
        </servlet-init-param>
    </servlet>
```

❍ C.

```
    <servlet>
        <name>Authentication03</name>
        <class>org.apache.tester.Authentication03</class>
        <servlet-init-param>
              <param-name>debug</param-name>
              <param-value>0</param-value>
        </servlet-init-param>
    </servlet>
```

❍ D.

```
    <servlet>
        <servlet-name>Authentication03</servlet-name>
        <servlet-class>org.apache.tester.Authentication03
</servlet-class>
        <servlet-init>
              <name>debug</name>
              <value>0</value>
        </servlet-init>
    </servlet>
```

Answer A is correct. The `init-param` element contains a name/value pair as an initialization parameter of the servlet. The other options are incorrect.

Question 10

Which two statements are true regarding the order in which the container loads servlets? (Choose two.)

- ❑ A. The container loads servlets in the order it finds them in /WEB-INF/.
- ❑ B. The container loads servlets in the order indicated by the **load-on-startup** element.
- ❑ C. If there is no **load-on-startup** element for a given servlet, there is no guarantee when it will be loaded.
- ❑ D. The container loads servlets in the order indicated by the **load-order** element.

Answers B and C are correct. The `load-on-startup` element indicates when a given servlet should be loaded (instantiated and have its `init()` method called) upon startup of the Web application.

Need to Know More?

 **XML element definition**—www.w3.org/TR/REC-xml#dt-element

 **W3Schools DTD tutorial**—www.w3schools.com/dtd/default.asp

 **W3Schools XML tutorial**—www.w3schools.com/xml/default.asp

 **The Java Servlet 2.3 Specification**—jcp.org/aboutJava/communityprocess/first/jsr053/index.html

 **Deploying Web applications**—java.sun.com/webservices/docs/ea2/tutorial/doc/WebApp.html

 **Configuring Tomcat servlets**—java.sun.com/docs/books/tutorial/servlets/servletrunner/webappdd.html

The Servlet Container

Terms you'll need to understand:

- ✓ Context
- ✓ Web app deployment descriptor
- ✓ Initialization parameters
- ✓ Context and attribute listener
- ✓ Distributable

Techniques you'll need to master:

- ✓ Retrieve servlet context-initialization parameters.
- ✓ Use a servlet context listener.
- ✓ Use a servlet context attribute listener.
- ✓ Use a session attribute listener.
- ✓ Distinguish the behavior of listeners in a distributable.

Context Architecture

You can see how Tomcat employs an architecture that implements Sun's specifications carefully. It is hard to understand context, though, if you don't know the overall architecture.

When you see the word *application* on the exam, think context. So, the application-initialization parameters are really those defined in the deployment descriptor with the **context-param** element and retrieved with **ServletContext.getInitParameters**.

A nice snapshot of the architecture is seen in Tomcat's primary configuration file server.xml (CATALINA_HOME\conf\server.xml). Other vendor containers also use configuration schemes, so if you aren't using Tomcat to study for the exam, look at your product's configuration files. The component elements shown in this chapter are nested corresponding to their parent-child relationships with each other. Descriptive comments are edits from comments in the sample server.xml file (ships with Tomcat). This file is not on the exam, but the architecture that Listing 3.1 defines helps give a big picture.

Listing 3.1 Sample Configuration Illustrates Architecture

```
<!--
A "Server" is a singleton element. It represents the
entire JVM. The server in turn may contain one or more "Service"
instances. The Server listens for a shutdown command
on the indicated port. Notice:  A "Server" is not
itself a "Container".
 -->
<Server port="8005" shutdown="SHUTDOWN" debug="0">

<!--
A "Service" is a collection of one or more "Connectors"
that share a single "Container" (and therefore the web
applications visible within that Container).  Normally,
that Container is an "Engine". Notice: A "Service" is
not itself a "Container".
-->

  <!-- Define the Tomcat Stand-Alone Service -->
  <Service name="Tomcat-Standalone">

<!-- A "Connector" represents an endpoint by which requests
are received and responses are returned.  Each Connector
passes requests on to the associated "Container" (normally
an Engine) for processing. By default, a non-SSL HTTP/1.1
Connector is established on port 8080.
```

(continued)

Listing 3.1 Sample Configuration Illustrates Architecture *(continued)*

```
    <!-- non-SSL HTTP/1.1 Connector on port 8080 -->
    <Connector className=
     "org.apache.catalina.connector.http.HttpConnector"
     port="8080" minProcessors="5" maxProcessors="75"
     enableLookups="true" redirectPort="8443"
     acceptCount="10" debug="0" connectionTimeout="60000"/>

<!-- You can also define an SSL HTTP/1.1 Connector on port
8443, an AJP 1.3 Connector on port 8009, a Proxied HTTP/1.1
Connector on port 8081, and non-SSL test connectors
on other ports such as 8082. -->


<!-- An Engine represents the entry point (within Catalina)
that processes every request.  The Engine implementation
for Tomcat stand alone analyzes the HTTP headers included
with the request, and passes them on to the appropriate
Host (virtual host). -->


      <!-- Define the default virtual host -->
      <Host name="localhost" debug="0" appBase="webapps"
       unpackWARs="true">


<!-- Logger shared by all Contexts related to this virtual
host.  By default (when using FileLogger), log files are
created in the "logs" directory relative to $CATALINA_HOME.
If you wish, you can specify a different directory with the
"directory" attribute.  Specify either a relative (to
$CATALINA_HOME) or absolute path to the desired directory.
-->
        <Logger
         className="org.apache.catalina.logger.FileLogger"
         directory="logs"  prefix="localhost_log."
         suffix=".txt"  timestamp="true"/>

<!-- Define properties for each web application such as
document roots in places other than the virtual host's
appBase directory.  -->

        <!-- Tomcat Examples Context -->
        <Context path="/examples" docBase="examples" debug="0"
                 reloadable="true">
          <Logger className="org.apache.catalina.logger.FileLogger"
                     prefix="localhost_examples_log." suffix=".txt"
           timestamp="true"/>
        </Context>
      </Host>
    </Engine>
  </Service>
```

The word *context* is really just a name that gets mapped to the document root of a Web application. For example, the context of the examples application is /examples. The request URL **http://localhost:8080/examples/welcome.html** retrieves the file welcome.html from CATALINA_HOME\webapps\examples\welcome.html.

Context-Initialization Parameters

The exam expects you to know the interface and methods to get context-initialization parameters. To understand these, remember that a Web application is a combination of JSP pages, servlets, tag libraries, JavaBeans, and other class files. The Java Virtual Machine creates a memory box for all of these called a `ServletContext` object that maintains information (context) about your Web application. You access the `ServletContext` for information about the application state. As the API states, the `ServletContext` grants you access to many types of information. You can get application-level initialization parameters. You can also set and get application attributes, as well as the major and minor version of the Servlet API that this servlet container supports. One very interesting capability refers to a `RequestDispatcher` object to forward requests to other application components within the server, or to include responses from certain components within the servlet and to log a message to the application log file. The `ServletContext` object enables you to set, get, and change application-level (not session-level) attributes and talk to the servlet container.

Context means application scope. The `getInitParameter` and `getInitParameterNames` methods retrieve context-wide, application-wide, or "Web application" parameters. The `getInitParameter` method returns a string containing the value of the parameter (you provide the name), or null if the parameter does not exist.

Some parameters have no information, so this method returns a string containing at least the servlet container name and version number. The `getInitParameterNames` method retrieves the names of the servlet's initialization parameters as an Enumeration of string objects. If there aren't any, it returns an empty Enumeration. Be careful; don't confuse this with session-wide attributes. The following snippet is how you might define a couple context-initialization parameters in the deployment descriptor:

```
<web-app>
    ...
    <context-param>
        <param-name>publisher</param-name>
        <param-value>QUE</param-value>
    </context-param>
    <context-param>
        <param-name>exam</param-name>
        <param-value>SCWCD</param-value>
    </context-param>
    ...
</web-app>
```

Refer to Chapter 2, "Deploying Web Applications," for more information about the deployment descriptor. Presently, realize that the `context-param` (with subelements `param-name`, `param-value`) declares the Web application's servlet context-initialization parameters for your application. You can access these parameters in your code using the `javax.servlet.ServletContext.getInitParameter()` and `javax.servlet.ServletContext.getInitParameterNames()` methods. Remember that the name specified in the `param-name` element must be unique in the Web application.

Given the previous deployment descriptor snippet, you would retrieve the two pairs of parameters with the following:

```
        // servlet configuration initialization parameters
        Enumeration params =
                getServletConfig().getInitParameterNames();
        while (params.hasMoreElements())
        {
            String param = (String) params.nextElement();
            String value =
                getServletConfig().getInitParameter(param);
            PrintWriter.println(param + "=" + value);
        }
//client would receive:
//publisher=QUE
//exam=SCWCD
```

Using Listeners

You also must know how to use the servlet context attribute listener and the session attribute listener. You can write code that responds to servlet events by defining listener objects. These objects have methods that the container invokes when life-cycle events occur. The event is triggered by a change in the application. For example, the session listener is invoked by the container when a session attribute changes. Also, this happens if an attribute in the application object changes and when the context or session is created and destroyed. You take advantage of this event model by defining a listener class that implements a listener interface. The container invokes the listener method and passes it information about that event. Notice that the methods in the `HttpSessionListener` interface are passed an `HttpSessionEvent`.

You can expect to see four listener interfaces on the exam. The following two tables describe them. Table 3.1 lists the context (Web application) events and the interface/method that your class must implement to respond to the event.

Table 3.1 Servlet Context Events

Event	Interface	Method
Servlet context has just been created	**javax.servlet.ServletContextListener**	**contextInitialized()**
Just before killing servlet context	**ServletContextListener**	**contextDestroyed()**
Adding an attribute	**javax.servlet. ServletContextAttributesListener**	**attributeAdded()**
Removing an attribute	**ServletContextAttributesListener**	**attributeRemoved()**
Replacing an attribute	**ServletContextAttributesListener**	**attributeReplaced()**

Table 3.2 lists the session events and the interface/method that your class must implement to respond to the event.

Table 3.2 Servlet Session Events

Event	Interface	Method
Session has just been created	**javax.servlet.http. HttpSessionListener**	**sessionCreated()**
Just before passivating session	**HttpSessionListener**	**sessionDestroyed()**
Adding an attribute	**javax.servlet.http. HttpSessionAttributesListener**	**attributeAdded()**
Removing an attribute	**HttpSessionAttributesListener**	**attributeRemoved()**
Replacing an attribute	**HttpSessionAttributesListener**	**attributeReplaced()**

The following is a short commentary on the methods mentioned previously:

- When a servlet is initialized or destroyed, you listen with `javax.servlet.ServletContextListener`:
  - `contextDestroyed(ServletContextEvent sce)`—Notification that the servlet context is about to be shut down
  - `contextInitialized(ServletContextEvent sce)`—Notification that the Web application is ready to process requests

- When a session is initialized or destroyed, you listen with `javax.servlet.http.HttpSessionListener`:
  - `sessionCreated(HttpSessionEvent se)`—Notification that a session was created
  - `sessionDestroyed(HttpSessionEvent se)`—Notification that a session became invalid or timed out
- When a context attribute is added, removed, or replaced you listen with `javax.servlet.ServletContextAttributeListener`:
  - `attributeAdded(ServletContextAttributeEvent scab)`—Notification that a new attribute was added to the servlet context
  - `attributeRemoved(ServletContextAttributeEvent scab)`—Notification that an existing attribute was removed from the servlet context
  - `attributeReplaced(ServletContextAttributeEvent scab)`—Notification that an attribute on the servlet context was replaced
- When a session attribute is added, removed, or replaced you listen with `HttpSessionAttributeListener`:
  - `attributeAdded(HttpSessionBindingEvent se)`—Notification that an attribute was added to a session
  - `attributeRemoved(HttpSessionBindingEvent se)`—Notification that an attribute was removed from a session
  - `attributeReplaced(HttpSessionBindingEvent se)`—Notification that an attribute was replaced in a session

Obvious similarities exist between context and session interfaces and methods. Use `javax.servlet.ServletContextAttributeListener` when a context attribute is added, removed, or replaced. On the other hand, use `HttpSessionAttributeListener` when the same is done in a session. Both of these are public interfaces (they extend `java.util.EventListener`) and have the same method names but different parameters.

Suppose that you wanted to mark the times when your Web application started and ended. The following code snippet shows how you could use the initialization and destruction events to do that:

```
public final class ContextListener
   implements ServletContextListener
{
   public void contextInitialized(
                              ServletContextEvent event)
   {
      ServletContext context = event.getServletContext();
      String IP = "209.83.3.142";
      context.setAttribute("DefaultAddress", IP);
   }

   public void contextDestroyed(ServletContextEvent event)
   {
      ServletContext context = event.getServletContext();
      String IP = context.getAttribute("DefaultAddress");
      //do something with IP
      //context.removeAttribute("DefaultAddress");
   }
}
```

The attribute `DefaultAddress` is set when the container initializes the application. Of course, you could dynamically get the IP. Then when the application quits, the same attribute is retrieved. When you have this IP, you could log it and then delete it, for example. For an excellent article that provides an overview of application life-cycle events, see "Servlet App Event Listeners," by Stephanie Fesler (April 12, 2001, `www.onjava.com/pub/a/onjava/2001/04/12/listeners.html`).

For a better example, Listing 3.2 demonstrates a simplified approach to how you could listen to an application and record what is going on.

Listing 3.2 Listening to Context and Session Events

```
package com.companyname.listening;

import java.io.*;
import java.util.Date;
import javax.servlet.*;
import javax.servlet.http.*;

/**
 * A custom listener for session events.
 * All events that occur are monitored.
 */

public class MySessionListener
    implements HttpSessionListener, HttpSessionAttributeListener
{
  private StringBuffer log = new StringBuffer("MySessionListener log\n");

  public void attributeAdded(HttpSessionBindingEvent event)
  {
     log.append(event.getName() + "," + event.getValue() +
                 "," + new Date() + "\n");
  }
```

(continued)

Listing 3.2 Listening to Context and Session Events *(continued)*

```
  public void attributeRemoved(HttpSessionBindingEvent event)
  {
     log.append(event.getName() + "," + event.getValue() +
                "," + new Date() + "\n");
  }

  public void attributeReplaced(HttpSessionBindingEvent event)
  {
     log.append(event.getName() + "," + event.getValue() +
                "," + new Date() + "\n");
  }

  public void sessionCreated(HttpSessionEvent event)
  {
     log.append("sessionCreated: " + new Date() + "\n");
  }

  public void sessionDestroyed(HttpSessionEvent event)
  {
     HttpSession session = event.getSession();
     if (session!=null)
     {
       log.append("Session Id:" + session.getId());
       log.append("Current Time: " + new Date());
       log.append("Created Time: " +
                  session.getCreationTime());
       log.append("Last Accessed: " +
                  session.getLastAccessedTime());
     }

     //permanently record the events; something like:
     //myLogger.record( log.toString() );
  }
}
```

The listener architecture in servlets is based on the event model. The container automatically calls certain methods when an event occurs. For example, the container calls **attributeRemoved** in a servlet that implements **HttpSessionAttributeListener** when an attribute is removed from a session object.

Before you can listen to events, you must configure your Web application to have an event listener. Most containers have default listeners already configured, so most likely you don't have to change the configuration. However, you should understand the steps involved. You would edit the web.xml (located in the WEB-INF) deployment descriptor of the Web application for which you are creating an event listener; you would add the `<listener>` element. Among containers, the required order of top-level elements varies. I recommend placing the `<listener>` element directly after the `<filter>`

and `<filter-mapping>` elements and before the `<servlet>` element. You can specify many listeners, and usually the container invokes the event listeners in the order in which they appear in the deployment descriptor. Conversely, most containers invoke these events in the reverse order during shutdown. The following snippet is an example of two listener declarations:

```
<listener>
  <listener-class>myContextListener</listener-class>
</listener>
<listener>
  <listener-class>
        mySessionAttributeListener
  </listener-class>
</listener>
```

Remember that the `listener` element indicates the deployment properties for a Web application listener bean. The `listener-class` element declares that a class in the application must be registered as a Web application listener bean. The value is the fully qualified class name of the listener class.

Context and Attributes within a Distributable

The behavior of these listeners in a distributable is exactly the same as the behavior of the listeners discussed in the previous section, with one notable exception: Event notification of addition, removal, or replacement affects the listener for only that context. No other context, even in the same JVM, knows about the listener events. However, some vendors do provide cross-context event capabilities.

The deployment descriptor contains the configuration for a Web application. The `distributable` element, by its presence in a Web application deployment descriptor, indicates that a given Web application is programmed appropriately to be deployed into a distributed servlet container. It is the only indication within the descriptor that the application is distributable. The syntax for the `distributable` element is shown in the following snippet:

```
<web-app>
        <distributable />
</web-app>
```

When a Web application is marked as distributable, the servlet container may distribute the application to multiple JVMs. There are advantages for clustering, scalability, and failover. Because the context exists locally in the

JVM (where created), the `ServletContext object` doesn't share memory space with other JVMs. Therefore, to manually share information between contexts, you should store this information externally in a DB or an EJB. Notice that the session is scoped to the service handling requests. However, the context is scoped to the Web container's JVM. Be careful—events and sessions are not propagated to other containers automatically. That is how you should answer any test questions about distributed applications. Vendors are free to improve on this, but answer according to how it works by default.

Practice Questions

Question 1

Read the following code snippet:

```
<listener>
  <listener-class>myContextListener</listener-class>
</listener>
<listener>
  <listener-class>
        mySessionAttributeListener
  </listener-class>
</listener>
```

Which two statements are true regarding this snippet? (Choose two.)

- ❑ A. The container calls the appropriate methods, such as **attributeAdded** and **attributeRemoved**, in the classes specified in the **listener-class** element.
- ❑ B. The methods in the classes specified in the **listener-class** element call the **attributeAdded** and **attributeRemoved** methods.
- ❑ C. The methods such as **attributeAdded** and **attributeRemoved** are defined in the classes specified in the **listener-class** element.
- ❑ D. The **listener-class** element goes in server.xml.

Answers A and C are correct. The `listener-class` element declares that a class in the application must be registered as a Web application listener bean. The value is the fully qualified class name of the listener class. In these classes, you can add the `attributeAdded` and `attributeRemoved` methods.

Question 2

What is the correct declaration of a context parameter?

❍ A.

```
<context-param>
    <name>publisher</name>
    <value>QUE</value>
        </context-param>
```

❍ B.

```
<context_param>
    <param_name>publisher</param_name>
    <param_value>QUE</param_value>
        </context_param>
```

❍ C.

```
<context>
    <name>publisher</name>
    <value>QUE</value>
</context>
```

❍ D.

```
<context-param>
    <param-name>publisher</param-name>
    <param-value>QUE</param-value>
</context-param>
```

Answer D is correct. This is the correct way to declare a context parameter named `publisher` with a value of `QUE`. All the other options have incorrect elements.

Question 3

What parameter is passed to the **attributeAdded** method for a session attribute?

❍ A. **HttpSessionListenerEvent**

❍ B. **HttpSessionEventEvent**

❍ C. **HttpSessionBindingEvent**

❍ D. **HttpSessionAttributeEvent**

Answer C is correct. Only the `HttpSessionBindingEvent` object is passed to `attributeAdded` by the container when an attribute is added to a session.

Question 4

Regarding the Web application directory structure, what is the root directory?

- ❍ A. CATALINA_HOME\webapps\
- ❍ B. CATALINA_HOME\webapps\WEB-INF\
- ❍ C. CATALINA_HOME\WEB-INF\webapps\
- ❍ D. CATALINA_HOME\WEB-INF\

Answer A is correct. Option A is the root directory for the Web application also known as the context.

Question 5

Which two of the following are elements of the Web application descriptor? (Choose two.)

- ❑ A. **init-type**
- ❑ B. **init-param**
- ❑ C. **listener-class**
- ❑ D. **error-class**

Answers B and C are correct. There is neither an `init-type` element nor an `error-class` element.

Question 6

What interface do you implement if you want to use the **attributeAdded** method?

- ❍ A. **HttpSessionListener**
- ❍ B. **HttpSessionAttributeListener**
- ❍ C. **SessionAttributeListener**
- ❍ D. **SessionAttributeListener**

Answer B is correct. The `HttpSessionAttributeListener` interface enables you to override the `attributeAdded` method, which is called by the container when an attribute is added to a session. `HttpSessionListener` enables you to listen to the notification that a session is created or destroyed. The other two options are not valid interfaces.

Question 7

Given the **contextInitialized(ServletContextEvent event)** method, how do you get the context (assuming that the request object is properly assigned)?

❍ A.

```
ServletContext context = request.getServletContext();
```

❍ B.

```
ServletContext context = event.getServletContext();
```

❍ C.

```
ServletSession context = event.getContext();
```

❍ D.

```
ServletContext context = request.getSessionContext();
```

Answer B is correct. This option is the only correct syntax shown. The others have incorrect syntax.

Need to Know More?

Writing Web Application Deployment Descriptors—edocs.bea.com/wls/docs70/webapp/webappdeployment.html

The Java Servlet 2.3 Specification—jcp.org/aboutJava/communityprocess/first/jsr053/index.html

Deploying Web applications—java.sun.com/webservices/docs/ea2/tutorial/doc/WebApp.html

Configuring Tomcat Servlets—java.sun.com/docs/books/tutorial/servlets/servletrunner/webappdd.html

Tomcat—An Implementation of the Java Servlet 2.3 and JavaServer Pages 1.2 Specifications—http://jakarta.apache.org/tomcat/index.html

Assembling and Configuring Web Applications—edocs.bea.com/wls/docs70/webapp/index.html

4

Servlet Exceptions

Terms you'll need to understand:

- ✓ Exception
- ✓ **sendError()**
- ✓ **setStatus()**
- ✓ RequestDispatcher
- ✓ Logging
- ✓ Status codes
- ✓ Error codes

Techniques you'll need to master:

- ✓ Identify correctly constructed code for handling business logic exceptions.
- ✓ Match that code with correct statements about the code's exception handling.
- ✓ Be able to return an HTTP error using the **sendError** response method.
- ✓ Return an HTTP error using the **setStatus** method.
- ✓ Identify the configuration that the deployment descriptor uses to handle each exception.
- ✓ Understand how to use a RequestDispatcher to forward the request to an error page.
- ✓ Specify error handling declaratively in the deployment descriptor.

- ✓ Identify the method used to write a message to the Web app log.
- ✓ Be able to write a message and an exception to the Web app log.

Handling Server-Side Exceptions

Server-side exceptions are harder to handle because the "action" is happening far from the user. You must be aware of both the severity and the type of error to properly tell the client what went wrong. Just how damaging is the problem? Your error-handling logic needs to determine the most appropriate severity for a particular error.

A servlet can throw the following exceptions during processing of a request:

- `IOExceptions` and subclasses of `IOException`
- Runtime errors
- Runtime exceptions
- `ServletExceptions` and subclasses of `ServletException`

After processing a request, the server responds and returns an HTTP response message. Part of this message is a numeric status code, which the browser reads and reacts to. This status code is what you are setting when you use `sendError` and `setStatus` methods. For example, when a resource is not found, most containers are configured to return the status of `404` and a `NOT FOUND` page. Table 4.1 provides a list of the HTTP status codes (only the first digit is significant).

Table 4.1 Status Codes

Number	Type	Description
1XX	Informational	The request was received; the process is continuing.
2XX	Success	The action was successfully received, understood, and accepted.
3XX	Redirection	Further action must be taken to complete the request.
4XX	Client error	The request contains bad syntax or cannot be fulfilled.
5XX	Server error	The server failed to fulfill an apparently valid request.

Table 4.1 describes a five-part scheme for the status codes, but we will primarily be interested in the server error category (`5XX`) codes.

Internally, `sendError()` and `setStatus()` are closely related. In fact, they both set the error message to be displayed by the client and the status code used by the client. The default status code is `HttpServletResponse.SC_OK ="OK"`; however, there are a few dozen standard codes.

Table 4.2 provides a sample list of status codes. These codes are defined by the W3C. The constant names, quoted messages that get displayed in the browser, and code descriptions are a combination of the servlet specification and the container's implementation of that specification.

Table 4.2 HTTP Status Codes

Code	Constant	RFC	Message	Description
100	SC_CONTINUE	10.1.1	"Continue"	Client can continue.
200	SC_OK	10.2.1	"OK"	Request succeeded normally.
301	SC_MOVED_PERMANENTLY	10.3.2	"Moved Permanently"	Resource has permanently moved to a new location, and future references should use a new URI with their requests.
302	SC_MOVED_TEMPORARILY	10.3.3	"Moved Temporarily"	Resource has temporarily moved to another location, but future references should still use the original URI to access the resource.
404	SC_NOT_FOUND	10.4.5	"Not Found"	Requested resource is not available.
500	SC_INTERNAL_SERVER_ERROR	10.5.1	"Internal Server Error"	Error occurred inside the server that prevented it from fulfilling the request. This error represents many server problems, such as exceptions or perhaps a database hiccup.
503	SC_SERVICE_UNAVAILABLE	10.5.4	"Service Unavailable"	Server is temporarily over loaded and cannot handle the request.

Return an HTTP Error Using sendError

The `sendError` method sets the appropriate headers and content body for an error message to return to the client. You can use the optional `String` argument, which is added to the content body of the message.

The `sendError` method sends an error response to the client using the specified status. Using this method clears the buffer. The server creates an

HTML-formatted server error page. This error page contains either a default message or one that you provide as an argument. It also sets the content type to `text/html`, even if you changed this, but it leaves cookies and other headers unmodified.

Using this method commits the response (if not already committed) and terminates it. The message in the output stream added before calling the `sendError()` method is ignored.

If the response has already been committed, this method throws an **IllegalStateException**. When you use this method, consider the response committed and do not attempt to send anything else to the client. The same is true for **sendRedirect**. However, the **setStatus** method does not commit the response.

Servlets must catch all exceptions except those that are a subclass of `ServletException`, `IOException`, and `RuntimeException`. Of course, they don't catch runtime errors.

Remember the difference between an `Error` and an `Exception`: An `Error` is a subclass of `Throwable` that indicates serious problems that a reasonable application should not try to catch. Most such errors are abnormal conditions. Although the `ThreadDeath` error is a "normal" condition, it is also a subclass of `Error` because most applications should not try to catch it.

A method is not required to declare in its `throws` clause any subclasses of `Error` that might be thrown during the execution of the method but that were not caught; this is because these errors are abnormal conditions that should never occur. For example, `OutOfMemoryError` is thrown when the Java Virtual Machine cannot allocate an object because it is out of memory and no more memory could be made available by the garbage collector. An `Error` differs from an `Exception` because the class `Exception` and its subclasses are a form of `Throwable` indicating conditions that a reasonable application might want to catch. For example, the `ArithmeticException` exception is thrown when an exceptional arithmetic condition has occurred, such as an integer divided by zero.

Return an HTTP Error Using setStatus

The `setStatus` method sets the status code for a given response. Use this method instead of `sendError` when there is no exception or serious error (such as a `Forbidden` page). If a serious error has occurred, use the `sendError` method; otherwise use `setStatus`. As with the `sendError` method, using this method clears the buffer but leaves cookies and other headers unmodified.

The same status codes used for the `sendError` method can be used for the `setStatus` method. The primary difference is that the `sendError` prevents any further response to the client and throws an exception if you try. This is not so for `setStatus`. One point of confusion arises with the `setStatus` method: The specification says that the buffer is cleared when called. In other words, you should set this first before you send anything back to the client. However, I looked in Tomcat and did not observe the buffer being cleared. The following snippet:

```
out.println("pre setStatus message.");
response.setStatus(HttpServletResponse.SC_OK);
out.println("post setStatus message.");
```

produced this:

```
pre setStatus message.
post setStatus message.
```

Exception Handling in the Deployment Descriptor

The container matches the exception thrown with the list of `exception-type` elements. If there is a match, the container returns the resource defined by the `location` element. The following snippet is such a definition in the deployment descriptor:

```
<web-app>
   <error-page>
        <error-code>404</error-code>
        <location>/404.html</location>
   </error-page>
   <error-page>
        <exception-type>MyException</exception-type>
        <location>/myException.html</location>
   </error-page>
</web-app>
```

If the error is a status error—say, **404** for a "not found" error—the container returns the resource at **error-code/location**. If the error or exception is a runtime problem—say, an **IOException**—the container returns the resource at **error-type/location**. Generally, the **error-type** exceptions are more serious.

Write a Message to the Web App Log

By default, log files are created in the log's directory relative to the home directory of the Tomcat installation ($CATALINA_HOME). You can specify a different directory using either a relative path (to $CATALINA_HOME) or an absolute path, with the `directory` attribute in the server.xml file. Different containers handle this in various ways, but Tomcat creates two new files, named access and activity, every time you start the server.

The following snippet shows how you would save a message to the log file using `ServletContext`:

```
    Context context = request.getContext();
    ServletContext context = getServletContext();
    String logMessage = "Something is wrong!";
    context.log(logMessage);
//You can pass an exception object to the log method.
//  context.log(logMessage, new ServletException() );
```

Using a RequestDispatcher to Forward to an Error Page

You can pass the responsibility for responding to the client request to another resource by using the RequestDispatcher object's `forward()` method. For example, you could handle the login generically and then pass off the client request to the appropriate page, such as a new customer registration page if no orders from this user are found. Remember, if you have already accessed a `ServletOutputStream` or `PrintWriter` objects, you cannot use this method; it throws an `IllegalStateException`. If you have already started replying to the user, you must use the `include` method instead.

Notice that **forward()** "transfers" the request to another resource. It doesn't take any HTML from one resource to another; it is as if the user went directly to the resource being forwarded to. **include**, on the other hand, *does* insert the result of an include. For example, the include might be a servlet that returns database results and appends it in place. Some say this is an inline include.

The following code snippet is an example of using the RequestDispatcher to forward to an error page:

```
// get request parameters
String userid = request.getParameter("userid");
String password = request.getParameter("password");
String nextAttemptURL = "/login/LoginErrorServlet";
String successfulLogin = "/customer/welcome.jsp";
String path = "";
if ((from == null) || (password == null) ||
{
   path = nextAttemptURL;
   request.setAttibute("exception", new UserNotFoundException());
} else
{
   path = successfulLogin;
}
RequestDispatcher rd =
getServletContext()
.getRequestDispatcher(path);
rd.forward(request, response);
```

Why use RequestDispatcher to forward a request to another resource instead of using a `sendRedirect`? It prevents a round trip because an HTTP redirect requires sending a message to the client telling it to request a new URL. Forwarding the request to another resource is much more efficient than using `sendRedirect`. Another important consideration is how the dispatcher preserves the state of the request object; the HTTP redirect loses this state information. Also be aware that, internally, the `sendRedirect` is really this:

```
setStatus(SC_MOVED_TEMPORARILY);
setHeader("Location", newURL);
```

Practice Questions

Question 1

Given the following code snippet:

```
//request for http://localhost/examples/WEB-INF/web.xml
//request = The servlet request we are processing
//response = The servlet response we are creating

        String path = getRelativePath(request);

        if ((path.toUpperCase().startsWith
("/WEB-INF")) ||
            (path.toUpperCase().startsWith
("/META-INF"))) {
            response.sendError(HttpServletResponse.
SC_FORBIDDEN);
            return;
        }
```

Which two statements are true regarding this snippet? (Choose two.)

- ❑ A. An exception is thrown by **sendError**.
- ❑ B. It compiles and an error status is set in the header, but no HTML body is returned to the client.
- ❑ C. It compiles and an error status is set in the header, and an error message is returned to the client.
- ❑ D. WEB-INF is a forbidden directory. A client can't request a resource directly from it.

Answers C and D are correct. It compiles and returns an error message in the body of the response because WEB-INF is not accessible to clients. This directory doesn't contain any resources that can be requested directly.

Question 2

The **sendError()** method creates which two kinds of information? (Choose two.)

- ❑ A. Response footer
- ❑ B. Response header
- ❑ C. Response content body
- ❑ D. Message for Web app log

Answers B and C are correct. The `sendError()` method creates a response header and content body that are returned to the client. There is no response footer. The Web app log is written to with the `ServletContext` object.

Question 3

Which of the following is a correct **sendError()** call?

- ❍ A. **response.sendError(HttpServletResponse.SC_FORBIDDEN, "Sorry, restricted to geeks.");**
- ❍ B. **request.sendError(HttpServletResponse.SC_FORBIDDEN, "Sorry, restricted to geeks.");**
- ❍ C. **request.sendError(HttpServletResponse.SC_FORBIDDEN);**
- ❍ D. **response.sendError("Sorry, restricted to geeks.");**

Answer A is correct. This option is the only correct syntax. Notice that `sendError` is a method of the response object, not the request object.

Question 4

The Status-Code element is a three-digit integer code. The first digit of the Status-Code defines the class of response; the last two digits do not have categories, although they are defined in the standard. What code would you use to represent a severe error—say, an exception thrown in a servlet?

- ❍ A. **SC_INTERNAL_SERVER_ERROR**
- ❍ B. **SC_NO_CONTENT**
- ❍ C. **SC_GONE**
- ❍ D. **SC_BAD_REQUEST**

Answer A is correct. A `500` error is an internal server error. This usually means that an exception has been thrown. The other three options also represent a problem, but not as severe as a thrown exception.

Question 5

You need to terminate the request because the client's request has a flaw. What method should your servlet respond with?

- ❍ A. **addHeader(String name, String value)**
- ❍ B. **response.sendError(HttpServletResponse.SC_BAD_REQUEST)**
- ❍ C. **response.sendError("SC_BAD_REQUEST")**
- ❍ D. **response.setStatus("SC_BAD_REQUEST")**

Answer B is correct. This is the proper way to return an error message to the client regarding a poorly formed request. Option A is not appropriate for this action, and options C and D are not valid method calls.

Question 6

What two methods commit the response, effectively terminating it? (Choose two.)

- ❑ A. **setStatus()**
- ❑ B. **setHeader()**
- ❑ C. **sendRedirect()**
- ❑ D. **sendError()**

Answers C and D are correct. The `sendError()` and `sendRedirect()` methods commit the response. An attempt to send further response to the client will throw an error. The other options do not commit the response.

Question 7

In the deployment descriptor, which of the following snippets is the correct way to declare a given error page for the **ArithmeticException** exception?

❍ A.

```
<web-app>
   <error-page>
        <error-code>ArithmeticException</error-code>
        <location>/ArithmeticException.html</location>
   </error-page>
</web-app>
```

❍ B.

```
<web-app>
   <error-page>
        <error>ArithmeticException</error>
        <location>/ArithmeticException.html</location>
   </error-page>
</web-app>
```

❍ C.

```
<web-app>
   <error-page>
        <exception>ArithmeticException</exception>
        <location>/ArithmeticException.html</location>
   </error-page>
</web-app>
```

❍ D.

```
<web-app>
   <error-page>
        <error-code>404</error-code>
        <location>/404.html</location>
   </error-page>
   <error-page>
        <exception-type>MyException</exception-type>
        <location>/myException.html</location>
   </error-page>
</web-app>
```

Answer D is correct. This is the correct syntax that tells the container what page to return to the client upon throwing an `ArithmeticException`. Option A has correct syntax, but it expects an integer value such as `404`, not `ArithmeticException`. Options B and C have incorrect syntax.

Need to Know More?

 **Hypertext Transfer Protocol—HTTP/1.1**—ftp://ftp.isi.edu/in-notes/rfc2616.txt

 **jGuru's Servlet FAQ**—www.jguru.com/faq/Servlets

 **The Java Servlet 2.3 Specification**—http://jcp.org/aboutJava/communityprocess/first/jsr053/index.html

 **Sun's servlet tutorial**—java.sun.com/docs/books/tutorial/servlets/TOC.html

 **"Servlet Essentials," by Stefan Zeiger**—www.novocode.com/doc/servlet-essentials/index.html

Session Management

Terms you'll need to understand:

✓ Session
✓ Session ID
✓ Session timeout
✓ Servlet attribute
✓ Session events
✓ Listeners
✓ URL rewriting

Techniques you'll need to master:

✓ Retrieve a session object across multiple requests to the same servlet or different servlets within the same Web app.
✓ Store objects in a **session** object.
✓ Retrieve objects from a **session** object.
✓ Respond to the event when a particular object is added to a session.
✓ Respond to the event when a session is created and destroyed.
✓ Expunge a **session** object.
✓ Know when a **session** object will be invalidated.
✓ Understand URL rewriting.

Session Management Overview

This section of the exam focuses on how servlets create and manage sessions. The container stores state information locally on the server, which is where the session information actually goes. It also places an ID on the client (in a cookie or appended to the URL). The server tracks the user with this ID, associating it with the data stored on the server. How long does the container keep this information? How long does a session last? These two questions refer to session longevity; to answer them, you must understand the life-cycle events and user actions, such as a configurable timeout, a user exiting the browser, and client inactivity.

The exam requires familiarity with `session` objects within servlets. You must know how to retrieve a `session` object across multiple requests to the same servlet or different servlets within the same Web app. You can store and later retrieve objects from the `session` object. Also, you need to know how you can respond to triggers that fire upon a change to the `session` object state (such as adding an object to or removing an object from a session).

One likely type of question will be reading a scenario and answering a question about whether the session becomes invalid. Other questions will ask you about URL rewriting, which is a way to get around clients who turn off their cookies by passing the session identifier in the query string. When you do this, you are rewriting the URL to include the identifier.

The most common techniques to maintain state are listed here:

- Query string
- Cookies
- Hidden form fields
- Session and application variables
- Database or file

All these methods work, and each has its pros and cons. For example, using hidden form fields is very simple—and this technique works whether the user has cookies turned on or off. However, every page needs a form with hidden form fields where you keep the state information. This gets ugly. Worse, you can't store objects this way—only text and numbers. A very nice snapshot of these five techniques is provided by Microsoft at `http://support.microsoft.com/default.aspx?scid=KB;EN-US;Q175167`.

The best way to maintain state is to use sessions. The `session` objects and attributes are stored on the server. The client gets a session ID, and the server stores the actual data. The session ID uniquely identifies each user's session. At the beginning of a new session, the container generates the ID and stores it in the user's Web browser as a cookie. Storing the session ID on the client requires users to turn on their browser cookies. The session ID is actually stored in an in-memory cookie (Mozilla, IE, and many others do this with session IDs); you won't find it on the hard drive with the other cookies. Actually two types of browser cookies exist: One uses files, and the other is an in-memory cookie. Session IDs are stored in the latter.

Session Methods

The primary methods associated with sessions belong to the `HttpSession` interface. The `session` object enables you to manage sessions by looking at the date stamp of the last time the session was accessed, for example. You can also get the maximum time interval that the servlet container will keep this session open between client accesses. You can even find out whether the client knows about the session (to see if the client has or hasn't acknowledged receiving the session ID). Although several methods are available, the following are the methods most likely to be on the exam:

- `getAttribute(java.lang.String name)`—Returns an `Object` associated with the name that was stored in the `session` object.
- `getAttributeNames()`—Returns an `Enumeration` object that lists the names of the objects stored in the `session` object.
- `invalidate()`—Destroys a session. The session can't be referenced after this method has been called.
- `removeAttribute(java.lang.String name)`—Removes an attribute. It deletes it from the `session` object.
- `setAttribute(java.lang.String name, java.lang.Object value)`—Used to add objects to a session. If you add an object to a session that has the same name as another object previously added to that session, the final object replaces the previous one.

getValue, **getValueNames**, **removeValue**, and **putValue** are deprecated so don't study these. Instead use **getAttribute**, **getAttributeNames**, **removeAttribute** and **setAttribute** methods, respectively.

The following servlet snippet shows you some of the methods you must know for the exam:

```
HttpSession session = request.getSession(false);
//you can retrieve information about the session such as:
//Current Session Id = session.getId()
//Session Created Time = session.getCreationTime()
//but the exam requires attribute get/set familiarity:

Enumeration enum = session.getAttributeNames();
while (enum.hasMoreElements())
{
        String key = (String) enum.nextElement();
        Object val = session.getAttribute(key);
        out.println(val.toString());
}

//and:
String key = request.getParameter("key");
String value = request.getParameter("value");
session.setAttribute(key, value);
String value = (String)session.getAttribute(key);

//You can add any object to a session:
Double account = new Double(1000);
session.setAttribute("Account", account);
Double account = (Double) session.getAttribute("Account");
//you are not likely to set-get the same session variable
//in the same servlet. This is just an example.
```

Be careful about Sun's language. The exam will use the word *expunge*, so you might see a question about expunging a **session** object. You can do this by calling the **invalidate** method. This method invalidates this session and then unbinds any objects bound to it.

Event Listeners

JDK 1.1 introduced a new event-handling paradigm for Java, allowing the generation and handling of AWT events. These events include a delegation event model, including events such as `ActionEvent`, `AdjustmentEvent`, and `FocusEvent`. Similar functionality exists in version 2.3 of the servlets specification. Four interfaces and several methods comprise the primary event-related methods that you need to know for the exam.

We will first look at how objects bound to a session can listen to container events, notifying them that sessions will be passivated and that sessions will be activated. This interface is `HttpSessionActivationListener extends java.util.EventListener`. The methods are listed here:

- `sessionDidActivate(HttpSessionEvent se)`—Notification that the session has just been activated

- `sessionWillPassivate(HttpSessionEvent se)`—Notification that the session is about to be passivated

These two methods call the method by the same name in the listener when the session is created or destroyed.

The listener interface that allows an object to monitor changes to the attribute lists of sessions within a given Web application is `HttpSessionAttributeListener extends java.util.EventListener`. The methods that concern us here are as follows:

- `attributeAdded(HttpSessionBindingEvent se)`—Notification that an attribute has been added to a session
- `attributeRemoved(HttpSessionBindingEvent se)`—Notification that an attribute has been removed from a session
- `attributeReplaced(HttpSessionBindingEvent se)`—Notification that an attribute has been replaced in a session

You use these methods when monitoring attributes within a session. If you build a shopping cart, you'll no doubt use sessions. Although some big players such as Amazon have steered toward URL variables, session variables are still a valid way to go. This is a nice way to keep track of what the user has added to his cart so that when he requests his total, you can easily provide it.

The last group of listeners is concerned with binding and unbinding to a session. This event listener notifies an object when it is bound to or unbound from a session. The interface `HttpSessionBindingListener` extends `java.util.EventListener`. This is triggered when a servlet is coded to explicitly unbind an attribute from a session because a session has been invalidated or because a session has timed out. The methods that concern us here are as follows:

- `valueBound(HttpSessionBindingEvent event)`—Notification to the object that it is being bound to a session, and identifies the session
- `valueUnbound(HttpSessionBindingEvent event)`—Notification to the object that it is being unbound from a session, and identifies the session

You might want to know when an object is added or removed from a session. For example, that shopping cart can store user selections, such as products chosen from your online store.

The following snippet creates a session, binds and unbinds attributes to it, and then destroys the session. These actions trigger the listeners discussed next.

```
// These activities trigger listener events
HttpSession session = request.getSession(true);
session.setAttribute("attributeName", "firstValue");
session.setAttribute("attributeName", " firstValue");
session.removeAttribute("attributeName");
session.invalidate();
```

When the previous lines of code execute, the container calls certain methods in classes that implement the listener interfaces, like so:

```
public class MySessionListener
    implements HttpSessionListener,
    HttpSessionAttributeListener
{
    public void attributeAdded(HttpSessionBindingEvent event)
    {
       //do something with event.getName() & event.getValue()
    }

    public void attributeRemoved(HttpSessionBindingEvent event) {
    {
       //do something with event.getName() & event.getValue()
    }

    public void attributeReplaced(HttpSessionBindingEvent event) {
    {
       //do something with event.getName() & event.getValue()
    }

    public void sessionCreated(HttpSessionEvent event) {
    {
       //do something with event.getName() & event.getValue()
    }

    public void sessionDestroyed(HttpSessionEvent event) {
    {
       //do something with event.getName() & event.getValue()
    }
}
```

When the line `request.getSession(true)` executes, the container searches for any class that implements the `HttpSessionListener` interface. The container then calls the `sessionCreated` method. Likewise, when attributes are added with `session.setAttribute`, the container calls `attributeAdded`, and so on.

Invalidating Sessions

The exam will ask you about what invalidates a session. It will present a scenario and ask you whether a `session` object will be invalidated. This can be tricky. For example, what happens to the session if a user abandons the computer for the night? In that case, the session timeout will invalidate it.

These six scenarios are common ways to invalidate a session:

- You call the `HttpSession.setMaxInactiveInterval(int secs)` method, explicitly setting how many minutes the session will last. This doesn't invalidate the session at the time of the call, but it does directly affect when a session will time out.
- The session automatically is invalid after a certain time of inactivity (most containers use a default of 20 or 30 minutes).
- When the user closes all browser windows, the client doesn't send a message to the server. There is no explicit cancellation signal when a client is no longer active. Instead, the session times out rather than directly triggering a session invalidation. This timeout is configurable. You can set it in the deployment descriptor (web.xml: `<web-app><session-config><session-timeout>30</session-timeout></session-config></web-app>`) or by calling `HttpSession.setMaxInactiveInterval(int secs)`. A negative value indicates the session should never time out.
- The session expires when it is explicitly invalidated by a servlet by calling `invalidate()`.
- The server is stopped or crashes. Notice that this event might not trigger session invalidation. A Web container that permits failover might persist the session and allow a backup Web container to take over when the original server fails.
- You set the default timeout in the web.xml file (`<web-app><session-config><session-timeout>`). (See Chapter 10, "Custom Tag Libraries," more information about the deployment descriptor file, web.xml.)

These four scenarios do not invalidate a session:

- The user browses to another Web site.
- The user jumps around on your Web site.
- In code, you query the `session` object, setting and getting attributes.
- The user leaves his computer for a while but requests another page later, and the time of inactivity is less than the timeout value.

Session Tracking Through a URL Rather Than a Cookie

As said earlier, the container associates session information stored on the server with a client through a session ID. Normally, this client identifies itself by sending this session ID along with the request. What happens if the client has cookies turned off or the client doesn't have the cookie feature (such as a Web-enabled cell phone)? The Servlet specification defines a way to pass the session ID in the query string by including it in every URL that is returned to the client.

You append the session ID in URLs by calling the `response` object's `encodeURL(URL)` (or `encodeRedirectURL()`) method on all URLs returned by a servlet. This method includes the session ID in the URL only if cookies are disabled; otherwise, it returns the URL unchanged. The following snippet demonstrates the `encodeURL` method that returns `myURL;jsessionid=2337L7E37975F305B07555859780E423?name=que&value=reader`:

```
HttpSession session = request.getSession(true);
out.print(response.encodeURL("myURL?name=que&value=reader"));
```

The **encodeURL** method does not use **jsessionid** if the client specifies in the request header that it will handle cookies because the session ID would then be returned as a cookie (for example, **Set-Cookie:JSESSIONID=12ae8%33dk22KKLdk39jKK9; path=/**). If the client's cookie feature is turned off, `encodeURL` appends **jsessionid** to the base path, as in **http://localhost:8080/bookstore1/cashier;jsessionid=f3s34zsefb2?sport=golf/**.

Internally, the container parses the URL and inserts the session ID between the path and the query; the pseudo code is something like this:

```
//parse URL into path and query components
String id = request.getSession().getId();
newURL = path + ";jsessionid=" + query + id;
```

Practice Questions

Question 1

What method deletes an object from a given session?

- ❍ A. **sessionRemoveAttribute**
- ❍ B. **removeAttribute**
- ❍ C. **httpSessionremoveAttribute**
- ❍ D. **deleteAttribute**

Answer B is correct. `removeAttribute(java.lang.String name)` removes an attribute and deletes it from the `session` object.

Question 2

How would you retrieve a collection of session attributes?

- ❍ A. **getAttributeCollection**
- ❍ B. **getSessionAttributes**
- ❍ C. **getAttributes**
- ❍ D. **getAttributeNames**

Answer D is correct. The `getAttributeNames` method returns an Enumeration object that lists the names of the objects stored in the session object.

Question 3

What interface do you implement to react to when a session is created?

- ❍ A. **HttpSessionActivationListener**
- ❍ B. **SessionActivationListener**
- ❍ C. **HttpSessionListener**
- ❍ D. **SessionListener**

Answer A is correct. `HttpSessionActivationListener` is the interface that you implement so that the container will notify your class when sessions are created or destroyed.

Question 4

What event method is called when a new attribute is created in a session object?

- ❍ A. **session.attributeAdded()**
- ❍ B. **attributeCreated**
- ❍ C. **session.newAttribute**
- ❍ D. **attributeAdded**

Answer D is correct. `attributeAdded(HttpSessionBindingEvent se)` is the notification that an attribute has been added to a session. It is called by the container, but it is a method in your class that implements the `HttpSessionAttributeListener` interface.

Question 5

What two scenarios will result in the container invalidating the session of a given user? (Choose two.)

- ❑ A. The user closes all browser windows.
- ❑ B. The user deletes cookies from the disk.
- ❑ C. The user browses to another Web site.
- ❑ D. The user leaves the computer overnight.

Answers A and D are correct. The session ID is stored by the browser as an in-memory cookie. If the user closes all the browsers, that ID is lost and the session becomes invalid. The session will time out overnight (unless you change the default configuration to an unusually long limit value).

Question 6

If cookies are turned off on the client, what two ways can you continue to return a session ID? (Choose two.)

- ❑ A. **encodeURL()**
- ❑ B. **response.getSessionId()**
- ❑ C. **encodeRedirectURL()**
- ❑ D. **sessionRedirectURL()**

Answers B and C are correct. The session ID is stored by the browser as an in-memory cookie. If the cookies are turned off, you must store the session ID in the URL. The URL-rewriting mechanism keeps track of a given session ID with the `jsessionid` parameter added to the query string, as in `www.mycompany.com;jsessionid=37979547975F305B07555859780E423?name=que&value=reader`.

Question 7

What two ways are used to store the session ID? (Choose two.)

- ❑ A. Hidden form field
- ❑ B. In-memory cookie
- ❑ C. URL
- ❑ D. File

Answers B and C are correct. The session ID is stored by the browser as an in-memory cookie. If cookies are turned off, you must store the ID in the URL.

Question 8

How do you get the session Id?

- ❍ A. **request.getSession().getId()**
- ❍ B. **request.getSessionId()**
- ❍ C. **ServletConfig().getSessionID()**
- ❍ D. **ServletContext.getSessionId()**

Answer A is correct. The `request` object returns the `session` object with `getSession()`. Then the `session` object returns the ID with `getId()`. All other options are invalid.

Need to Know More?

"Session Tracking," tutorial by Sun—http://java.sun.com/docs/books/tutorial/servlets/client-state/session-tracking.html

The Java Servlet 2.3 Specification—http://jcp.org/aboutJava/communityprocess/first/jsr053/index.html

Java Developer Journal's "Servlet Session Display," cool session code example—www.sys-con.com/java/source.cfm?id=760

jGuru's servlet session FAQs—www.jguru.com/faq/subtopic.jsp?topicID=52021

"Take Control of the Servlet Environment, Part 2," a nice workaround to session limitations in Web farm, by Thomas E. Davis and Craig Walker—www.javaworld.com/javaworld/jw-12-2000/jw-1221-servlets.html

Sun's J2EE API—http://java.sun.com/j2ee/sdk_1.3/techdocs/api/index.html

Web Application Security

Terms you'll need to understand:

- ✓ Authentication
- ✓ Authorization
- ✓ Data integrity
- ✓ Auditing
- ✓ Malicious code
- ✓ Web site attacks
- ✓ Security constraint
- ✓ Login configuration
- ✓ Security role

Techniques you'll need to master:

- ✓ Define authentication.
- ✓ Identify BASIC, DIGEST, FORM, and CLIENT-CERT authentication types.
- ✓ Define data integrity.
- ✓ Define auditing.
- ✓ Describe malicious code and Web site attacks.
- ✓ Identify the deployment descriptor element names, and their structure, that declare a security constraint, a Web resource, the login configuration, and a security role.

Web Application Security Overview

A Web application is fundamentally built to invite many people to access it. At least one of these people is a jerk or, worse, a malicious malcontent. That is not your fault. Still, you can't ignore this fact, so it is paramount that you design security into your Web site.

Fortunately, Sun has much experience in this area and designed security into Java from the beginning. They also added a minimum security feature set in the servlet specification. This area of the exam tests your familiarity with these features for Web applications.

You can protect a resource with a defined security constraint. You use this restraint to define the user roles that can access the protected resource. This is part of the specification, so compliant containers, including Tomcat, have this mechanism in place. Basically, a set of usernames, passwords, and their associated roles can be defined as part of your Web application.

You can use the Java Authentication and Authorization Service (JAAS) in your Web application. This is an excellent foundation upon which to build security into an application. However, you do not need to study JAAS for this exam. I expect future servlet specifications to integrate JAAS, a set of packages that enables services to authenticate and enforce access controls upon users. JAAS supports user-based authorization. It is for authentication of users to reliably and securely determine who is currently executing Java code, regardless of whether the code is running as an application, an applet, a bean, or a servlet; and for authorization of users to ensure that they have the access control rights (permissions) required to do the actions performed. If you want to know about this promising technology, see Sun's JAAS page at `java.sun.com/products/jaas/`.

Let's walk through the steps necessary to secure a directory under Tomcat, the reference implementation for servlets. We'll create a simple form-based secure directory. Some of the code is edited from a sample that ships with Tomcat. You need to work through this exercise even if it seems too simple because you will have to take these steps to understand how to implement security in a Web application.

1. Create the directory where you want to store resources that will be secured. For example, you can add the directory:

   ```
   TOMCAT_HOME\webapps\scwcd\jsp\que\secureArea
   ```

2. Open the deployment descriptor to the application to which you want to add security; here it is scwcd. Making sure that the elements are in the

right order, you can start your modifications by adding the `security-constraint` element, as shown here:

```
<security-constraint>
  <display-name>Que Security Constraint</display-name>
  <web-resource-collection>
     <web-resource-name>Secured Area</web-resource-name>
    <!-- context-relative URL(s) to be protected -->
     <url-pattern>/jsp/que/secureArea/*</url-pattern>
    <!-- Only those http methods are protected -->
    <http-method>DELETE</http-method>
     <http-method>GET</http-method>
     <http-method>POST</http-method>
    <http-method>PUT</http-method>
  </web-resource-collection>
  <auth-constraint>
     <!-- Anyone with one of the listed roles may access this area -->
    <role-name>queReader</role-name>
  </auth-constraint>
</security-constraint>
```

3. Add the `login-config` element to the deployment descriptor:

```
<login-config>
  <auth-method>FORM</auth-method>
  <realm-name>Form-Based Authentication for Que Area</realm-name>
  <form-login-config>
    <form-login-page>/jsp/que/secureArea/login.jsp</form-login-page>
    <form-error-page>/jsp/que/secureArea/error.jsp</form-error-page>
  </form-login-config>
</login-config>
```

4. Define the user, including name, password, and role in the TOMCAT_HOME\conf\tomcat-users.xml configuration file. Each vendor handles this differently, but in Tomcat you would add this element:

```
<tomcat-users>
  <user name="que" password="genesis" roles="queReader" />
</tomcat-users>
```

5. Define the default page that the container will use after a successful login using the `welcome-list` element:

```
<welcome-file-list>
        <welcome-file>welcome.jsp</welcome-file>
</welcome-file-list>
```

6. Write a login page and place it where it was defined in the deployment descriptor's `login-config` element. (See step 3.) The following is edited from a sample that ships with Tomcat:

```
<html>
<head>
<title>Que Login Page</title>
<body>
```

```
<form method="POST"
   action='<%= response.encodeURL("j_security_check") %>' >
  <table border="0" cellspacing="5">
    <tr>
      <th align="right">Username:</th>
      <td align="left"><input type="text"
                              name="j_username"></td>
    </tr>
    <tr>
      <th align="right">Password:</th>
      <td align="left"><input type="password"
                              name="j_password"></td>
    </tr>
    <tr>
      <td align="right"><input type="submit"
                               value="Log In"></td>
      <td align="left"><input type="reset"></td>
    </tr>
  </table>
</form>
</body>
</html>
```

7. Write an error page and place it where it was defined in the deployment descriptor's `login-config` element. (See step 3.)

```
<html>
<head>
<title>Que Secure Error Page</title>
</head>
<body bgcolor="white">
<p>Invalid Login Credentials</p>
<p>Try
  <a href='<%= response.encodeURL("login.jsp") %>'>
  again</a>.</p>
</body>
</html>
```

8. Write a JSP page that has a default name (such as index.jsp), and place it in the newly secured directory:

```
<%
  if (request.getParameter("logoff") != null) {
    session.invalidate();
    response.sendRedirect("welcome.jsp");
    return;
  }
%>
<html>
<head>
<title>Secured Area</title>
</head>
<body>
<p>
Logged in as: <b><%= request.getRemoteUser() %></b><br />
Session ID: <b><%= session.getId() %></b><br /><br />
Your principal name:
 <b><%= request.getUserPrincipal().getName() %></b><br />
Your role: <b><%= request.getParameter("role") %></b><br />
```

```
Using form-based authentication, log off by clicking
<% String url = response
                .encodeURL("welcome.jsp?logoff=true"); %>
<a href='<%= url %>'>here</a>.
This will return you to the logon page.
</p>
</body>
</html>
```

You can define the default pages where the container will look in your Web application by defining them in the `welcome-file-list` element of the deployment descriptor:

```
<welcome-file-list>
       <welcome-file>welcome.jsp</welcome-file>
</welcome-file-list>
```

9. You'll need to stop and start the container so that it will recognize the changes in the deployment descriptor.

10. Surf to the URL, such as `http://localhost:8080/scwcd/jsp/que/secureArea/welcome.jsp`. If you configured the Web application correctly, the container will redirect this request to the login as defined in the deployment descriptor. You should see the screen shown in Figure 6.1.

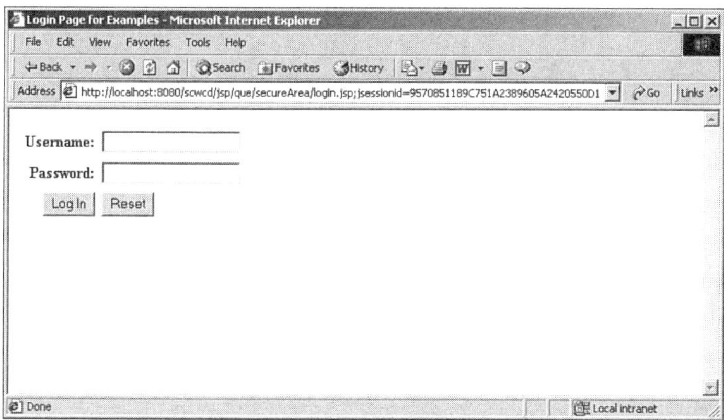

Figure 6.1 The login screen is presented to authenticate a user when **FORM** is specified in the auth-method deployment descriptor.

If you use the DIGEST authentication method, you should see the screen shown in Figure 6.2.

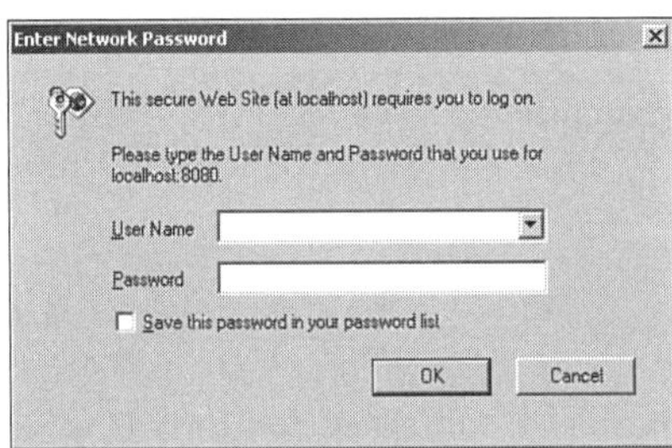

Figure 6.2 The login screen is presented to authenticate a user when **DIGEST** is specified in the **auth-method** deployment descriptor.

11. If you supplied the correct username and password (in this example, `que` and `reader`, respectively), you will arrive at the welcome.jsp page, which will look something like Figure 6.3.

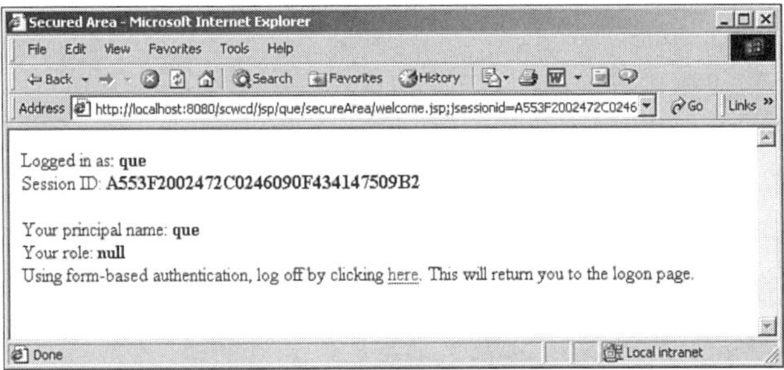

Figure 6.3 Welcome page, the default page for the application configured according to the previous steps, after a successful logon.

Deployment Descriptor Security Elements

As described in Chapter 2, "Deploying Web Applications," the deployment descriptor (web.xml) is your Web application's initialization file. This chapter reviews the security portion of this XML document. As you'll recall, the syntax for the web.xml file is as follows:

```
<!ELEMENT web-app (icon?, display-name?, description?, distributable?,
context-param*, filter*, filter-mapping*, listener*, servlet*,
servlet-mapping*, session-config?, mime-mapping*, welcome-file-list?,
error-page*, taglib*, resource-env-ref*, resource-ref*, security-
➥constraint*,
login-config?, security-role*, env-entry*, ejb-ref*,  ejb-local-ref*)>
```

The order of the deployment descriptors is important. You must have them in the right order or the application will throw an exception. The exam expects you to know the order, too—although there won't be many questions about this, there might be one.

The elements we will cover here are `security-constraint`, `login-config`, and `security-role`. They are listed in Table 6.1.

Table 6.1 Security Web App Elements

Element	DTD
security-constraint	<!ELEMENT security-constraint (display-name?, web-resource-collection+,auth-constraint?, user-data-constraint?)> <!ELEMENT auth-constraint (description?, role-name*)> <!ELEMENT web-resource-collection (web-resource-name, description?,url-pattern*, http-method*)> <!ELEMENT user-data-constraint (description?, transport-guarantee)>
login-config	<!ELEMENT login-config (auth-method?, realm-name?, form-login-config?)>
security-role	<!ELEMENT security-role (description?, role-name)>

To provide users with easier URLs, you can use the combination of servlet and servlet-mapping elements of the deployment descriptor. You can't have a servlet-mapping element without a servlet element because the servlet-mapping element refers to the name of a servlet specified in the preceding servlet element.

Listing 6.1 is a deployment descriptor example.

Listing 6.1 A Deployment Descriptor

```
<?xml version="1.0" encoding="ISO-8859-1"?>

<!DOCTYPE web-app
    PUBLIC "-//Sun Microsystems, Inc.//DTD Web Application 2.3//EN"
    "http://java.sun.com/j2ee/dtds/web-app_2_3.dtd">

<!-- Deployment Descriptor for a Web Application -->

<web-app>
    <security-constraint>
        <web-resource-collection>
            <web-resource-name>
                     General Protected Area
```

(continued)

Listing 6.1 A Deployment Descriptor *(continued)*

```
            </web-resource-name>
            <url-pattern>/protected/*</url-pattern>
        </web-resource-collection>
        <auth-constraint>
            <role-name>tomcat</role-name>
        </auth-constraint>
    </security-constraint>

    <login-config>
        <auth-method>FORM</auth-method>
        <realm-name>Authentication Servlet</realm-name>
    </login-config>

    <security-role>
        <description>Security role</description>
        <role-name>tomcat</role-name>
    </security-role>

</web-app>
```

Listing 6.1 is a valid deployment descriptor that includes only the security elements discussed in this chapter. Notice the order of the elements. You must comply with the DTD regarding the order, or the container won't work properly. For example, if you list the `security-role` element before the `login-config` element, Tomcat will report an error. The following elements are abbreviated from Chapter 2.

servlet

The following is the DTD for using the security portions of the `servlet` element:

```
<!ELEMENT servlet (icon?, servlet-name, display-name?, description?,
➥(servlet-class¦jsp-file), init-param*, load-on-startup?, run-as?,
➥security-role-ref*)>
<!ELEMENT security-role-ref (description?, role-name, role-link?)>
<!ELEMENT role-link (#PCDATA)>
<!ELEMENT role-name (#PCDATA)>
```

Within the `servlet` element, you can define the security for a servlet. The `security-role-ref` element contains the declaration of a security role. This element associates the name defined by `security-role` element to a servlet. The `role-link` element is a reference to a defined security role and must contain the name of one of the security roles defined in the `security-role` elements.

Example

The following is an example of using the `security-role-ref` element:

```
<web-app>
    ...
    <servlet>
        <servlet-name>
            customer
        </servlet-name>
        <servlet-class>
            Customer
        </servlet-class>
        <run-as>
            <description>Security for customer</description>
            <role-name>customer</role-name>
        </run-as>
    </servlet>
    ...
</web-app>
```

login-config

The following exemplifies the DTD for the `login-config` element:

```
<!ELEMENT login-config (auth-method?, realm-name?, form-login-config?)>
<!ELEMENT auth-method (#PCDATA)>
<!ELEMENT realm-name (#PCDATA)>
<!ELEMENT form-login-config (form-login-page, form-error-page)>
<!ELEMENT form-login-page (#PCDATA)>
<!ELEMENT form-error-page (#PCDATA)>
```

The `login-config` element is key to the security configuration. Remember the `auth-method` element in the previous section "Web Application Security Overview"? This element is how you define the level of authentication for your Web application. This is how you determine BASIC, DIGEST, FORM, or CLIENT-CERT types of security. If you use FORM authentication, you will also need the `form-login-config` element to specify the login and error pages that should be used. If form-based authentication is not used, these elements are ignored. See the previous section, "Web Application Security Overview."

security-role

The following illustrates the DTD for the `security-role` element:

```
<!ELEMENT security-role (description?, role-name)>
```

The `security-role` element contains the definition of a security role. The definition consists of an optional description of the security role, and the security role name.

```
<security-role>
   <description>
      This security role defines paid customers.
```

```
    </description>
    <role-name>customer</role-name>
  </security-role>
```

security-constraint

The following shows the DTD for the `security-constraint` element:

```
<!ELEMENT security-constraint (display-name?, web-resource-collection+,
➥auth-constraint?, user-data-constraint?)>
<!ELEMENT web-resource-collection (web-resource-name, description?,
url-pattern*, http-method*)>
<!ELEMENT web-resource-name (#PCDATA)>
<!ELEMENT url-pattern (#PCDATA)>
<!ELEMENT http-method (#PCDATA)>
<!ELEMENT auth-constraint (description?, role-name*)>
```

The `security-constraint` element is used to associate security constraints with one or more Web resource collections. The `web-resource-collection` element is used to identify a subset of the resources and HTTP methods on those resources within a Web application to which a security constraint applies. A Web resource collection is a pattern of URLs that, when requested, is subject to the constraint.

The `auth-constraint` element indicates the user roles that should be permitted access to this resource collection. The `role-name` must be listed in the `security-role` element or must be the specially reserved role name `*`, which is a compact syntax for indicating all roles in the Web application. If no roles are defined, no user is allowed access to the portion of the Web application described by the containing `security-constraint`. The container matches role names case sensitively when determining access. See the example in the previous section "Web Application Security Overview."

Security Concepts

The security of Web applications is under assault. More than ever, we need to master the issues of authentication, authorization, data integrity, and more. Fortunately, security is one area that Sun focused on early in its development of Java. This early effort has paid off: Java is more inherently secure than most other languages. Web applications that use Java benefit, too.

For this area of the exam, you must understand a few definitions. The following list defines each of the items in the objective:

- **Authentication**—The means by which communicating entities prove to one another that they are acting on behalf of specific identities. This proves that you are really you.
- **Authorization**—Access control in which interactions with resources are limited to collections of users or programs for the purpose of enforcing integrity, confidentiality, or availability constraints. This proves that you have permission to use a given page.
- **Data integrity**—The means used to prove that information was not modified by a third party while in transit. This proves that the data received is exactly the data that was sent.
- **Auditing**—Maintaining a record of Web application activity. For example, you can log resource accesses including times, requester IP, and ID. This usually involves a log somewhere.
- **Malicious code**—Code that causes harm to your computer's software or hardware.
- **Web site attack**—An overt attempt to compromise your Web site. The most popular attack is the denial-of-service attack, in which the attacker floods the server with requests, reducing its capacity to service legitimate requests.

Many users out there break the rules—the misguided hacker, hell-bent cracker, nonmeek phreak, meddling script kiddie, or code loader. These derelicts sometimes cause enough reaction to do some good, but it is like the malcontent who pulled the fire alarm to prove he was right about that sloth fire department. The fire department became a little better for the practice, but that idiot still cost us plenty. There is no getting around it: You have to be good at security if you build a commercial Web application. One area that you must understand on the exam is how servlet containers handle authentication.

Authentication Types

The exam will mention a few authentication types, mainly BASIC, DIGEST, FORM, and CLIENT-CERT. Authentication is the mechanism that makes sure the user is really who he claims to be. It is how your Web application will identify the user.

The following list defines each of the authentication types required for the exam:

- **HTTP BASIC authentication**—Authentication based on a username and password. This is the authentication mechanism defined in the HTTP/1.0 specification. A Web server requests a Web client to authenticate the user. The Web client obtains the username and the password from the user and transmits them to the Web server. The Web server then authenticates the user. The Web server stores the usernames and passwords in a database. When a protected resource is accessed, the Web server requests a username and password pair. This pair is sent back to the server. The server checks these against its database. It is not a secure authentication protocol because the passwords are sent in simple base64 encoding. Notice that the usernames and passwords are normally stored in clear text in the database, another weakness of this approach. The advantage is how easy it is to set up.
- **HTTP DIGEST authentication**—The password is encrypted. As with HTTP BASIC authentication, HTTP DIGEST authentication authenticates a user based on a username and a password. The authentication is achieved by sending the username and password in an encrypted form. Using encryption improves security dramatically over the simple base64 encoding used by BASIC authentication. However, this authentication is not supported by very many browsers.
- **HTTPS CLIENT-CERT authentication**—End user authentication using HTTPS (HTTP over SSL). This mechanism uses public key encryption, which requires the user to possess a public key certificate (PKC). This is the highest level security of the four here.
- **FORM authentication**—Similar to BASIC, except that a form is used with predefined fields. These fields must be named `j_username` and `j_password`, respectively, and the form method and action must be named `POST` and `j_security_check`, respectively. See the steps outlined in the section "Web Application Security Overview," for an example that includes a form with these required items: 1) a form with the `method` attribute set to `POST` and the `action` attribute set to `j_security_check`, 2) a textbox with the `name` attribute set to `j_username`, and 3) a `password` field with the `name` attribute set to `j_password`.

BASIC and DIGEST authentication types use the base64 algorithm. See RFC 1521 section 5.2 for details about this. Because the details of base64 encoding are not on the exam, a quick note will suffice to explain what it is. This is a simple encoding and decoding algorithm. After data is encoded, it is about 33 percent larger than the unencoded data. A 65-character subset of US-ASCII is used (A = 0, …, Z = 25, a = 26, …, z = 51, 0 = 52, …, 9 = 61, + = 62, / = 63, and = is a pad; there are 64 bits altogether, hence its name). This encoding converts three 8-bit bytes into four 6-bit characters. There is no attempt to hide the information; it is only a change in alphabet.

The very best security, by far, is SSL, which uses RSA public key cryptography for security over the Internet. Each browser and container vendor implements the Secure Sockets Layer (SSL) protocol slightly differently, but almost all of them use RSA, so it is rock solid. Public key cryptography is the most reliable mechanism for authentication and encryption in the computer industry. Public key encryption is a technique that uses a pair of asymmetric keys for encryption and decryption. Its name comes from the fact that each pair of keys consists of a public key and a private key. As the name implies, the public key is distributed widely, while the private key is kept secret by the owner. The amazing trick is that data that is encrypted with the public key can be decrypted only with the private key—and the other way around works, too. That you have two keys that don't have to be traded (asymmetry) is the gem of it all.

Well, you don't have to know SSL details for the exam, but it is a fascinating study if you care to challenge yourself. One last if-you-were-wondering fun fact: You encrypt with the public key and decrypt with the private key to hide your information. But, if you want to authenticate the original author, you can reverse this process and encrypt with the private key and decrypt with the public key; only the owner of the private key can encrypt a message that the public key can decrypt. This reverse process is used in digital signatures.

Practice Questions

Question 1

Read the following code snippet:

```
<form method="POST" action="j_security_check">
        <input type="text" name="j_username">
        <input type="password" name="j_password">
</form>
```

Which statement is true regarding this snippet?

- ❍ A. This is used for BASIC authentication.
- ❍ B. This is not part of servlet security.
- ❍ C. This is used for form-based authentication.
- ❍ D. This is used for HTTP CLIENT-CERT authentication.

Answer C is correct. This is similar to BASIC authentication, except that a form is used with predefined fields. These fields must be named `j_username` and `j_password`, respectively, and the form method and action must be named `POST` and `j_security_check`, respectively.

Question 2

What is the correct declaration of a **security-role**?

❍ A.

```
<security-role>
        <description>Security role we are testing for
➥</description>
        <role-name>tomcat</role-name>
</security-role>
```

❍ B.

```
<security-role>
        <description>Security role we are testing for
➥</description>
        <name>tomcat</name>
</security-role>
```

❍ C.

```
<security>
        <description>Security role we are testing for
➥</description>
        <role-name>tomcat</role-name>
</security>
```

❍ D.

```
<security-role>
        <description>Security role we are testing for
➥</description>
        <role>tomcat</name>
</security-role>
```

Answer A is correct. This is the correct DTD for a `security-role`. All the other options have incorrect elements.

Question 3

Regarding the Web application directory structure, which statement is true about the security directory?

- ❍ A. This is where you place resources that you apply certain security restrictions upon.
- ❍ B. The WEB-INF directory is also referred to as the security directory when you use the deployment descriptor to define it as such.
- ❍ C. The security directory is a subdirectory of the WEB-INF directory.
- ❍ D. Security is defined in the deployment descriptor, not a security directory.

Answer D is correct. There is no security directory. You secure a directory by configuring the deployment descriptor and placing the secure resources at the correct path as configured.

Question 4

Which two of the following are elements of the Web Application Descriptor that declare some part of the security configuration?

- ❑ A. **security-role**
- ❑ B. **security-type**
- ❑ C. **security-param**
- ❑ D. **role-name**

Answers A and D are correct. The `security-role` element and its child element `role-name` are valid security elements. These are used to define security roles within a Web application.

Question 5

How do you declare DIGEST authentication for a given servlet?

❍ A.

```
<login>
    <auth-method>DIGEST</auth-method>
    <realm-name>Authentication Servlet
➥</realm-name>
</login>
```

❍ B.

```
<login-config>
    <method>DIGEST</method>
</login-config>
```

❍ C.

```
<security-config>
    <auth-method>DIGEST</auth-method>
    <realm-name>Authentication Servlet
➥</realm-name>
</security-config>
```

❍ D.

```
<login-config>
    <auth-method>DIGEST</auth-method>
    <realm-name>Authentication Servlet
➥</realm-name>
</login-config>
```

Answer D is correct. This option is the only correct syntax shown. The `login-config` element is used to configure the authentication method, the realm name for this application, and the attributes that are needed by the form login mechanism.

Question 6

How do you declare security parameters for a servlet?

❍ A.

```
    <servlet>
        <servlet-name>Authentication03
</servlet-name>
        <servlet-class>org.apache.tester.Authentication03
➥</servlet-class>
        <security-role>
            <role-name>alias</role-name>
            <role-link>tomcat</role-link>
        </security-role>
    </servlet>
```

❍ B.

```
    <servlet>
        <servlet-name>Authentication03</servlet-name>
        <servlet-class>org.apache.tester.Authentication03
➥</servlet-class>
        <security-role-ref>
            <role-name>alias</role-name>
        </security-role-ref>
    </servlet>
```

❍ C.

```
    <servlet>
        <name>Authentication03</name>
        <class>org.apache.tester.Authentication03</class>
        <security-role>
            <role-name>alias</role-name>
            <role-ref>tomcat</role-ref>
        </security-role>
             </servlet>
```

❍ D.

```
    <servlet>
        <servlet-name>Authentication03</servlet-name>
        <servlet-class>org.apache.tester.Authentication03
➥</servlet-class>
        <security-role-ref>
            <role-name>alias</role-name>
            <role-link>tomcat</role-link>
        </security-role-ref>
    </servlet>
```

Answer D is correct. The `security-role-ref` element contains the declaration of a security role assigned to a servlet. The other options have incorrect syntax.

Question 7

What is the action for an HTML form when you want to use FORM type authentication? (Fill in the blank.) ________________

`j_security_check` is the correct answer. This is how you use an HTML form for FORM type authentication. The other options mention other types of authentication that do not use the HTML form code shown.

Question 8

How would you specify which resource the container requests when a user first goes to a page secured by FORM authentication?

❍ A.

```
<form-login-config>
   <form-login-page>/jsp/que/secureArea/login.jsp
➥</form-login-page>
   <form-error-page>/jsp/que/secureArea/error.jsp
➥</form-error-page>
</form-login-config>
```

❍ B.

```
<form-login-config>
   <form-login-page>/jsp/que/secureArea/login.jsp
➥</form-login-page>
   <form-error-page>/jsp/que/secureArea/error.jsp
➥</form-error-page>
</form-login-config>
```

❍ C.

```
<form-login-config>
   <form-login-page>/jsp/que/secureArea/login.jsp
➥</form-login-page>
   <form-error-page>/jsp/que/secureArea/error.jsp
➥</form-error-page>
</form-login-config>
```

❍ D.

```
<form-login-config>
   <form-login-page>/jsp/que/secureArea/login.jsp
➥</form-login-page>
   <form-error-page>/jsp/que/secureArea/error.jsp
➥</form-error-page>
</form-login-config>
```

Answer A is correct. The `form-login-config` element contains the declaration of which resource to use when a user first enters a secure area. This points to a login form. This is not used with BASIC, DIGEST, or CLIENT-CERT types of authentication.

Need to Know More?

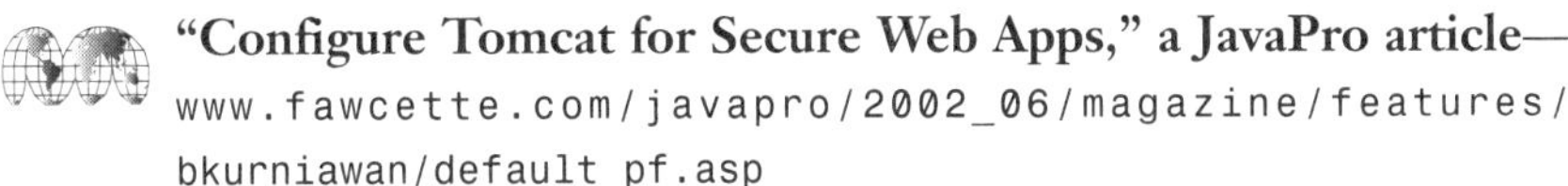

"Configure Tomcat for Secure Web Apps," a JavaPro article—www.fawcette.com/javapro/2002_06/magazine/features/bkurniawan/default_pf.asp

"Deploying Web Applications to Tomcat," an onJava article—www.onjava.com/pub/a/onjava/2001/04/19/tomcat.html

"Installing and Configuring Tomcat," an onJava article—www.onjava.com/pub/a/onjava/2001/03/29/tomcat.html

The Java Servlet 2.3 Specification—jcp.org/aboutJava/communityprocess/first/jsr053/index.html

"Deploying Web Applications"—java.sun.com/webservices/docs/ea2/tutorial/doc/WebApp.html

"Getting Started with Tomcat," a Sun tutorial—java.sun.com/webservices/docs/1.0/tutorial/doc/GettingStarted.html

Thread-Safe Servlets

Terms you'll need to understand:

- ✓ Threads
- ✓ Multithreads and single threads
- ✓ Thread-safe attribute scopes
- ✓ **SingleThreadModel**

Techniques you'll need to master:

- ✓ Identify which attribute scopes are thread-safe.
- ✓ Understand the differences between the multithreaded and single-threaded servlet models.
- ✓ Identify the interface used to declare that a servlet must use the single-threaded model.

This chapter provides an explanation of servlet threads and servlets that are considered thread-safe.

Servlet Threads

A thread is a single execution process, a single sequential flow of control within a given program. The container runs several threads at once. The way the server works begins with at least one thread listening to the port for HTTP requests. When a request arrives, something has to service that request. So, a new thread is spawned for it and each subsequent request. At the same time, another thread is listening to the port for the next incoming request. This is multithreading in action. Imagine how busy things get and how many threads are spawned when millions of users hit a popular Web site such as MSN, Amazon, and Google. Hopefully you'll be the one they call to help them improve their processing strategies—in the mean time, you need to understand how threads affect servlets for the exam.

A thread has a life cycle. When several are vying for the processor's resources, one of them gets top priority. How does the container prioritize threads? These are deeper questions that aren't required for the exam, but I encourage you to study them.

Sometimes several requests are made for the same servlet. The container can allow many threads to concurrently share access to a given servlet. For example, imagine a JavaBean that uses a file. This JavaBean is used by a servlet to write or read data from this file. What happens when two requests in that servlet try to write and read the file simultaneously? There must be a mechanism that allows threads to share a common resource in a synchronized way. This part of the exam concerns writing servlets that can handle multithreaded situations.

Normally, servlets implement a `service` method in a non–thread-safe manner. This is the default. There is a way to tag a servlet so that it can execute in a thread-safe manner, however. If you write a servlet that implements the `javax.servlet.SingleThreadModel` interface, the container is prevented from calling the servlet's `service` method concurrently from multiple threads. This servlet is said to be thread-safe. Notice that this interface is empty; it does not contain any methods. According to the specification, when implementing the `SingleThreadModel` interface "the servlet programmer is guaranteed that no two threads will concurrently execute the service method of that servlet." It only tags that servlet as not being thread-safe. The following is a snippet that illustrates how you would do this:

```
public class SingleThreadedServlet extends HttpServlet
        implements SingleThreadModel
{
   void doGet(HttpServletRequest req,
                          HttpServletResponse res)
        throws ServletException, IOException
   {
      // Never called concurrently from
      // HttpServlet's service method.
      // Process request:
   }
}
```

You can make a JSP page thread-safe by writing the code in such a way that there's no problem if two threads execute it simultaneously. If you don't write your code that way, you can make your JSPs thread-safe with the `page` directive, like this:

```
<%@ page isThreadSafe="false" %>
```

It sounds a little strange to say that you want to make the JSP thread-safe, but then you set **isThreadSafe** to **false**. Actually, making something thread-safe is to write its code so that two or more threads can execute it simultaneously.

When the container translates this directive, it implements the `SingleThreadModel` interface on the resultant servlet. Without it, the container loads a single instance of the servlet in memory allowing many threads (read requests) to access that one servlet. With this interface, many instances of the servlet are loaded and initialized, with the `service` method of each instance effectively synchronized. Some containers enable you to specify the number of instances instantiated for servlets that implement the `SingleThreadModel` interface.

Notice that although the servlet instance is thread-safe in the `SingleThreadModel`, the resources it accesses are not affected by this interface, so you'll need to be careful to synchronize access to other shared resources. Consider the `HttpSession` object. It is not single-threaded, so its contents are changed and updated in a multithreaded environment while your servlet is living in a single-threaded environment.

Worse, both the request (`HttpServletRequest`) and the response (`HttpServletResponse`) objects are not guaranteed to be thread-safe. Be very careful when you pass these from a `service` or `doXXX` method that implements the `SingleThreadedServlet` interface. These objects are passing from single-threaded to multithreaded situations; their behavior could cause surprises, so they should be used only in the scope of the request-handling thread.

Object Scope Affects Thread Safety

One thing that is highly likely to appear on the exam is thread safety. For example, is an instance variable thread-safe? What about the response object? The thread safety of objects is tricky at times, especially in an environment that pools servlets for performance gains. The following list defines each of the primary object scopes regarding their thread safety:

- **Local variables**—Local variables are thread-safe.
- **Instance variables**—Instance variables are not thread-safe because a single servlet instance can be accessed by multiple service requests simultaneously.
- **Class variables**—Class variables are not thread-safe because multiple servlet instances may access a class variable concurrently.
- **Request object**—Both request (`HttpServletRequest`) and response (`HttpServletResponse`) objects are not thread-safe.
- **Session attributes**—Session attributes are not thread-safe because sessions have Web application scope and may be accessed by multiple servlets simultaneously.
- **Context attributes**—Context attributes are not thread-safe because the context object has Web application scope and may be accessed by multiple servlets simultaneously.

Implementing the `SingleThreadModel` interface ensures that servlets handle only one request at a time. In other words, the container restricts access to that servlet in such a way that no two threads will execute concurrently in the servlet's service method. Normally, this is accomplished two ways. Some containers or configurations invoke the `service` method on the single instance of the servlet sequentially with each incoming request. In other setups, the container employs a servlet pool where the servlet engine dispatches a free servlet instance for each new request.

Although implementing the `SingleThreadModel` interface makes your servlet instance single-threaded (that is, each request gets its own copy because they don't share a servlet), you still have to worry about accessing resources (for example, the `session` object) outside that servlet. Also, besides needing to synchronize access to shared resources, using this interface mitigates high performance within a multithreaded environment. This probably won't be on the exam, but notice that the container is not required to synchronize event calls to listener classes; you have to manually handle this. Instance variables also can't be used as globals, in case you want them to be such.

Listing 7.1 illustrates a simple servlet that implements the `SingleThreadModel` interface.

Listing 7.1 Thread-Safe Servlet

```
/*
 * ThreadSafeServlet.java, v 1.0
 */

import java.io.IOException;
import java.io.PrintWriter;
import javax.servlet.*;
import javax.servlet.http.*;

/**
 * A simple implemetation of SingleThreadModel.
 * SCWCD Exam Objective 7.1 = thread-safety
 *
 * @author Reader@Que
 */

public class ThreadSafeServlet extends HttpServlet
    implements SingleThreadModel
{
    //class variables, not thread-safe:
    static int counterSum = 0;

    //instance variable, not thread-safe:
    //int counter = 0;

    //Class method, normally not thread-safe
    //synchronized makes it thread-safe
    synchronized static int getCounter()
    throws ServletException
    {
    return counterSum++;
    }

    public void doGet(HttpServletRequest req, HttpServletResponse res)
    throws ServletException, IOException
    {
        //local variables, thread-safe:

    res.setContentType("text/html");
    PrintWriter out = res.getWriter();
    out.println("<html>");
    out.println("<head>");
    out.println("<title>SingleThreadServlet</title>");
    out.println("</head>");
    out.println("<body>");
    out.println("<h1>SingleThreadServlet</h1>");
    out.println("counter: " + getCounter());
    out.println("</body>");
    out.println("</html>");
    }
}
```

Listing 7.1 shows an example of how you can implement the `SingleThreadModel` interface. The following snippet is the result of hitting this servlet several times:

```
<html>
<head>
<title>SingleThreadServlet</title>
</head>
<body>
<h1>SingleThreadServlet</h1>
counter: 23
</body>
</html>
```

In multithreaded situations, each servlet has only one instance. Normally, the server spawns a separate thread that executes the servlet's **service** method for each request, so you must synchronize access to instance variables and methods to make it thread-safe. On the other hand, single threading creates a pool of servlet instances. This ensures that no two threads execute concurrently in the servlet's **service** method, but you lose some performance. Therefore, you don't have to synchronize access to instance variables and methods. You still must synchronize objects outside the scope of the servlet (for example, with **HttpSession** and **ServletContext**) and static variables.

Practice Questions

Question 1

What is the correct declaration of a single-threaded servlet?

❍ A.

```
public class ThreadSafeServlet extends
SingleThreadModel
```

❍ B.

```
public class ThreadSafeServlet extends HttpServlet
    implements SingleThreadModel
```

❍ C.

```
public class ThreadSafeServlet extends HttpServlet
    implements SingleThread
```

❍ D.

```
public class ThreadSafeServlet
    implements ThreadSafeServlet
```

Answer B is correct. This is the correct way to implement a thread-safe servlet by implementing the `SingleThreadModel` interface. All the other options have incorrect syntax. Should you make your servlet thread-safe or single-threaded? The difference is very important and really needs to be considered. Making the whole servlet single-threaded is overkill in the vast majority of situations. Making the servlet single-threaded is the most extreme form of making it thread-safe.

Question 2

Which option includes elements that are thread-safe by default?

❍ A. Session and context attributes

❍ B. Instance and class variables

❍ C. Local variables

❍ D. Class variables

Answer C is correct. Local variables are the only inherently thread-safe variables. The others are not thread-safe. Instance variables become thread-safe if you implement the `SingleThreadModel` interface. The class variables, request object, session attributes, and context attributes are all thread-dangerous, even if you implement the `SingleThreadModel` interface: They exist outside the servlet even if you declare a local variable that refers to them.

Question 3

What is a thread?

- ❍ A. It is the complete processing of a request.
- ❍ B. It is the memory space taken by a variable.
- ❍ C. It is an execution process that occurs because of the **SingleThreadModel** object.
- ❍ D. It is a single execution process, a single sequential flow of control within a given program.

Answer D is correct. Options A and B are completely wrong. The `SingleThreadModel` interface does not spawn a thread, but it addresses how many threads can simultaneously access a servlet. Option D is correct as a thread is a single execution process, a single sequential flow of control within a given program.

Question 4

How can you make a JSP page thread-safe?

- ❍ A. **<%@ page SingleThreadModel="true" %>**
- ❍ B. **<%@ page isThreadSafe="false" %>**
- ❍ C. **<%@ page isThreadSafe="true" %>**
- ❍ D. **<%@ page SingleThreadModel="false" %>**

Answer B is correct. Use the `page` directive and set the `isThreadSafe` attribute to `false`. This tells the container that your servlet is not thread-safe so that when it translates your JSP page into a servlet, it implements the `SingleThreadModel` interface. However, making the whole page single-threaded is extreme. It is usually better to synchronize methods than to make the whole page single-threaded. Also, notice that if the page is not thread-safe, you are setting `isThreadSafe` to `false`, not `true`. It is easy to make this mistake.

Question 5

What can you do to make variables thread-safe in a servlet without using the **SingleThreadModel** interface?

- ❍ A. You use the **synchronized** keyword.
- ❍ B. You declare the servlet thread-safe in the deployment descriptor.
- ❍ C. You can't do this.
- ❍ D. You use the **threadSafe** keyword.

Answer A is correct. When multiple threads access the same variables, problems can easily occur. To avoid this thread-dangerous situation, you can block access to all but one. You do this by declaring a variable or method with the `synchronized` keyword. The Java platform then associates a lock with every object that has synchronized code.

Question 6

Which two statements are true about servlet thread safety? (Choose two.)

- ❑ A. Instance variables are thread-safe by default.
- ❑ B. Implementing the **SingleThreadModel** interface does not ensure that servlets handle only one request at a time.
- ❑ C. The request (**HttpServletRequest**) and response (**HttpServletResponse**) objects are not guaranteed to be thread-safe.
- ❑ D. Context attributes are not thread-safe because the context object has Web application scope and may be accessed by multiple servlets simultaneously.

Answers C and D are correct. Request (`HttpServletRequest`) and response (`HttpServletResponse`) objects and context attributes are not thread-safe. A context object has Web application scope and may be accessed by multiple servlets simultaneously.

Question 7

Consider the following code snippet:

```
public class SingleThreadedServlet extends HttpServlet
        implements SingleThreadModel
{
   void doGet(HttpServletRequest req,
                       HttpServletResponse res)
        throws ServletException, IOException
   {
      // Never called concurrently from
      // HttpServlet's service method.
      // Process request:
   }
}
```

Which two statements are true regarding this snippet? (Choose two.)

- ❑ A. Two threads can access the same **SingleThreadedServlet** instance at the same time.
- ❑ B. The servlet that implements the **SingleThreadModel** interface is thread-safe.
- ❑ C. The container can't allow two requests to access the **SingleThreadedServlet** instance at the same time.
- ❑ D. The **doGet** method is not thread-safe.

Answers B and C are correct. Implementing the `SingleThreadModel` interface guarantees that no two threads execute concurrently the `service` method of that servlet; it makes the `service` method and the subsequent invoking of the `doGet` method thread-safe. Be careful about making the whole program thread-safe because this kills performance. It is almost always better to make specific blocks or methods thread-safe by synchronizing them.

Need to Know More?

 **Sun tutorial on synchronizing threads**—java.sun.com/docs/books/tutorial/essential/threads/multithreaded.html

 **jGuru FAQ on synchronizing servlets**—www.jguru.com/faq/subtopic.jsp?topicID=52028

 **My favorite multithread example at Sun**—java.sun.com/docs/books/tutorial/essential/threads/

 **The Java Servlet 2.3 Specification**—jcp.org/aboutJava/communityprocess/first/jsr053/index.html

 **Deploying Web applications**—java.sun.com/webservices/docs/ea2/tutorial/doc/WebApp.html

8

JavaServer Pages (JSP)

Terms you'll need to understand:

- ✓ JavaServer Pages (JSP)
- ✓ Servlet
- ✓ Directive
- ✓ Expression
- ✓ Scriptlet
- ✓ Implicit object
- ✓ JSP container
- ✓ JSP page life cycle
- ✓ Tag library
- ✓ Web application

Techniques you'll need to master:

- ✓ Write and use JSP tags.
- ✓ Given a JSP tag type, use the equivalent XML-based tags.
- ✓ Use the **page** directive.
- ✓ Import a Java class into the JSP page.
- ✓ Use a session in a JSP page.
- ✓ Declare that a JSP page is or uses an error page.
- ✓ Understand the JSP page life cycle.
- ✓ Use JSP's implicit objects: **request**, **response**, **out**, **session**, **config**, **application**, **page**, **pageContext**, and **exception**.
- ✓ Write scriptlet code.

JavaServer Pages is Sun's technology for giving nonprogrammers a way to contribute to a Web application on the J2EE platform. It makes up a large section of the exam; this chapter explains everything you need to know for it.

JavaServer Pages Introduction

In a Web application, the container only invokes servlets. What does it do with JavaServer pages? It converts them into servlets. Later, you'll find more information about the JSP life cycle, but right now you should understand that JSP is a convenience format for Web page authors.

As noted throughout the book, vendors implement their containers differently. Here, I use Tomcat to show you how the standard container implements JSP technology. Normally, on Tomcat, you place JSP pages in the directory CATALINA_HOME\APPLICATION_HOME\ or in a subdirectory beneath this one.

Let's start with a simple example. Listing 8.1 demonstrates how you can use a JSP page to dynamically build HTML, get form field values, call a method, forward to another resource, set and get session attributes, and get the age of a session.

Listing 8.1 JSP Example Using Session and Request Objects

```
//localhost:8080/examples/jsp/que/examcram/login.jsp

<%@ page language="java" contentType="text/html" %>

<%
  String welcomePage = "welcome.jsp";
  String username = request.getParameter("username");
  String password = request.getParameter("password");
  String securityMessage = "Your Security Message";

  // session is how old?
  long now  = System.currentTimeMillis();
  long born  = session.getCreationTime();
  int ageInMinutes = (int)(now - born) / 60000;

  if( isValidLogin(username, password, ageInMinutes) )
  {
      session.setAttribute("username", username);
      session.setAttribute("password", password);
      %>
      <jsp:forward page="<%=welcomePage %>"/>
      <%
  } else
  {
    securityMessage = "Invalid Crendtials!";
  }
%>
```

(continued)

Listing 8.1 JSP Example Using Session and Request Objects *(continued)*

```
<%!
  public boolean isValidLogin(String username,
                String password,
                int ageInMinutes)
  {
    //check against DB or LDAP
    //for now, simple check
    if ((username == null || username.length() == 0) ||
      (password == null || password.length() == 0) ||
      (ageInMinutes > 60) )
    {
      return false;
    } else {
      return true;
    }
  }
%>

<html>
<head>
  <title>JSP Login Example</title>
</head>
<body>
  <h1>JSP Login Example</h1>

  <table valign="center" align="center" width="400"
        cellpadding="0" cellspacing="0" border="0">
    <tr>
      <td colspan="3" bgcolor="gray"> </td>
    </tr>
    <tr>
      <td rowspan="5" width="1"></td>
      <td width="400">
        <table cellpadding="0" cellspacing="0"
               border="0">
            <tr>
              <td></td>
              <td><b>User Login</b></td>
            </tr>
              <tr>
               </td>
                <td rowspan="5" width="1"></td>
              </tr>
              <tr>
                <td ><hr /></td>
              </tr>
              <tr>
                <td width="400">
                  <form action='login.jsp' method='post'>
                  <table width="400" cellpadding="0"
                        cellspacing="0" border="0">
            <tr>
              <td width="80" align="right" height="20">
                                  user name: </td>
              <td width="100" align="left">
                               <input type="text"
                               name="username" size="10" >
              </td>
```

(continued)

Listing 8.1 JSP Example Using Session and Request Objects *(continued)*

```
            </tr>
            <tr>
              <td width="80" align="right" height="20">
                                    password: </td>
              <td width="100" align="left">
                                <input type="password"
                                name="password" size="10" >
                                <input type="submit"
                                value="Login" />
              </td>
            </tr>
            <tr>
              <td colspan="4"></td>
            </tr>
        </table>
        </form>
       </td>
      </tr>
      <tr>
        <td ><hr /></td>
      </tr>
      <tr>
        <td colspan="3" align="center">
                       <i><%=securityMessage %></i>
        </td>
      </tr>
      <tr>
        <td colspan="3" bgcolor="gray"> </td>
      </tr>
     </table>
</body>
</html>

/**************************************/

// login posted from:
// localhost:8080/examples/jsp/que/examcram/login.jsp

<%@ page language="java" contentType="text/html" %>
<%
String welcomePage = "welcome.jsp";
String username = (String)session.getAttribute("username");
String password = (String)request.getAttribute("password");
%>

<html>
<head>
  <title>Successful Login</title>
</head>
<body>
  <h1>Successful Login</h1>
Welcome <%=username %>
</body>
</html>
```

Listing 8.1 shows you an example of a JSP-driven login process. Figure 8.1 illustrates what the page first looks like. Figure 8.2 shows you what the user sees upon successfully logging in.

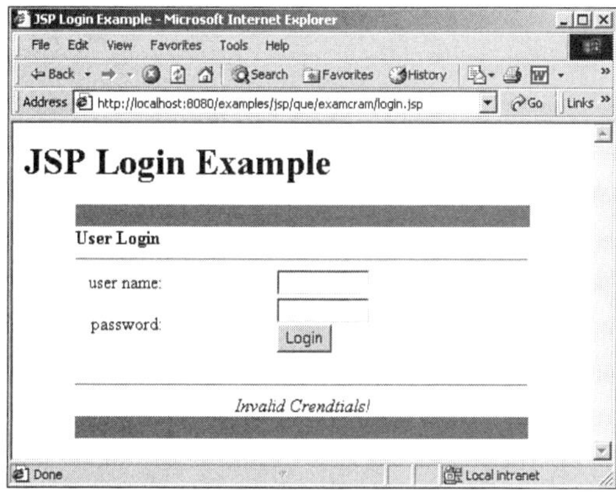

Figure 8.1 JSP login screen.

Figure 8.2 Successful login screen.

JavaServer Pages enables Web authors to easily develop and maintain dynamic Web pages. This technology enables you to create Web-based applications that are server and platform independent. An interface was created specifically for dynamic HTML content: the Common Gateway Interface, or CGI. CGI is a simple interface for running external programs and software on an HTML server. It was created by Robert Denny as part of the HTTPd Web server running on Windows 3.1. CGI scripts can be written in Perl and a wide variety of other languages.

CGI hit the World Wide Web in 1993. One of the first popular script languages to generate dynamic Web pages was Perl (the Practical Extraction and Report Language, an interpreted language optimized for handling text files). CGI suffered from significant scalability problems because each CGI request launches a new process on the server.

The next champion was Microsoft's Active Server Pages (ASP). Microsoft's server-side solution was a boon. However, it suffers from its proprietary nature because it works only with Microsoft IIS natively. Vendors have stepped in and created virtual environments for ASP so that it now can run on many platforms, but the performance isn't great. The most popular are PHP, ColdFusion (CFML), ASP (written in VBScript or JScript), and JSP (Java), all widely used server-side scripting languages. There are many more, but these are the most popular.

ASP (now ASP.NET) has the most developers. It is based on scripting languages, especially VBScript and JScript, which make it dynamic. With these languages you can instantiate server-side objects and build loops. ASP was originally tightly coupled with Windows Internet Information Server, Microsoft's Web server of choice. I started using ASP when it first came out, and I'm still using it; I'm currently building an intranet with it for a client.

Other vendors have entered the market as well. Of the current crop, ColdFusion is a strong alternative because it is easy to learn and, for many tasks, accomplishes in just hours what once took days. ColdFusion gives developers shortcuts by eliminating the need to create or destroy objects. When you put a CFML tag on a page, the ColdFusion server instantiates it. ColdFusion also takes care of the cleanup. However, it is hardly portable and the vendor traded away some power for simplicity.

One convenience to ASP, ColdFusion, and JSP is that you can edit the page at will, and the engine either interprets the new file on the fly (in ASP and ColdFusion) or figures out when to recompile (JSP into a servlet).

Servlets are the server-side kings currently, and that is good news to JSP fans. JavaServer Pages are harder to work with than ColdFusion—and even a little harder than ASP, although they're a lot easier than servlets. The trade-off here is power, portability, and scalability. Technically, whatever you can do in servlets can be done in JSP pages. However, the point in JSP is to focus on presentation, leaving complex processing to servlets, JavaBeans, and tag handlers. As you know, JSP pages and Java servlets run on the server (as opposed to an applet, which runs in the browser).

JSP pages can simply generate HTML or manage a complex Web application. The structure of a Web application is covered in Chapter 2, "Deploying Web Applications." Remember where the JSP pages go: in the Web application root directory or one of its subdirectories besides WEB-INF. The following shows you the location of two JSP pages in a Web application structure:

```
/login.html
welcome.jsp
```

```
jsp/security/login.jsp
/WEB-INF/web.xml
/WEB-INF/classes/ProcessOrder.class
```

The actual path to the login.jsp (assuming that the Web application is orders) would be TOMCAT_HOME\webapps\orders\jsp\security\login.jsp, called, for example, by `http://localhost:8080/orders/jsp/security/login.jsp` (replace `localhost:8080` with a real URL, such as `www.que.com`).

You can't place any JSP files (or any static file to be requested directly) in the WEB-INF directory or one of its subdirectories. This will likely be on the exam. JSP pages go in the application root, along with plain HTML files described with the forward slash alone (/).

JSP Life Cycle

Each page has a life cycle within the servlet engine. You need to understand each step of the cycle and know the order of the steps. The following are the elements of the JSP page life cycle in the correct sequence:

1. Translate page.
2. Compile JSP page.
3. Load class.
4. Create instance.
5. Call `jspInit`.
6. Call `_jspService`.
7. Call `jspDestroy`.

The exam will ask you about translating JSP code into servlets. Remember that scriptlets, expressions, directives, and declarations are all translated into servlet code and then compiled into a servlet class.

The JSP page sits idle until it is first requested. If there are any JSP errors (HTML errors won't be detected by the container), they will go unnoticed until it is first compiled. The servlet container parses the JSP, creates a servlet, runs the servlet, handles responding to the request, and manages servlet persistence. Table 8.1 offers a quick review of the steps in the JSP page life cycle that you need to know.

Table 8.1 JSP Page Life Cycle

JSP Process Step	Explanation
Translate page.	JSP: **<%=expression%>** Translated to: Servlet: **out.print(expression)**;
Compile page.	Compiles the servlet Java source code into the class file.
Load class.	Loads the servlet class upon first request.
Create instance.	Instantiates the servlet class.
Call **jspInit.**	Initializes the servlet instance by calling the **jspInit** method.
Call **_jspService**.	Invokes the **_jspService** method, passing a request and a response object.
Call **jspDestroy.**	If the container needs to remove the JSP page's servlet, it calls the **jspDestroy** method.

Notice that a JSP page is always converted to a servlet. The response for a JSP page is slow the first time it is requested because of translation and compilation. Afterward it is a servlet and loads just as fast. This life cycle also is repeated entirely when you change the JSP file because the container keeps track of file dates.

The container translates the various parts of a JSP page differently. For example, HTML (or `<jsp:text>template data</jsp:text>`) is simply passed through to the current output stream. All other text, such as scriptlets and XML-equivalent actions, is converted to Java.

JSP Syntax

Let's look at the syntax. Shown in Table 8.2 is a snapshot of JSP syntax that you are expected to know for the exam.

Table 8.2 JSP Syntax Snapshot

Element	Syntax	Example
HTML comment	**<!-- comment -->**	**<!-- HTML comments are passed through as is -->**
JSP comment	**<%-- comment --%>**	**<%-- JSP comments are not translated --%>**
page directive	**<%@ page [key]="[value]" %>**	**<%@ page import="com.myClasses.*" %>**

(continued)

Table 8.2 JSP Syntax Snapshot *(continued)*

Element	Syntax	Example
Declaration	**<%! Declaration %>**	**<%! String name = new String ("Devyn"); %>**
Expression	**<%= expression %>**	**<%= myProduct.getColor() %></b>**
Scriptlet	**<% code %>**	**<% int count = 10; String URL = "www.que.com"; %>**
Static include, parsed at compile time	**<%@ include file="myFile" %>**	**<%@ include file="loginCheck.jsp">**
Dynamic include, at request time and not parsed	**<jsp:include page="file" />**	**<jsp:include page="wel come.html" />**

The following is a template for JSP that includes examples of non-XML syntax:

```
<%--@ page
   [ language="java" ]
   [ extends="package.class" ]
   [ import="{package.class ¦ package.*}, ..." ]
   [ session="true¦false" ]
   [ buffer="none¦8kb¦sizekb" ]
   [ autoFlush="true¦false" ]
   [ isThreadSafe="true¦false" ]
   [ info="text" ]
   [ errorPage="relativeURL" ]
   [ contentType="mimeType [ ; charset=characterSet ]" ¦
     "text/html ; charset=ISO-8859-1" ]
   [ isErrorPage="true¦false" ]
   [ pageEncoding="characterSet ¦ ISO-8859-1" ]
--%>
<%@ page import="java.util.*, java.lang.*" %>

<%--! declaration; [ declaration; ]+ ... --%>
<%! int count = 0; %>

<%-- some HTML --%>
<html>
<head><title>A Comment Test</title></head>
<body>

<%--@ include file="relativeURL" --%>
<%@ include file="banner.jsp" %>

<%--= expression --%>
<%= count %>
```

```
<%-- code fragment --%>
<%
   String customer = request.getParameter("customer");
%>

<%-- implicit objects -----
request, response, out, session
config, application, page
pageContext, exception
------------------------ --%>
<%
   String customer = (String)session.getAttribute("customer");
%>

<%-- final HTML --%>
</body>
</html>
```

Directive

The directive affects the JSP page overall. The syntax is given here:

```
<%@ directive attribute="value" %>
```

These directives have page scope, so what you declare in a directive is available throughout the page. You don't nest a directive in a code block; it goes at the top of the page (some people place it at the bottom, but I don't like it there).

include Directive

The `include` directive is processed during translation. Other languages refer to this as a server-side include. The text that this directive gets is placed directly inline *before* compilation. The syntax is as follows:

```
<%@ include file="relativeURLspec" %>
```

It is good form to break your pages into several files. Notice that because the included text is translated before compilation, these includes don't degrade performance. You can use the XML equivalent, which has a very elegant feature: If the resource pointed to is another servlet or JSP, the container invokes the resource first and then uses the results. So, the advantage of using the `include` action over the directive is that the resource is called dynamically and is not compiled. That means you can change the resource without forcing a recompilation of the JSP page including it.

taglib Directive

The `taglib` directive syntax is shown here:

```
<%@ taglib uri="tagLibraryURI" prefix="tagPrefix" %>
```

Although JSP makes it easy to mix Java and HTML, it is architecturally suspect. One way to improve the situation is to collect functionality into a Bean (encapsulate) and expose a few methods to JSP. You can then compose a JSP page with HTML and XML. The XML elements are custom tags used in JSP by way of the tag library facility. Although this is more work initially, using tag libraries is a cleaner implementation that enables you to separate presentation from business logic.

page Directive

This directive is the most loaded of the three directives. Its nine attributes cover a lot of ground. The following is the `page` directive syntax:

```
<%@ page
   [ language="java" ]
   [ extends="package.class" ]
   [ import="{package.class ¦ package.*}, ..." ]
   [ session="true¦false" ]
   [ buffer="none¦8kb¦sizekb" ]
   [ autoFlush="true¦false" ]
   [ isThreadSafe="true¦false" ]
   [ info="text" ]
   [ errorPage="relativeURL" ]
   [ contentType="mimeType [ ; charset=characterSet ]" ¦
     "text/html ; charset=ISO-8859-1" ]
   [ isErrorPage="true¦false" ]
   [ pageEncoding="characterSet ¦ ISO-8859-1" ]
%>
```

Importing Classes

You import classes for the same reason you do elsewhere in Java: to reuse functionality already available in other classes rather than duplicating code. Notice that imports are cumulative. The following is an example of how you would import several packages:

```
<%@ page import="com.myCompany.*,java.util.*" %>
```

The classes are specified in a comma-separated list. As with an import declaration in the Java programming language, the value is either a fully qualified type name or a package name followed by the `".*"` string, denoting all the public types declared in that package.

Declare a Session

You can set this attribute to `true` (default) or `false` like this:

```
<%@ page session="true" %>
```

If this attribute is set to `true` or is absent, the translation step instantiates an implicit variable named `session` (`javax.servlet.http.HttpSession`) that you can refer to in the current page or another within the same session. You might set it to `false` to reduce overhead if you don't need to use the `session` object.

Declare an Error Page

The `errorPage` attribute specifies a page that should be called when an uncaught exception occurs within the current page. It works only with throwable objects (exceptions) and won't help if a fatal error occurs (if the server crashes). The syntax is as follows:

```
<%@ page errorPage="loginError.jsp" %>
```

Notice that the error page has access to the implicit exception object, which gives access to information about the exception.

language

This attribute defines the scripting language. The syntax is shown here:

```
<%@ page language="java" %>
```

This declaration applies to all content that is translated, compiled, and included during the processing of a request for this JSP page. This attribute is largely for forward compatibility because JSP 1.2 allows only Java; perhaps a future version will allow other languages. Sun also is trying to model JSP so that many features are not language specific.

The source code used during the translation is required to be Java. However, nothing prevents a vendor from using another language that somehow complies with the JSP model. An alternative scripting language must support the Java Runtime Environment (JRE) and expose the Java technology object model to the script environment, especially implicit variables, JavaBeans component properties, and public methods. Currently, it is a fatal translation error for a directive with a non-Java language attribute to appear after the first scripting element has been encountered.

extends

The `extends` attribute works just like it does in regular Java. It enables you to inherit a class by naming the superclass of the class created by runtime compiling this JSP page. It looks like this:

```
<%@ page extends="package.class" %>
```

Be careful: It enables the developer to circumvent the JSP engine.

buffer

This attribute defines memory size for the initial buffer. This `buffer` is for the `out` object, which is a `JspWriter` type of object. The syntax is shown here:

```
<%@ page buffer="16kb" %>
```

The contents of the buffer are dumped to the output stream when the buffer becomes full. Setting it to `none` makes the container send all output directly to the output stream as the request is processed; hence, no buffer. The default size is 8KB.

autoFlush

A `true` setting (default) means that the buffered output should be flushed automatically when the buffer is full. If this is set to `false`, an exception is raised when the buffer overflows. Be aware that you cannot set `autoFlush` to `false` when the buffer is set to `none`. This, too, throws an exception.

isThreadSafe

A value of `true` (default) means that multiple requests can be processed simultaneously with a single servlet instance. In this case, you must synchronize access to instance variables. A value of `false` implements `SingleThreadModel` and causes the container to process requests serially or by giving separate servlet instances to each request.

info

The `info` attribute stores an arbitrary string that can subsequently be retrieved with the `Servlet.getServletInfo()` method. It is used like this:

```
<%@ page info="myPageInfo" %>
```

contentType

This defines the MIME type of the returned stream. The default is `text/html`. The syntax is shown here:

```
<%@ page contentType="text/html" %>
```

The duplicate way of accomplishing the same thing is with the following scriptlet:

```
<% response.setContentType("text/html"); %>
```

Expression

Expressions are a shortcut for appending output to the output stream. The syntax is this:

```
<%="some text" %>
```

Notice that you do not use the semicolon terminator in an expression.

JSP Scriptlets

Scriptlets enable you to add Java code to an otherwise HTML page. This is simple to do when you delimit the Java by opening the section with `<%` and closing it with `%>`. You will spend the majority of your time between these two delimiters.

JSP Implicit Objects

JSP gives you access to several objects implicitly (that is, you don't have to declare them—they are already accessible by predefined names). The following sections cover required material for the exam. Each section defines the object and gives a small code example.

request

This is the `HttpServletRequest` object that represents the client request. This object enables you to inspect that request message, which has a surprising amount of information stored in it. The following is an example:

```
<%= request.getContentType() %>
```

The following are the `request` methods you can use to get information about the request using the syntax shown: `getMethod`, `getRequestURI`, `getProtocol`, `getServletPath`, `getPathInfo`, `getPathTranslated`, `getQueryString`, `getContentLength`, `getContentType`, `getServerName`, `getServerPort`, `getRemoteUser`, `getRemoteAddr`, `getRemoteHost`, `getAuthType`, and `getHeader`.

You can get and set variables with request scope using request.setAttribute("myName",object) and request.setAttribute("myName",object) syntax.

The most used methods are the getParameter, getParameterNames, and getParameterValues methods. So, to retrieve the value of the form field firstName, you would use <%= request.getParameter("firstName"); %>.

response

This object is in the HttpServletResponse class and manages the response to the client. The five primary things that you do with it are add cookies (addCookie), add a header (addHeader), return an error (sendError), redirect a browser to another URL (sendRedirect), and set the HTTP status (setStatus).

session

This is the HttpSession object automatically created for a request that remains alive for subsequent requests by the same client until the session times out or another event kills that session. The session stores state between page views. Remember that the session is on by default; if you don't want it on, add "session=false" to the JSP page directive.

The following are the methods of the session object in JSP that you are most likely to see on the exam:

- getAttribute
- removeAttribute
- setAttribute

The following is a snippet showing how to use these methods, although you will not likely be setting, getting, and removing an attribute all in the same block:

```
<% session.setAttribute("firstname", firstname); %>
<input type="text" value="<%=session.getAttribute("firstname")%>">
<% session.removeAttribute("firstname"); %>
```

config

The config implicit object is an instance of the class javax.servlet.ServletConfig. It is usually used in servlets rather than JSP pages. The methods of this object return initialization parameters for the page that are declared in the web.xml file. You define initialization parameters by setting the property when you register a servlet in the web.xml file, the deployment descriptor. The most used methods of this object are `getInitParameter` and `getInitParameterNames`. The following snippet demonstrates how to use this object:

```
<% String parameter_one = config.getInitParameter("first_parameter"); %>
```

application

The session object shares information between JSP pages for a given user, but an `application` object shares information among all users of a currently active JSP application. When you need to store information for use throughout an application, you can store it in the servlet context. This is sometimes referred to as the `application` object. The `application` object is automatically created for you in JavaServer pages representing the servlet context. Whatever information you store in the servlet context remains until the Web application itself is invalidated. The methods germane to JSP that you should know for the exam are the same as the methods of the session object. The syntax of this object looks like this:

```
<% application.setAttribute("firstname", firstname); %>
<input type="text" value="<%=application.getAttribute("firstname")%>">
<% application.removeAttribute("firstname"); %>
```

pageContext

JSP has an object called `pageContext` that gives you access to server functionality, such as getting the session or `out` objects. The following is an example of its use:

```
HttpSession session = pageContext.getSession();
JspWriter   out     = pageContext.getOut();
```

The `PageContext` encapsulates the complete state of a single request execution of a single JSP page.

page

`page` is JSP's version of Java's `this` keyword, but I've never seen it used; I doubt that this will be on the exam. The JSP designers created it to address JSP's support for other scripting languages beside Java. We recommend that you use the Java `this` keyword instead.

out

You use this object to append output to the stream. Internally, this is how the container declares and instantiates the out object:

```
JspWriter out = out = pageContext.getOut();
```

You can use this object to print to the client like this:

```
<% out.println("welcome to the customer page!"); %>
```

Declaration

You must declare a variable before you use it. You can do this in a scriptlet or a declaration. The only difference between the two involves using an exclamation mark in the opening delimiter like this:

```
<%! int count = 0; %>
<%! MyClass teamScores = new MyClass(); %>
```

If you use a declaration (with an exclamation mark) to declare a variable, it gets translated as a class member (class scope). If you do so in a scriptlet, the variable is translated as being declared within the _jspService method. This difference shows up if you try to access a variable declared in a scriptlet from a method; you'll get an error in this case. The following JSP page generates a servlet error because the getPassword method is trying to access an undefined variable (password).

```
<%@ page language="java" contentType="text/html" %>
<% String password = "que"; %>
<%! String Name = "reader"; %>

<%! String getName(){return Name;} %>
<%! String getPassword(){return password;} %>

<html>
<head>
  <title>Successful Login</title>
</head>
<body>

<%=getName() %><br />
<%=getPassword() %>

</body>
</html>
```

So, using a declaration declares an instance variable, and using a scriptlet declares a local instance. You must use a declaration to declare methods.

Using XML to Create JSP Actions

Much of JSP syntax has an XML equivalent. These equivalents are usually handled the same way as the JSP syntax, but a few elements are handled differently.

You need to know the syntax of the XML versions of the JSP actions. JSP enables you to use two forms of certain tag types. Table 8.3 offers a quick review of these XML equivalents.

Table 8.3 XML Equivalents for Certain JSP Tag Types

JSP Tag Type	Syntax	XML
Expression	**<%=expression%>**	**<jsp:expression> expression </jsp:expression>**
Scriptlet	**<% yourCode %>**	**<jsp:scriptlet> yourCode </jsp:scriptlet>**
Declaration	**<%! yourCode %>**	**<jsp:declaration> yourCode </jsp:declaration>**
page directive	**<%@ page att="val" %>**	**<jsp:directive.page att="val"/>**
include directive	**<%@ include file="url" %>**	**<jsp:directive.include file="url"/>**
Actions	None (XML only)	**<jsp:useBean /> <jsp:setProperty /> <jsp:getProperty /> <jsp:include /> <jsp:forward /> <jsp:plugin />**
Tag library	**<%@ taglib uri="URIFor Library" prefix="tagPrefix" %>**	No equivalent
Bean	**<jsp:useBean />**	**<jsp:useBean id="customer" scope="page" class= "session.Customer" />**
Bean property	**<jsp:setProperty />**	**<jsp:setProperty name= "customer" property="lastName" />**
Bean property	**<jsp:getProperty />**	**<jsp:getProperty name= "customer" property="firstName" />**

(continued)

Table 8.3 XML Equivalents for Certain JSP Tag Types *(continued)*

JSP Tag Type	Syntax	XML
Dispatch	**<jsp:forward />**	**<jsp:forward page=“partner.jsp”/>**
Include	**<jsp:include />**	**<jsp:include page=“banner.inc” />**
Plug-in	**<jsp:plugin />**	**<jsp:plugin type=applet code=“Customer.class” codebase=“/html”> <jsp:params> <jsp:param name=“debt” value=“large” /> </jsp:params> <jsp:fallback> <p>Unable to load applet</p> </jsp:fallback> </jsp:plugin>**

The following is a template for using a tag library and a JavaBean:

```
<%--@ taglib uri="URIForLibrary" prefix="tagPrefix" --%>
<%@ taglib uri="/myCustomerCare" prefix="customerCare" %>

<%--jsp:useBean id="beanInstanceName"
   scope="page¦request¦session¦application"
{
   class="package.class" [ type="package.class" ]¦
   beanName="{package.class ¦ <%= expression %>}"
      type="package.class" ¦
   type="package.class"
}
{ /> ¦ > other elements </jsp:useBean> }
--%>
<jsp:useBean id="cart" class="cart.ShoppingCart" scope="session"/>
    <% cart.add("lamp"); %>
  <jsp:setProperty name="cart" property="itemCount" value="<%=count%>" />

<%-- mixing tag library with bean --%>
<customerCare:present parameter="cartItems">
    <jsp:getProperty name="cart" property="itemCount"  />
 </customerCare:cartItems>
```

Practice Questions

Question 1

What option shows a correct sequence of the JSP page life cycle? The correct option might not show all of the elements, but those it does list are in the correct order.

❍ A. Load class, translate page, compile JSP page, create instance, call **jspInit**, call **_jspService**

❍ B. Load class, create instance, call **_jspService**, call **jspInit**, call **jspDestroy**

❍ C. Translate page, compile JSP page, create instance, load class, call **jspInit**, call **_jspService**, call **jspDestroy**

❍ D. Compile JSP page, load class, create instance, call **jspInit**, call **_jspService**, call **jspDestroy**

Answer D is correct. All the others have valid steps, but they are in the wrong order.

Question 2

What is the XML equivalent for an expression?

❍ A.

```
<myPrefix:expression>
expression
</myPrefix:expression>
```

❍ B.

```
<jsp:expression>
expression
</jsp:expression>
```

❍ C.

```
<myPrefix:expression>
<%=expression%>
</myPrefix:expression>
```

❍ D.

```
<jsp:expression>
<%=expression%>
</jsp:expression>
```

Answer B is correct. This is the correct XML equivalent for an expression. All the other options have incorrect syntax.

Question 3

How do you declare a JavaBean in a JSP page?

- ❍ A. **<jsp:useBean name="customer" scope="page" class="session.Customer" ></jsp:useBean>**
- ❍ B. **<jsp:useBean class="session.Customer" scope="page" />**
- ❍ C. **<jsp:Bean id="customer" scope="page" class= "session.Customer" />**
- ❍ D. **<jsp:useBean id="customer" scope="page" class= "session.Customer" />**

Answer D is correct. This is the correct way to declare a JavaBean in a JSP page. All the other options have incorrect syntax.

Question 4

What is the XML equivalent for a tag library?

- ❍ A. **<%@ tag-library url="URIForLibrary" prefix="tagPrefix" %>**
- ❍ B. **<%@ tag-lib uri="URIForLibrary" prefix="tagPrefix" %>**
- ❍ C. **<%@ taglib uri="URIForLibrary" prefix="tagPrefix" %>**
- ❍ D. **<%@ taglib uri="URIForLibrary" %>**

Answer C is correct. This is the proper syntax for a directive that loads a tag library. All the other options have incorrect syntax.

Question 5

Which of the following is a valid expression?

- ❍ A. **<%! String name="Patricia" %>**
- ❍ B. **<%! String name="Patricia"; %>**
- ❍ C. **<%= (new java.util.Date()).toLocaleString() %>**
- ❍ D. **<expression: name="color" type=String>blue</expression>**

Answer C is correct. This is the only expression in the group. All the other options have incorrect syntax or are not expressions.

Question 6

Which two options correctly describe the following code snippet? (Choose two.)

```
<%
  String firstname = request.getParameter("firstname");
  String lastname = request.getParameter("lastname");
  String address = request.getParameter("address");
%>
```

- ❑ A. Three variables are declared.
- ❑ B. The **getParameter** method retrieves data from the request object that was assigned to it earlier in the page.
- ❑ C. The request object must be declared before this scriptlet.
- ❑ D. These parameters were provided by the client making the request.

Answers A and D are correct. The `firstname`, `lastname`, and `address` variables are declared and then assigned values provided by the client. The request object is implicit; if you declare it the container, you cause an error.

Question 7

How would you import classes into a JSP page?

- ❍ A. You can declare outside classes with fully qualified names, but you can't import them into a JSP page.
- ❍ B. You can't import; you use JavaBeans and tag libraries instead.
- ❍ C. **<%@ page import="java.util.*, java.lang.*" %>**
- ❍ D. **<%@ page-import="java.util.*; java.lang.*" %>**

Answer C is correct. A JavaServer Page is like any other servlet, but it starts life as a script. Therefore, you can import classes using the syntax in option C. A `page` directive is an instruction to the container that carries it out at translation time, not execution time.

Question 8

What objects can preserve information across two requests by the same user? (Choose two.)

- ❑ A. **application**
- ❑ B. **page**
- ❑ C. **request**
- ❑ D. **session**

Answers A and D are correct. Both the `application` and `session` objects can preserve information through two requests by the same user. The `page` object holds information only for the duration of that page. The `request` object holds information only for the duration of that page and one other if the first page forwards to another one. Remember, the `application` object is visible to multiple users.

Question 9

What does the following code snippet do?

```
<%--@include file="companyBanner.html" --%>
```

- ❍ A. It includes the file companyBanner.html before compilation.
- ❍ B. It is ignored during the translation step.
- ❍ C. It includes the file companyBanner.html at the time of a request.
- ❍ D. This generates an error.

Answer B is correct. This `include` directive is ignored because it is inside JSP comment delimiters. It includes the file companyBanner.html before compilation if it is `<%@include file="companyBanner.html" %>`.

Need to Know More?

JSP syntax—java.sun.com/products/jsp/tags/12/syntaxref12.html

Servlets and JavaServer Pages: A Tutorial—www.apl.jhu.edu/~hall/java/Servlet-Tutorial/

JavaServer Pages: A Developer's Perspective—developer.java.sun.com/developer/technicalArticles/Programming/jsp/

The Java Servlet 2.3 Specification—jcp.org/aboutJava/communityprocess/first/jsr053/index.html

JSP Downloads & Specifications—java.sun.com/products/jsp/download.html

Sun's JavaServer Pages resources—java.sun.com/products/jsp/technical.html#faqs

JSP and JavaBeans

Terms you'll need to understand:

- ✓ JavaBean
- ✓ Bean properties
- ✓ XML
- ✓ Bean and attribute scope
- ✓ Attribute get/set methods

Techniques you'll need to master:

- ✓ Declare the use of a JavaBean component within the page.
- ✓ Specify, for **jsp:useBean** or **jsp:getProperty** tags, the name of an attribute.
- ✓ Specify, for a **jsp:useBean** tag, the class of the attribute.
- ✓ Specify, for a **jsp:useBean** tag, the scope of the attribute.
- ✓ Access or mutate a property from a declared JavaBean.
- ✓ Specify, for a **jsp:getProperty** tag, the property of the attribute.
- ✓ Specify, for a **jsp:setProperty** tag, the property of the attribute to mutate and the new value.
- ✓ Code JSP page attributes including their scopes.
- ✓ Identify techniques that access a declared JavaBean component.

JavaBean Overview

What is the purpose of JavaBeans in JavaServer Pages? One way to answer this question is to say that a JavaBean acts like a simplified state machine that stores attributes. Using tags, the JSP page can be written so that it can operate on input (such as a request form field value) to change the attributes. Each JavaBean tag is an instruction that changes one or more of these attributes and can cause other actions to take place. Each attribute stores a state. Each JavaBean begins with some initial state that can change as the JSP page is executed and processes the request. If you care to give your mind a little tug, investigate finite-state machines. Presently, it is enough to understand that the primary purpose of a JavaBean is how it stores attributes and exposes `get/set` methods to change those attributes' values.

You can use JavaBean tags to instantiate the Bean and then set or get attribute values. Actually, you can use either XML notation or scriptlets to do this. The exam will expect you to know how to do both. You use XML to instantiate a Bean and get and set the Bean's properties by using the `useBean`, `getProperty`, and `setProperty` standard tags. The scriptlet equivalent is easy to master, as shown later in the chapter.

The two major topics that you could benefit from when using JavaBeans, but that are not on the exam, are calling ad-hoc JavaBean methods from scriptlets and creating JavaBean classes. Writing JavaBeans is an important aspect of Web application development, but because writing Beans is not on the exam, I won't discuss this directly. For the curious, a Java class can be a JavaBean if it satisfies the following requirements:

- The class contains a no-argument constructor.
- The class uses standardized method names for property accessors and mutators.
- There are no public instance variables.

Sun has positioned JavaBeans as a plug-and-play development standard for Java. These are reusable components. The core idea behind JavaBeans is the component architecture. This architecture exposes a component's (JavaBean's) properties and methods, has events and listeners, and has a standard way for containers to manipulate them.

Don't confuse Web application JavaBeans with Enterprise JavaBeans. JavaBeans and Enterprise JavaBeans (EJB) are two entirely different things that share the same name because they are used for similar purposes. An Enterprise Bean is a server-side component just like a JavaBean. So, JavaBeans and EJBs encapsulate the business logic of an application. However, because EJBs are not used with JSP, they are not on the exam.

Mixing HTML (presentation) and scriptlets (logic) in a JSP page is both the beauty and the bane of JSP architecture. This mixture of presentation and logic requires less expensive skill sets to create pages. But mixing like this is poor architecture. Why? It quickly becomes unwieldy, and not having a clear separation between presentation and logic makes it hard to change one without disturbing the other. Using Beans is better than using complex scriptlets because Beans separate display and logic. Even servlets can be a problem in that they also mix the two. Beans are a valuable tool that can trade lines of scriptlet code for clean XML notation (covered later).

A JavaBean itself is an ordinary class. JavaBeans do not extend any specific class. Instead, the JSP specification defines how the container will allow a JSP page to access a JavaBean through XML notation and scriptlets.

Each JavaBean component has the expected class structure but follows a convention that includes `get` and `set` methods. This convention is what transforms a regular class into a JavaBean. A class becomes a JavaBean if it is public, has a public constructor with no arguments, follows the `set`/`get` paradigm, and is placed where the container can access it. Once you meet these criteria, you can take advantage of the JavaBean by writing the XML tags in JSP that bring that Bean into play.

Look at Figure 9.1, which illustrates how the container processes a request to a JSP page that employs a JavaBean. This is a high-level process diagram, but it shows you how a JSP page accesses a JavaBean.

Now that you see the high-level architecture, let's look at some code. Listing 9.1 demonstrates how you access a JavaBean class from a JSP page.

Listing 9.1 Accessing a JavaBean from a JSP Page

```
<%-- exam.jsp that uses a JavaBean --%>

<%@ page session="false"%>
<jsp:useBean id="exam" class="com.myCom.ExamBean"/>

<!--carries forward question number from previous page-->
<jsp:setProperty name="exam" property="questionCount"/>

<%
   if (exam.isComplete())
   {
%>
```

(continued)

Listing 9.1 Accessing a JavaBean from a JSP Page *(continued)*

```
    <jsp:forward page="completedExam.jsp"/>
<%
   }
%>

<html>
<head>
<title>JavaBean Driven Exam</title>
</head>
<body>

<h1>Exam</h1>
<form method="POST" action="exam.jsp">
<!--Where was George Washington born?--?
<%=exam.getQuestion()%><br />
<input type="radio" name="answer" value="1">
                        // New Hampshire
                        <%=exam.getAnswer(1)%><br />
<input type="radio" name="answer" value="2">
                        // New York
                        <%=exam.getAnswer(2)%><br />
<input type="radio" name="answer" value="3">
                        // Virginia
                        <%=exam.getAnswer(3)%><br />
<input type="radio" name="answer" value="2">
                        // Massachusetts
                        <%=exam.getAnswer(4)%><p />
<input type="submit" value=" Login ">
<input type="hidden" name="questionCount"
     value="<%=exam.getQuestionCount()%>">

</form>
</body>
</html>
```

Listing 9.1 shows a JavaBean accessed from a JSP page. All the code for keeping track of the question counter and the question and answer texts, and the code for determining whether the exam has been completed is placed in the JavaBean. This cleans up the JSP page considerably. In the JavaBean, the question counter is a simple private instance variable (`questionCount`) that is set and gotten with regular methods (`getQuestionCount/setQuestionCount`).

When you start creating JavaBeans for your JSP pages, the JavaBean must belong to a Java package. You *must* place your JavaBeans in a package, or the servlet engine (such as Tomcat) will throw an exception because it won't find the JavaBean.

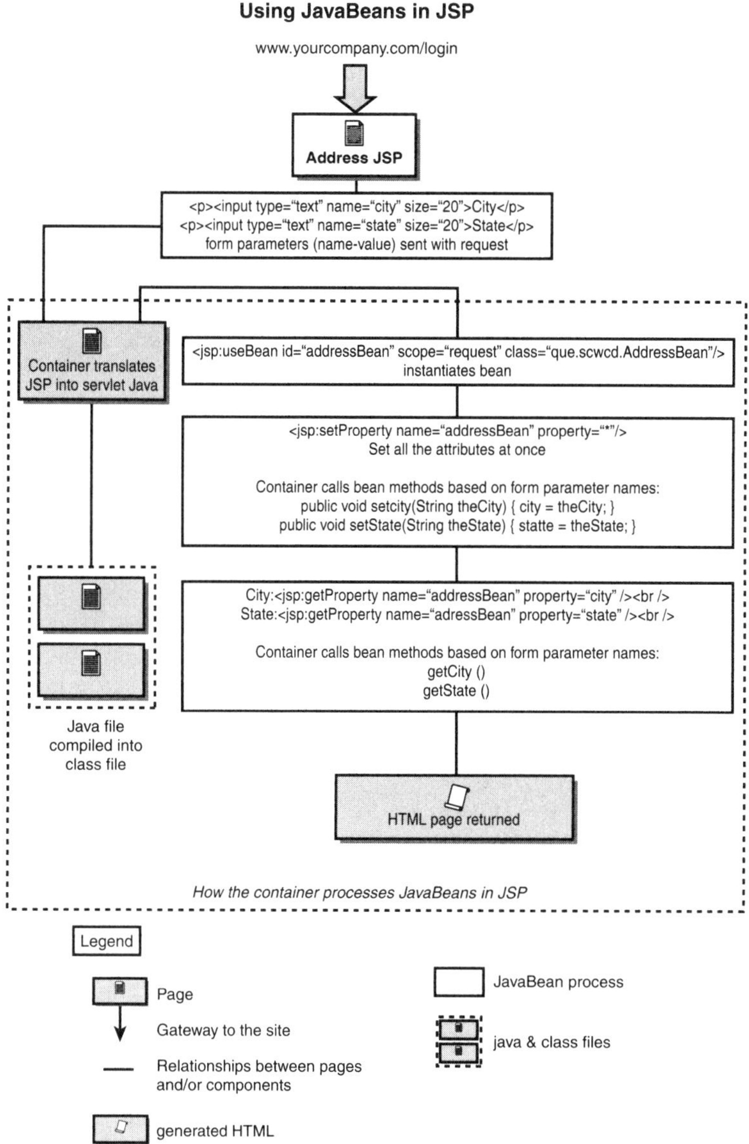

Figure 9.1 How a JSP page accesses a JavaBean.

jsp:useBean

The jsp:useBean JSP element declares that a Bean is stored within and is accessible from the specified scope (application, session, request, or page). When you use jsp:useBean, the container performs several actions. Basically, it instantiates the object in memory and provides a variable name for you to use within the scope that you set in the tag. The value of the id attribute determines the name of the Bean within the object scope. Also, you use that name to refer to the object in other JSP elements and scriptlets.

The syntax is shown here:

```
<jsp:useBean id="name"
      scope="page¦request¦session¦application" typeSpec />
typeSpec ::= class="className" ¦
class="className" type="typeName" ¦
type="typeName" class="className" ¦
beanName="beanName" type="typeName" ¦
type="typeName" beanName="beanName" ¦
type="typeName"
```

The id and scope are easy. The confusion arises over the typeSpec. The container always looks for the Bean. However, if the typeSpec is used one way, the container throws an exception if it can't find that Bean (because it is not already instantiated). If it is used another way, it creates a new instance of the Bean if one hasn't been created already.

The typical use of the jsp:useBean element is this:

```
<jsp:useBean ...>
    Body
</jsp:useBean>
```

This is a way to instantiate a Bean. Table 9.1 explains the syntax. The body is executed upon instantiation, but not after the Bean is loaded. Be careful about this. So, there are two behaviors of useBean: to instantiate an object and to retrieve an object as a Web application attribute.

The body portion of the jsp:useBean element is executed only when the Bean is first instantiated. If the Bean instance has already been loaded into memory from a previous jsp:useBean (for example, in the previous page with session scope), the body of the jsp:useBean element is not executed. Because Beans can be shared, jsp:useBean doesn't always newly instantiate a Bean. The body is executed only once for a given Bean, regardless of how many jsp:useBean elements refer to it.

To get you started, Table 9.1 offers a quick overview of the useBean attributes.

Table 9.1 useBean Attributes

Attribute	Definition
id	The case-sensitive name used to identify the object instance in the specified scope. This name doubles as the scripting variable name declared and initialized with that object reference.
scope	The scope within which the reference is available. The default value is **page**. The options are **page**, **request**, **session**, and **application**.
class	The fully qualified name of the class. If the **class** and **beanName** attributes are not specified, the object must be present in the given scope. The class must not be abstract (or an interface) and must have a public, no-argument constructor, but the implicit **no args** constructor will suffice.
beanName	The name of a Bean, as expected by the **instantiate()** method of the **java.beans.Beans** class. This name can be set dynamically by an expression as a value.
type	If specified, it defines the type of the variable defined. The type is required to be the class itself, a superclass of the class, or an interface implemented by the class specified. If unspecified, the value is the same as the value of the **class** attribute.

The following is an example of how you would declare a JavaBean in a JSP page:

```
<jsp:useBean id="customer" scope="request" class="que.scwcd.Customer">
```

This XML snippet is how you create an instance of the `Customer` class in the container. After you do that, the Bean is in memory, but the attributes are initially null. To change these attributes, you can use scriptlets or XML. Generally, XML is preferred over scriptlets.

When you use `jsp:useBean`, the container performs several actions. Basically, it loads the object in memory and instantiates it, providing a variable name for you to use within the scope you specified in the tag. If this JavaBean doesn't yet exist in memory, the container will try to create it. The container does a lot of work for you, so you need only a few tags to perform helpful work.

As you can see, employing a JavaBean is easy with the `useBean`, `getProperty`, and `setProperty` actions to get and set the attributes of the Bean. Also, you can refer to the Bean like any other object in scriptlets by the name specified in the `id` attribute of the `useBean` element. The `id` attribute specifies an instance name that you can refer to in your scriptlets.

jsp:setProperty Action

You use `jsp:setProperty` to set the property values of Beans that have been referenced earlier in the JSP page. For example, the following snippet shows you how to set the `color` attribute of the product Bean:

```
<jsp:useBean id="product" scope="request"
                          class="que.scwcd.Product" />
<jsp:setProperty name="product"
                     property="color" value="green"  />
```

Notice that a shortcut to assigning values to many JavaBean attributes simultaneously is to set the property to the wildcard value, like so: **<jsp:setProperty name="myBean" property="*" />**.

If you want to set a property only during the Bean's initialization, you can place it in the body of the useBean tag. For example, the `jsp:setProperty` is executed only the first time the JavaBean is instantiated. It is ignored if the JavaBean has already been loaded in memory, as would happen if the JavaBean was loaded on a previous page with application scope or session scope by the same client.

```
<jsp:useBean id="beanName" ... >
<jsp:setProperty name="beanName"
                 property="propertyName" ... />
</jsp:useBean>
```

Values can be assigned to JavaBean properties in three ways: using the `value` attribute of the `jsp:setProperty` element, using the `param` attribute using a named parameter, and using the `param` attribute with the wildcard. You can set the property directly with the `value` attribute of the `setProperty` action. The following element sets a property from a value:

```
<jsp:setProperty name="addressBean" property="phone" value="<%= "714-" +
phone %>" />
```

The container assigns the value from the JSP page to the JavaBean attribute variable.

Another way to assign values to JavaBean properties is to use the `param` attribute using a named parameter. The container then takes the value of the given request parameter assigning it in the JavaBean property. These two names don't have to match, but it is easier to maintain an application if they do. When using the `jsp:setProperty` element, the container assigns the parameter value to the JavaBean `property` variable. You do this like so:

```
<jsp:setProperty name="addressBean" property="state" param="state" />
```

The `property` is the name of the attribute in the JavaBean, while the `param` is the name of the parameter in the `request` object. Notice that the `param` attribute is optional if it is the same as the `property` attribute.

The third manner to assign a value to a JavaBean property looks like this:

```
<jsp:setProperty name="addressBean" property="*"/>
```

You'll notice that the property is set to the wildcard star. That tells the container to match as many request parameters with JavaBean properties as possible. If the request parameter is named `color`, the container will assign its value to the JavaBean property of the same name through the `setColor` method in the JavaBean. If several request parameter names have matching JavaBean property names, only one `jsp:setProperty` tag is needed to transfer all the form field values to the corresponding JavaBean properties. Notice that the HTML field names must match exactly—even the case.

Table 9.2 offers a quick overview of the `setProperty` attributes. The definitions are slightly edited from the specification.

Table 9.2 setProperty Attributes

Attribute	Definition
name	The case-sensitive name of a Bean instance defined by a **<jsp:useBean>** element. The Bean instance must contain the property that you want to set. The defining element must appear before the **<jsp:setProperty>** element in the same file.
property	The name of the Bean property whose value you want to set. If you set **propertyName** to *, the tag iterates over the current **ServletRequest** parameters, matching parameter names and value type(s) to property names and setter method type(s), and setting each matched property to the value of the matching parameter. If a parameter has a value of "", the corresponding property is not modified.
param	The name of the request parameter (Web form or query string) whose value you want to give to a Bean property. If you omit **param**, the request parameter name is assumed to be the same as the Bean property name. If the **param** is not set in the **request** object, or if it has the value of "", the **jsp:setProperty** element has no effect. An action may not have both **param** and **value** attributes.
value	The value to assign to the given property. This attribute can accept a **request-time** attribute expression as a value. An action may not have both **param** and **value** attributes.

jsp:getProperty Action

A <jsp:getProperty> action places the value of a Bean instance property into the implicit out object. The String representation is sent to the HTTP response stream. Unlike a scriptlet, which can get a value and assign it to a variable, the getProperty action converts the Bean property value to a String and immediately adds that String to the output stream. You cannot assign the value from this tag to a variable in most containers.

You use jsp:getProperty to get the property values of Beans that have been referenced earlier in the JSP page. In the following case, the jsp:getProperty is executed regardless of whether a new Bean was instantiated or an existing Bean already exists in memory.

```
<jsp:useBean id="beanName" ... />
<jsp:getProperty name="beanName"
                 property="propertyName" ... />
```

However, in the next case, jsp:getProperty is executed only the first time the JavaBean is instantiated. It is ignored if the JavaBean has already been loaded in memory.

```
<jsp:useBean id="beanName" ... >
<jsp:getProperty name="beanName"
                 property="propertyName" ... />
</jsp:useBean>
```

Table 9.3 offers a quick overview of the getProperty attributes. There are only two, less than with the more complicated setProperty element.

Table 9.3 getProperty Attributes

Attribute	Definition
name	The case-sensitive name of a Bean instance defined by a **<jsp:useBean>** element. The Bean instance must contain the property you want to set. The defining element must appear before the **<jsp:setProperty>** element in the same file.
property	The name of the Bean property whose value you want to get. If you get a **propertyName** that doesn't exist, you will generate an error.

Scope of JavaBeans in JSP

Given JSP page attribute scopes request, session, and application, how are JavaBeans affected? You define the scope of the Bean in the jsp:useBean element. For example, if you declare the Bean in session scope, all JSP pages within that session have access to the same JavaBean. The following list describes the four scopes, including page, request, session, and application.

Page

The address Bean is instantiated as a local variable. Because its scope is page, the reference disappears once the JSP page is processed. It can't be referenced by another JSP or servlet, even if a forward or include is used. The syntax is shown here:

```
<jsp:useBean id="address" class="que.scwcd.AddressBean" scope="page" />.
```

Request

The address Bean is instantiated into the current request object. It can be accessed by any JSP or servlet within the same request. This reference remains alive in any other servlets/JSPs called by `jsp:include` and `jsp:forward`, or in ones called via a `RequestDispatcher` object. The syntax is `<jsp:useBean id="address" class="que.scwcd.AddressBean" scope="request" />`. The following snippet demonstrates how Tomcat translates this JSP action into servlet code:

```
que.scwcd.AddressBean address =
    (que.scwcd.AddressBean)request.getAttribute("address");
if (address == null)
{
  address = new que.scwcd.AddressBean();
  request.setAttribute("address", address);
}
```

Session

The address Bean is instantiated in the current session. It can then be accessed by any JSP or servlet responding to requests by the current user. The syntax is `<jsp:useBean id="address" class="que.scwcd.AddressBean" scope="session" />`. The following snippet demonstrates how Tomcat translates this JSP action into servlet code:

```
HttpSession session = request.getSession(true);
que.scwcd.AddressBean address =
(que.scwcd.AddressBean)session.getAttribute("address");
if (address == null)
{
  address = new que.scwcd.AddressBean();
  session.setAttribute("address", address);
}
```

Application

The AddressBean Bean is instantiated within the servlet context. It can be accessed by any JSP or servlet within the servlet context and, thus by any user. The syntax is `<jsp:useBean class="que.scwcd.AddressBean" scope="application" />`. The following snippet demonstrates how Tomcat translates this JSP action into servlet code:

```
que.scwcd.AddressBean address = (que.scwcd.AddressBean)
                                getServletContext()
                                .getAttribute("address");
if (address == null)
{
  address = new que.scwcd.AddressBean();
  getServletContext().setAttribute("address", address);
}
```

Accessing JavaBeans with Scriptlets

When you declare a Bean in JSP code, you can access it with both XML elements (called an action) and scriptlets. The previous discourse demonstrated how to access JavaBeans with XML. After the Bean has been declared, you can also access it by the name specified in the `id` attribute of `<jsp:useBean>` by using scriptlets and expressions.

Table 9.4 gives you a list of three examples representing the three ways to access Beans.

Table 9.4 JavaBean Access Techniques

Access	Example
XML	**<jsp:getProperty name="addressBean" property="city" ... />**
Scriptlet	**<% String city = myAddress.getCity()%>**
Expression	**<%= myAddress.getCity()%>**

A JavaBean can be referenced in three ways: through an expression, a scriptlet, or an XML tag.

The following is how you would access attributes of the player JavaBean in XML:

```
<jsp:useBean id="playerBean" scope="request"
                       class="que.scwcd.PlayerBean"/>
First Name:<jsp:getProperty name="playerBean"
                             property="firstName" /><br />
Last Name:<jsp:getProperty name="addressBean"
                             property="lastName" /><br />
Position:<jsp:getProperty name="addressBean"
                             property="position" /><br />
```

Now this is how you would get the same result accessing the JavaBean using expressions:

```
<jsp:useBean id="playerBean" scope="request"
                       class="que.scwcd.PlayerBean"/>
First Name:<%=playerBean.getFirstName() %><br />
Last Name:<%=playerBean.getLastName() %><br />
Position:<%=playerBean.getPosition() %><br />
```

Practice Questions

Question 1

Which two statements describe JavaBeans? (Choose two.)

- ❑ A. JavaBeans are powerful components, but they make it harder for non-programmers to write JSP pages.
- ❑ B. A JavaBean is a self-contained component. JavaBeans are compiled as servlets, making them easy to use in Web applications.
- ❑ C. JavaBeans are reusable components. You can encapsulate business logic and properties in them.
- ❑ D. A JavaBean is a self-contained component. JavaBeans are easy to reuse and share among developers.

Answers C and D are correct. JavaBeans are reusable, self-contained components. You can encapsulate business logic and properties in them. They also make it easier to write JSP pages, with consistent XML notation. Although you can use scriptlets to access them, it is better to use XML. Finally, JavaBeans are easy to reuse and share among developers.

Question 2

Which two of the following are part of what makes a class a JavaBean? (Choose two.)

- ❑ A. Public constructor with no arguments
- ❑ B. Public class
- ❑ C. Private **set** and **get** methods
- ❑ D. Public instance variables

Answers A and B are correct. Four things make a class a JavaBean in JSP: a public class, a public constructor with no arguments, public `set` and `get` methods to simulate properties, and the declaration of a JavaBean within a JSP page.

Question 3

When you access a JavaBean from a scriptlet, what object do you pass to the Bean so that it has the request information?

❍ A. **HttpServletRequest**

❍ B. **HttpServletResponse**

❍ C. **HttpSession**

❍ D. **HttpContext**

Answer D is correct. You don't pass objects to a JavaBean. You change a JavaBean property using either the `setProperty` action (XML) or the equivalent scriptlet.

Question 4

If a JavaBean instance is shared by different users, what scope was it declared with?

❍ A. Page

❍ B. Request

❍ C. Session

❍ D. Application

Answer D is correct. If different users can access the same JavaBean, it must have Web application scope.

Question 5

How do you tell the container to assign all the values from a request to corresponding JavaBean attributes?

❍ A. **<jsp:setProperty name="myBean" property="*" />**

❍ B. **<jsp:property name="myBean" property="*" />**

❍ C. **<jsp:getProperty name="myBean" property="*" />**

❍ D. **<jsp:useBean name="myBean" setProperty="*" />**

Answer A is correct. The JavaBean attributes are set when the container captures the form field name-value pairs and then calls the setter methods in the Bean for the attributes that have the same name as the form fields. Option A is the only correct syntax among the options.

Question 6

Read the following code:

```
HttpSession session = request.getSession(true);
que.scwcd.AddressBean address =
➥(que.scwcd.AddressBean)session.getAttribute
➥("address");
if (address == null)
{
  address = new que.scwcd.AddressBean();
  session.setAttribute("address", address);
}
```

Which statement is true regarding the code?

❍ A. The address instance of this Bean can be accessed by many users.

❍ B. The code is invalid because you can instantiate a Bean only using the XML notation.

❍ C. The address instance of this Bean can be accessed by the same user over several requests.

❍ D. This Bean has an **address** attribute.

Answer C is correct. The `address` instance of this Bean has session scope, so it can be accessed by the same user across multiple requests. However, access by multiple users requires application scope.

Question 7

How would you change the size attribute of a JavaBean instance if it was declared with the following:

```
<jsp:useBean id="product" scope="session"
                       class="que.scwcd.ProductBean">
```

❍ A. **<%=product.setSize() %>**

❍ B. **<%=productBean.setSize() %>**

❍ C. **<%=product.size() %>**

❍ D. **<%=productBean.size() %>**

Answer A is correct. In scriptlets, you name the JavaBean by its declared ID and then, using the dot notation, call the `setProperty` method, as is done in option A. Option B is wrong because it did not refer to `product` with its declared ID. Options C and D both call the wrong method.

Question 8

What is the element name (prefix:name) for declaring a JavaBean (do not use "<" nor ">" and do not include the id, scope, or class attributes)?

____

The correct answer is `jsp:useBean`.

Need to Know More?

 **JavaBeans home page**—http://java.sun.com/beans

 **JavaBeans Component Architecture FAQ**—http://java.sun.com/products/javabeans/FAQ.html

 **JavaBeans specification**—http://java.sun.com/products/javabeans/docs/spec.html

 **JavaBeans API Definitions (javadoc generated)**—http://java.sun.com/j2se/1.3/docs/api/java/beans/package-summary.html

 **Guidelines for Bean development**—http://java.sun.com/products/javabeans/docs/initial.html

 **Sun's JavaBeans Tutorial**—http://java.sun.com/docs/books/tutorial/javabeans/

Custom Tag Libraries

Terms you'll need to understand:

- ✓ Custom tags
- ✓ Tag libraries
- ✓ Tag library descriptor
- ✓ Web deployment descriptor
- ✓ Nested tags
- ✓ Tag attributes and bodies
- ✓ taglib directive
- ✓ Custom tag life cycle

Techniques you'll need to master:

- ✓ Know the tag library descriptor elements for tag libraries.
- ✓ Be able to write a tag library descriptor in XML notation.
- ✓ Understand the tag life cycle.
- ✓ Identify triggers for event methods (**doStartTag**, **doAfterBody**, and **doEndTag**).
- ✓ Identify valid return values for the event methods.
- ✓ Understand how to use **BODY** or **PAGE** constants in event methods.
- ✓ In the custom tag handler, know how to access a given JSP page's implicit variable and the page's attributes.
- ✓ Identify methods that return an outer tag handler from within an inner tag handler.

Custom Tag Library Overview

Tag libraries and JavaBeans are closely related. JavaBeans provide a way to encapsulate functionality in classes accessible via tags in JSP pages using XML notation. Tag libraries provide this functionality, too. JavaBeans provides easy access to `get/set` methods, but tag libraries provide access to any method via XML notation. In fact, you can completely eliminate scriptlets in JSP by replacing them with custom tags.

Tag libraries are really an extension of JavaBeans in JSP. Although they get and set attributes like JavaBeans, they do much more if you want them to. You can access this extra functionality with XML tags that you define in JSP; that is why they're called custom tags.

Many commercial and free tag libraries are available on the market. In fact, the tag library technology is deep enough to merit its own book. However, the exam restricts us to the main aspects of the technology covered in this chapter.

A terrific way to learn tag libraries is to use and dissect the JavaServer Pages Standard Tag Library (JSTL). This encapsulates core functionality that JSP page authors normally implement with scriptlets—for example, flow control, XML processing, number and date formatting, and even database querying and result set handling. I predict the JSTL will slowly replace scriptlets and myriad tags from numerous vendors. The same thing is happening with XML: The J2SE 1.4 version's included XML/XSL processors are killing off proprietary implementations. The JSTL defines a standard tag set. Of course, with every tag library there is a new set of tags to learn, but the pressure is on to minimize scriptlets in the name of better architecture. Although JSTL is not on the exam, it represents the best of tag library technology. I recommend playing with the JSTL and even modifying it.

To use custom tags, you will need the following:

- **Tag handler**—A tag handler is a special JavaBean that is the compiled class referenced by the JSP page through custom tags. It has access to the same objects that your JSP page has. The JSP page passes in attributes of the custom tag and the body between opening and closing custom tags. The output from the tag handler replaces the tag in the JSP page.
- **Tag library descriptor (TLD)**—This XML file defines the properties and location of the tag handler class file.
- **Deployment descriptor (web.xml)**—This is your Web application configuration file. In it, you map a custom tag library URI to the TLD file location, which, in turn, defines the tag handler class location.

- **`taglib` directive**—You declare your tag library in your JSP page. This declaration maps a prefix (this is how you reference your tag library) to a URI that the container resolves to a TLD, directly if a path to the TLD file is given or indirectly if a name is declared. In the latter case, the container looks in the deployment descriptor to match this name to an actual TLD file location.
- **Custom tags in JSP**—Now you can use your tags in the JSP page code.

Table 10.1 lists and describes the four files that are involved in using a tag library.

Table 10.1 Files Comprising Tag Library Example

File	Description
YourTagHanlder.java	The tag handler class that does the work, similar to a JavaBean
YourTagLibraryDefinition.tld	The actual tag library that defines the tag names and associates them with classes
web.xml	The container's configuration file that tells the container where the tag libraries are located and what each one's URI is
yourJSP.jsp	The JSP page that uses XML (custom tags) to access classes defined in the tag library

Let's go through the steps necessary to build and use a tag library:

1. This step is required if you use a `taglib` directive in a JSP page that references a TLD by name (indirectly) rather than by location (directly). Open the WEB-INF/web.xml file and add a `taglib` element like this:

```
<taglib>
    <taglib-uri>
            http://www.yourcompany.com/yourTagLibrary
    </taglib-uri>
    <taglib-location>
       /WEB-INF/yourTagLibrary.tld
    </taglib-location>
</taglib>
```

2. Write a tag library descriptor, such as this:

```
<?xml version="1.0" encoding="UTF-8" ?>

<!DOCTYPE taglib PUBLIC
   "-//Sun Microsystems, Inc.//DTD JSP Tag Library 1.1//EN"
 "http://java.sun.com/j2ee/dtds/web-jsptaglibrary_1_1.dtd">

<taglib>
    <tlibversion>1.0</tlibversion>
```

```
<jspversion>1.1</jspversion>
<shortname>yourLibrary</shortname>
<uri>http://www.yourcompany.com/yourTagLibrary</uri>
<info>Your first tag library</info>

<tag>
    <name>whatColorIsIt</name>
    <tagclass>examples.ColorTagHandler</tagclass>
    <info>Echos back text to it through JSP</info>
    <attribute>
        <name>color</name>
        <required>true</required>
        <rtexprvalue>false</rtexprvalue>
               </attribute>
</tag>

</taglib>
```

3. Write and compile a tag handler (WEB-INF\classes\examples\ColorTagHandler.class), as in Listing 10.1.

Listing 10.1 The Source Code for a Tag Handler

```
//must be in a package or Tomcat won't find it
package examples;

import java.io.*;
import javax.servlet.jsp.*;
import javax.servlet.jsp.tagext.*;

/**
* Given a color, simply send back the value.
*
* @author      QUE reader
*/
public class ColorTagHandler
   extends javax.servlet.jsp.tagext.TagSupport
{   //     makes this a tag handler ^^^^^^^^^^


        /** color attribute */
        private String color;
        //access from JSP^^^^^through get/set methods

        public int doStartTag() throws JspException
        {//        ^^^^^^^^^^ is called automatically

            // build up some HTML
            String html = "The current color is: ";

            // add to output stream
            try {
                pageContext.getOut().write( html + color);
            } catch (IOException ioe) {
                throw new JspException(ioe.getMessage());
            }
```

(continued)

Listing 10.1 The Source Code for a Tag Handler *(continued)*

```
            return EVAL_BODY_INCLUDE;
        }

        /**
         * JavaBeans style property setter for color.
         *
         * @param s        a String representing the color
         */
        public void setColor(String s)
        //          ^^^^^^^^^called by container
        {
            this.color = s;
        }
}
```

4. Write a JSP page that includes a `taglib` directive and a custom tag. The JSP page (\webapps\examples\jsp\yourTagLibrary.jsp) that uses a tag library can be as simple as this:

```
<html>
<head>
<%@ taglib uri="http://www.yourcompany.com/yourTagLibrary"
                                   prefix="yourLibrary" %>
</head>

<body>
<b><yourLibrary:whatColorIsIt color="red"/></b>
<p />
Your first tag library works!
</body>
</html>
```

5. Restart your container.

6. Testing your tag library (localhost:8080/examples/jsp/yourTagLibrary.jsp) should produce this:

```
<html>
<head>

</head>

<body>
<b>red</b>
<br />
<p>Your first tag library works!</p>
</body>
</html>
```

taglib Directive

The exam expects you to identify a properly formatted taglib directive in a JSP page. The taglib directive has the following syntax:

```
<%@ taglib uri="tagLibraryURI" prefix="tagPrefix" %>
```

The taglib directive has only two attributes: uri and prefix. Remember that the uri attribute names the tag library with the same namespace as you use in the web.xml deployment descriptor. The container then maps the name to an actual location by looking in the web.xml file. You can also specify the actual location of the tag library descriptor directly. The prefix attribute is any legal identifier. Notice that you can use many taglib directives in a single page, but each prefix must be unique.

For example, you would declare a tag library with a "direct" URI in the JSP like this:

```
//pointing directly to TLD file
<%@ taglib uri="/WEB-INF/myTagLibrary.tld" prefix="myTag" %>
```

Alternatively (and these two have the same effect), you can declare a tag library with an "indirect" URI, like this:

```
//"indirect" uri points to name in web.xml
<%@ taglib uri="myTagLib" prefix="myTag" %>
```

For the previous taglib directive to work, the web.xml would include the following taglib element:

```
<webapp>
   <taglib>
     <taglib-uri>
         /myTagLib
     </taglib-uri>
     <taglib-location>
         /WEB-INF/myTagLibrary.tld
     </taglib-location>
   </taglib>
<webapp>
```

So, the JSP taglib declaration in a JSP page does two things. First, it points to a library, directly or indirectly. Second, it gives a prefix that is used to refer to that particular tag library. Whenever you use a tag with this prefix, the container knows which library to use.

Custom Tag

You will need to know how to use custom tags in a JSP page. Four variations exist, including an empty tag, a tag with attributes, a tag with body content, and a nested custom tag.

Table 10.2 lists the four ways to use a custom tag.

Table 10.2 Ways to Use Custom Tags

Tag	Description
<libraryPrefix:handlerName />	The custom tag with no body is said to be an empty custom tag.
<libraryPrefix:handlerName parameterName="value"/>	This tag causes the container to call the **setParameterName** method and pass the value to it.
<libraryPrefix:handlerName parameterName="value"> <%= 23 * counter %> <b>Congratulations!</b> </libraryPrefix:handlerName>	This is a custom tag with body. The body can contain core tags, scripting elements, HTML text, and tag-dependent body content between the start and end tags.
<library:outerTag> <library:innerTag/> </library:outerTag>	You nest custom tags with this syntax. The XML is easy, but the handler is more involved.

Tag Handler

A tag handler must implement either the `Tag` or the `BodyTag` interfaces or must extend `TagSupport` or `BodyTagSupport` classes. Interfaces can be used to make an existing Java object a tag handler. In most cases, you will extend the `TagSupport` or the `BodyTagSupport` classes. These classes and interfaces are contained in the javax.servlet.jsp.tagext package.

The `Tag` interface is the base interface for custom tag handlers. Useful for a simple tag handler that does not want to manipulate a custom tag's body, this interface defines the life cycle and the methods to be invoked at the start and end tags. The `BodyTag` interface implements `Tag` and is used to handle tags that do something with the body within a custom tag. The `TagSupport` and `BodyTagSupport` classes also can be extended to write your tag handler. Table 10.3 explains what each of these do.

Table 10.3 Interfaces and Classes for Tag Handlers

Interface or Class	Purpose
Tag	The **Tag** interface handles life-cycle methods to be invoked at a start and end tag. Fields: **EVAL_PAGE**, **SKIP_BODY**, **SKIP_PAGE** Methods: **doEndTag**, **doStartTag**, **getParent**, **release**
IterationTag	The **IterationTag** interface extends **Tag** by defining one additional method that controls the re-evaluation of its body. Field: **EVAL_BODY_AGAIN** Method: **doAfterBody**
BodyTag	The **BodyTag** interface extends **IterationTag** by defining additional methods that let a tag handler manipulate the content of evaluating its body. Fields: None Method: **doInitBody**
TagSupport	The **TagSupport** class is used as the base class for new tag handlers. Your tag handlers that don't alter the body of a custom tag extend this class. The **TagSupport** class implements the **Tag** and **IterationTag** interfaces and adds additional convenience methods, including getter methods for the properties in **Tag**. Methods: **doAfterBody**, **doEndTag**, **doStartTag**, **getParent**, **release**
BodyTagSupport	The **BodyTagSupport** class implements the **BodyTag** interface and adds additional convenience methods, including getter methods for the **bodyContent** property and additional methods to create a reference to the previous **out** JspWriter. Field: **bodyContent** Methods: **doAfterBody**, **doEndTag**, **doInitBody**, **doStartTag**, **getBodyContent**, **getParent**, **getPreviousOut**, **release**

The basic idea is to extend `TagSupport` if you don't need the tag body, but to extend `BodyTagSupport` if you do. As the container finds the tags listed in Table 10.2, the event model triggers the container to call certain tag-handler methods that you override from either `TagSupport` or `BodyTagSupport`. Table 10.4 lists the methods that get triggered when the container processes each custom tag.

Table 10.4 Event Methods of a Custom Tag

Element	Associated Tag Body Content
doStartTag()	This method is called when the container first starts to process the tag. Notice that when this method is invoked, the body has not yet been evaluated. It can return either the **EVAL_BODY_INCLUDE** or the **SKIP_BODY** fields.
doEndTag()	This method is called after the container completes the **doStartTag()** method. Notice that the body of your custom tag might or might not have been evaluated, depending on the return value of **doStartTag()**. It can return either the **EVAL_PAGE** or the **SKIP_PAGE** fields.
doAfterBody()	This method is used for iterations (**IterationTag**). It is called after every body evaluation to control whether the body will be re-evaluated. If this method returns **EVAL_BODY_AGAIN**, the body is re-evaluated. If it returns **SKIP_BODY**, the body is skipped and **doEndTag()** is invoked next.
release()	This is called on a **Tag** handler to release state.
PageConext.getOut()	This is how you add the output stream directly. This method returns **javax.servlet.jsp.JspWriter**.

Tag-handler methods are called by the JSP page's servlet during the evaluation of the tag. In your tag handler, you implement certain tags based on the type of tag you want to use. Table 10.5 shows which methods you need based on the tag type.

Table 10.5 Event Methods Necessary to Process a Given Tag Type

Tag Type	Required Methods
Basic and those with body	**doStartTag**, **doEndTag**, **release**
Body, iterative evaluation	**doStartTag**, **doAfterBody**, **doEndTag**, **release**
Body, interaction	**doStartTag**, **doInitBody**, **doAfterBody**, **doEndTag**, **release**
Attributes	**doStartTag**, **doEndTag**, **release**, **setAttribute1**, **getAttribute1...**, **setAttributeN**, **getAttributeN**

You've probably noticed that these methods don't add to the output stream with the `return` keyword. When you override these methods in your tag handler class, you add to the output stream directly with the `JspWriter` object. The return from these methods is reserved to tell the container what to do next. For example, if one of these methods returns the `SKIP_PAGE` constant, the container does not process anymore of the JSP code after that tag. This constant causes the container to ignore the page after that tag.

Table 10.6 lists the return values possible for the event methods described in more detail immediately after the discussion on these fields. These return constants tell the container what to do after processing the triggered method.

Table 10.6 Event Methods of a Custom Tag

Element	Returned from Which Method
EVAL_BODY_INCLUDE	Evaluates the body into an existing out stream (**doStartTag()**).
EVAL_BODY_AGAIN	Evaluates the body again. Used for iterations (**doAfterBody()**).
EVAL_PAGE	Continues to evaluate the page (**doEndTag()**).
SKIP_BODY	Skips body evaluation. Stops processing the JSP after the current custom tag (**doStartTag()**, **doAfterBody()**).
SKIP_PAGE	Stops processing the JSP after the current custom tag (**doEndTag()**).

When you write a tag handler, you need to tell the container what to do regarding the tag body and the remainder of the JSP page. You will likely see one of the constants in Table 10.6 on the exam.

Custom Tag Body

As you learned in the previous section, the body of a custom tag is significant. You will be required to understand how the tag body is processed for an empty tag, a scriptlet in the body of the tag, and text meant strictly for the tag handler.

As shown in Table 10.7, there are three ways to use the body of a custom tag. Table 10.7 matches examples that look like what you will encounter on the exam, with the appropriate descriptor `bodycontent` element.

Table 10.7 bodycontent Element of a Custom Tag

Element	TLD **bodycontent** Declaration
<tagLibrary:myTag firstName= "Patricia" lastName="Trottier" ... />	<bodycontent>empty</bodycontent>
<tagLibrary:myTag> <%= 23 * counter %> </tagLibrary:myTag>	<bodycontent>JSP</bodycontent>
<tagLibrary:myTag> SELECT * FROM CUSTOMER </tagLibrary:myTag>	<bodycontent>tagdependent </bodycontent>

The `empty` (tag with no body) and `JSP` (default and interpreted if present) options are straightforward. The `tagdependent` option is the strange one. This means that the text is sent to the tag handler, but the container ignores it otherwise.

Tag Library Descriptor

You must know how to write a tag library descriptor. The elements that you'll see questions about are the tag name, the tag handler location, the type of content that the tag accepts, and tag attributes (whether required and settable dynamically). Table 10.8 lists all these elements with descriptions.

Table 10.8 Ways to Use Custom Tags

Element	Description
<name>tagName</name>	This required element is the name of the tag and is referred to after the colon in a JSP file (**<libraryName:tagName>**).
<tagclass>packageName.className </tagclass>	This required element points to the tag handler class using the fully qualified package name of the class, as if you were using it in a class without the **import** statement. The package name is the directory structure under the WEB-INF/classes directory.

(continued)

Table 10.8 Ways to Use Custom Tags *(continued)*

Element	Description
<bodycontent>tagdependent | JSP | empty</bodycontent>	The **tagdependent** option means the tag will regard the contents of the body as non-JSP. The body is passed verbatim to the tag handler itself. The body of the action may be empty. The **JSP** option means that the body is interpreted before being made available to the tag handler. The body is considered JSP if the **<body-content>** element is missing. The **empty** option means that the tag can have no body.
taglib/tag/attribute	**Description**
<name>attributeName</name>	This required element is the name of the attribute in a tag.
<required>true | false</required>	This optional element within the attribute element tells the container whether you have to specify a value for this attribute when you use the custom tag in JSP.
<rtexprvalue>true | false</rtexprvalue>	The **rtexprvalue** element tells the container whether the attribute can take a scriptlet expression as a value (dynamically assigned).

Accessing JSP Objects from the Custom Tag Handler

The tag handler class can access a JSP page's implicit variables and its attributes. To use a JSP page's implicit variables and attributes from a tag handler, you need the `PageContext` object. An instance of this object provides access to all the namespaces and most attributes for a JSP page. You can grab the implicit objects with the following methods:

- `getOut()`—Returns the current `JspWriter` stream being used for client response
- `getException()`—Returns any exception passed to this as an error page
- `getPage()`—Returns the `Page` implementation class instance (`Servlet`) associated with this `PageContext`

- `getRequest()`—Returns the `ServletRequest` for this `PageContext`
- `getResponse()`—Returns the `ServletResponse` for this `PageContext`
- `getSession()`—Returns the `HttpSession` for this `PageContext` or `null`
- `getServletConfig()`—Returns the `ServletConfig` for this `PageContext`
- `getServletContext()`—Returns the `ServletContext` for this `PageContext`

Notice that to get servlet-initialization parameters, you need the **ServletConfig** object. To get the application-initialization parameters, you need the **PageContext** object.

The previous list details methods that you use to get JSP page objects. You use them in the tag handler as you would any servlet. Likewise, you can access the attributes of a JSP page. The following methods are used to access the attributes from your tag handler for a given JSP page:

- `setAttribute()`—Registers the name and object specified with appropriate scope semantics
- `getAttribute()`—Returns the object associated with the name in the page scope, or `null` if not found
- `findAttribute()`—Searches for the named attribute in page, request, session (if valid), and application scope(s), and returns the value associated or `null`
- `removeAttribute()`—Removes the object reference associated with the given name by looking in all scopes in the scope order
- `getAttributesScope()`—Returns the scope of the object associated with the name specified or `0`
- `getAttributeNamesInScope()`—Returns an Enumeration of names (`java.lang.String`) of all the attributes in the specified scope.

Returning a Tag Handler from a Method

Occasionally, you will want to nest tags. For example, you might have one tag that will return the price of the shopping cart. You could nest a location tag within it to provide locale-specific currency formatting. Within the inner tag's methods, you will need a method that returns a reference to the outer tag handler.

The following methods are most helpful when trying to reach another tag from an inner tag:

- `getParent()`—Finds the parent (closest enclosing tag handler) for this tag handler. You might use this to navigate the nested tag handler structure at runtime.

- `findAncestorWithClass()`—Finds the instance of a given class type that is closest to a given instance. This method uses the `getParent()` method from the `Tag` interface.

Practice Questions

Question 1

Given the following code snippet:

```
<tagLibrary:myTag>
   <%= 23 * counter %>
</tagLibrary:myTag>
```

Which of the following is the associated TLD declaration?

- ❍ A. **<bodycontent>tagdependentempty</bodycontent>**
- ❍ B. **<bodycontent>JSP</bodycontent>**
- ❍ C. **<bodycontent>empty</bodycontent>**
- ❍ D. **<bodycontent>scriptlet</bodycontent>**

Answer B is correct. The `tagdependent` option means that the tag regards the contents of the body as non-JSP. The body is passed verbatim to the tag handler itself. The body of the action may be empty. The `JSP` option means that the body is interpreted before being made available to the tag handler. The body is considered JSP if the `<bodycontent>` element is missing. The `empty` option means that the tag can have no body.

Question 2

Which two of the following in the tag library descriptor are part of the **tag** element? (Choose two.)

- ❑ A. **namespace**
- ❑ B. **name**
- ❑ C. **tagclass**
- ❑ D. **taguri**

Answers B and C are correct. The `tag` element includes the following elements: `name`, `tagclass`, `info`, and `attribute` (`attribute` has three child elements—`name`, `required`, and `rtexprvalue`).

Question 3

Which two of the following in the tag library descriptor are part of the tag's **attribute** element? (Choose two.)

- ❑ A. **rtexprvalue**
- ❑ B. **required**
- ❑ C. **tagclass**
- ❑ D. **uri**

Answers A and B are correct. The tag's `attribute` element includes the following elements: `name`, `required`, and `rtexprvalue` (attribute is a child element of `tag`).

Question 4

Which file is not used when the **taglib** directive in a JSP page includes a URI pointing directly to the tag library descriptor?

- ❍ A. web.xml
- ❍ B. yourPage.jsp
- ❍ C. YourTagLibraryDefinition.tld
- ❍ D. YourTagHanlder.java

Answer A is correct. All of these files are critical to using custom tags except the deployment descriptor, option A. This is because the `taglib` URI points directly to the TLD. If you used only a name in the `taglib` directive, the container would look in the web.xml file to map that name to an actual location for the TLD.

Question 5

What is a valid taglib directive within a JSP page?

- ❍ A. **<%@ page taglib="http://www.myCompany.com/jsp/JAXP" prefix="JAXP"%>**
- ❍ B. **<%@ taglib prefix="JAXP"%>**
- ❍ C. **<%@ page prefix="JAXP"%>**
- ❍ D. **<%@ taglib uri="http://www.myCompany.com/jsp/JAXP" prefix="JAXP"%>**

Answer D is correct. The `taglib` directive creates a reference to the prefix. The prefix tells the container which library you want. Option D is a valid `taglib` directive that might be typical for the JavaServer Pages standard tag library.

Question 6

What base interface does the **doStartTag()** method belong to?

- ❍ A. **TagSupport**
- ❍ B. **TagProcess**
- ❍ C. **Tag**
- ❍ D. **TagStart**

Answer C is correct. Your tag handler is a class that extends the `TagSupport` class, which implements the `IterationTag` interface, which implements the `Tag` interface if it has `doStartTag()` and `doEndTag()` methods.

Question 7

What is the correct order of life-cycle event calls by the container when it processes a custom tag that doesn't have a body?

- ❍ A. **doStartTag**, **doInitBody**, **doAfterBody**, **doEndTag**
- ❍ B. **doStartTag**, **doEndTag**, **doInitBody**, **doAfterBody**
- ❍ C. **doStartTag**, **doStartBody**, **doEndBody**, **doEndTag**
- ❍ D. **doInitTag**, **doInitBody**, **doAfterBody**, **doAfterTag**

Answer A is correct. These are the correct methods are in the correct order. Option B has the correct method names, but they are in the wrong order. Options C and D contain incorrect method names.

Question 8

Used in a custom tag, what is the **tagdependent** element?

- ❍ A. It is part of the **bodycontent** element.
- ❍ B. It tells the container to validate the custom tag.
- ❍ C. It is part of the **name** element.
- ❍ D. It is in the web.xml file.

Answer A is correct. It is part of the `bodycontent` element. The `tagdependent` option means that the tag regards the contents of the body as non-JSP. The body is passed verbatim to the tag handler itself.

Question 9

Used in a tag library descriptor to define a custom tag, what is the **rtexprvalue** element?

- ❍ A. It defines the attribute data type.
- ❍ B. It defines whether a custom tag can return a value.
- ❍ C. It is a custom tag return type.
- ❍ D. It is an attribute can take a scriptlet expression as a value.

Answer D is correct. The `rtexprvalue` element tells the container whether the attribute can take a scriptlet expression as a value (dynamically assigned).

Question 10

How would you implement the method(s) to handle a simple tag such as **<myTag:color />**?

❍ A.

```
public SimpleTag implements TagSupport {
  public int doStartTag() throws JspException {
      out.print("Hello.");
    return SKIP_BODY;
  }
  public int doEndTag() {
    return EVAL_PAGE;
  }
}
```

❍ B.

```
public SimpleTag implements TagSupport {
  public int doStartTag() throws JspException {
    try {
      pageContext.getOut().print("Hello.");
    } catch (Exception ex) {
      throw new JspTagException("SimpleTag: " +
        ex.getMessage());
    }
    return SKIP_BODY;
  }
  public int doEndTag() {
    return EVAL_PAGE;
  }
}
```

❍ C.

```
public SimpleTag extends TagSupport {
  public int doStartTag() throws JspException {
    try {
      pageContext.getOut().print("Hello.");
    } catch (Exception ex) {
      throw new JspTagException("SimpleTag: " +
        ex.getMessage());
    }
    return SKIP_BODY;
  }
  public int doEndTag() {
    return EVAL_PAGE;
  }
}
```

❍ D.

```
public SimpleTag extends Tag {
  public int doStartTag() throws JspException {
    try {
      pageContext.getOut().print("Hello.");
    } catch (Exception ex) {
      throw new JspTagException("SimpleTag: " +
        ex.getMessage());
    }
    return SKIP_BODY;
  }
}
```

Answer C is correct. Option C correctly extends `TagSupport`, and the rest of this class is right. Options A and B implement `TagSupport`, which is a class; you must extend `TagSupport`. Also, you don't just use `out`; you must get the `PrintWriter` object, as shown in option C. Option D is wrong mainly because it extends `Tag`, an interface that must be implemented.

Need to Know More?

A nice tutorial by Magnus Rydin—www.orionserver.com/taglibtut/lesson1/

A nice tutorial by Wrox—http://tutorials.findtutorials.com/read/category/82/id/233 and http://tutorials.findtutorials.com/read/category/82/id/234

A small but helpful introduction to tag libraries by Stardeveloper.com—www.stardeveloper.com:8080/articles/081301-1.shtml

A good overview of tag libraries from BEA (helpful because BEA uses its own excellent product weblogic, which differs somewhat from Tomcat used in this book)—http://edocs.bea.com/wls/docs61/taglib/overview.html#362351

Servlets and JavaServer Pages, by Marty Hall, an expert who is highly regarded—www.coreservlets.com/.

More Servlets and JavaServer Pages, by Marty Hall—www.moreservlets.com/

Designing JSP Custom Tag Libraries, by Sue Spielman, a very short but excellent snapshot of tag libraries—www.onjava.com/pub/a/onjava/2000/12/15/jsp_custom_tags.html

Sun's reference page, with many good links for tag libraries—http://java.sun.com/products/jsp/taglibraries.html

JavaServer Pages Standard Tag Library (JSTL) tutorial—java.sun.com/webservices/docs/1.0/tutorial/doc/JSTL.html

Design Patterns

Terms you'll need to understand:

- ✓ JFC/Swing architecture
- ✓ Design patterns
- ✓ Model-View-Controller
- ✓ Value objects
- ✓ Data Access Object
- ✓ Business Delegate
- ✓ Front controller

Techniques you'll need to master:

- ✓ Given a scenario description with a list of issues, select the design pattern that would best solve those issues.
- ✓ Match design patterns with their benefits.
- ✓ Know how to use these patterns: Value Objects, MVC, Data Access Object, and Business Delegate.

Servlet Design Patterns

In this chapter, you will study design patterns, a highly abstract approach to designing applications—here, Web applications. For example, Swing GUIs are built with the Model-View-Controller pattern. Your familiarity with the four patterns listed in the objectives will help you answer the related questions on the exam.

It is imperative that you understand how to apply patterns to software problems. Fortunately, many patterns are defined today, with many more published often. The purpose of this chapter is to define each of the four patterns listed in the objectives so that you can answer any exam question about them. The style of question for patterns on the exam is matching statements and benefits and then choosing the best pattern for a given situation.

Object-oriented modeling languages started gathering momentum in the 1980s. A few dozen methodologists systematized the approach and documentation of object-oriented analysis and design. It was chaos because there was no one modeling language—at least, not one clearly prominent language. Then in 1994, Grady Booch and Jim Rumbaugh of Rational Software Corporation started unifying the Booch and OMT (Object Modeling Technique) methods: UML was born. In 1996, a Request for Proposal (RFP) was issued by the Object Management Group (OMG) for the Unified Modeling Language (UML). In 1997, it was adopted and it has only recently become popular. Design patterns stand to have as big an impact (if not a bigger impact) on object-oriented analysis and design. We still don't have a real champion, although Sun is positioning itself as the chief evangelist. Who else has so publicly immersed design patterns into its wares?

I leave it to the reader to review the history of this movement. I'll just mention that it started with Alexander, a building architect who invented patterns. Afterward, the Gang of Four, as Erich Gamma, Richard Helm, Ralph Johnson, and John Vlissides are now known, applied his patterns to software in their classic book *Design Patterns: Elements of Reusable Object-Oriented Software* (Addison-Wesley, 1995). These four people laid the foundation; there are many good sites and books to fill in the rest.

The following section is divided into four parts, one for each design pattern that will be on the exam. I use the classical way to define patterns: I describe each pattern's elements using a prettied version of GOF.

The pattern elements used in this chapter are listed here:

- Benefits
- Purpose

- Solution
- Reference

Patterns on the Exam

As mentioned previously, you must know five patterns for the exam: Value Objects, Data Access Object, Business Delegate, MVC, and Front Controller. The following five definitions cover all you need to know about each one. Of course, I hope you get curious and study them deeper, but that is not the purpose of this book. Rather, you'll read the essential material about each one, enough to ace this portion of the exam.

Value Object

This pattern provides the best way to exchange data across tiers or system boundaries. It is an object that encapsulates a set of values (namesake) and is itself moved across the boundary so that attempts to get the values of those attributes are local calls.

If you get a question regarding an advantage in a network situation, the Value Object should be your first guess, unless something else in the question statement gives preference to another pattern.

Benefits and Gotchas

- Improves response time (local not remote calls)
- Reduces the load on the remote object itself because access to the attributes of the Value Objects becomes local
- Reduces network traffic by acting as a caching proxy of a remote object
- Allows data to become outdated

Purpose

This pattern attempts to reduce the network overhead by minimizing the number of network calls to get data from the business tier. It provides a mechanism for exchanging many remote calls to local, direct calls.

Solution

This pattern is useful when you need a collection of data from a remote source or, more likely, when a client has to make several calls for data from entity beans. J2EE applications often use enterprise beans. All calls to these beans are performed via remote interfaces to the bean due to Java's architecture.

Sun suggests using `getData()` and `setData()` methods on certain entity beans as a way to get and set a value object containing the set of attribute values. Calling the `getData()` method once replaces multiple calls to get methods. Likewise, the `setData()` method replaces many set calls.

Reference

Sun's Value Object page: `http://developer.java.sun.com/developer/restricted/patterns/ValueObject.html`

Data Access Object

This pattern provides the connection between the business logic tier and the resource (usually database or file) tier. The Data Access Object represents a general interface to the resources layer: It handles all calls to it. JDBC is an example of this.

This pattern is an object that encapsulates a set of behaviors for accessing databases, files, and other resources. This way you have only one API to deal with rather than a different one for every type of resource.

Benefits and Gotchas

- Clients and components can now access data with the same API, which makes the variety of sources transparent and reduces complexity.
- Easy changing of data sources, with reduced errors.
- Greater deployment flexibility.
- Vendor and implementation independence.
- More extensibility.
- Increased complexity.

Purpose

The problem being attacked here is that applications often need to use persistent data. This data persists in many forms, such as files, relational database, XML storage, and other types of repositories. All these stores have different APIs. Interfacing with so many APIs presents a problem when designing clients. This pattern will provide a uniform API to any persistent data storage. It attempts to reduce the network overhead by minimizing the number of network calls to get data from the business tier.

Solution

There needs to be a layer that has a uniform API to access these disparate data sources. The pattern applies to any application that requires access to several data source types, or even an application that accesses only one but that may switch between sources in the future. You use this pattern to design a Data Access Object that abstracts the access API to various data sources. For example, JDBC represents this pattern.

Reference

Sun's Data Access Object page: `http://java.sun.com/blueprints/patterns/j2ee_patterns/value_object/index.html`

Business Delegate

This pattern reduces the dependency between tiers. It is an attempt to make tiers interchangeable so that one can access the services of any other. It is the mediator between services. The Business Delegate pattern makes it easier to communicate requests and results from one layer to another.

Benefits and Gotchas

- Caching is always good between parts that exchange a lot of data.
- This pattern changes the interface, with the intent of making the API more stable from the presentation tier's perspective.
- This pattern will now handle any exceptions, whether from the business tier itself or from the plumbing between it and the requester.
- This pattern isolates the presentation and business tiers from each other by adding a mediator between the two, making it easier to manage changes on either side.
- This pattern offers reduced coupling and improved manageability.

Purpose

This pattern isolates the presentation layer from changes in the business-tier API. Usually, the presentation tier interacts directly with the business logic layer. This sounds fine. However, what if the business services change and the old API becomes invalid? If this happens, the presentation tier will break. The problem is that the access code in the presentation tier is vulnerable. This delegate is responsible for reliably transporting messages between the two.

Solution

Large systems change components often. A change in the business tier often occurs, which breaks the access portion of clients. Sun offers this advice:

> Use a Business Delegate to reduce coupling between presentation-tier clients and business services. The Business Delegate hides the underlying implementation details of the business service, such as lookup and access details of the EJB architecture.

B2B systems usually employ an XML exchange for communicating between disparate systems. Proxy services and lookup services also usually represent this pattern.

Reference

Sun's Business Delegate page: `http://developer.java.sun.com/developer/restricted/patterns/ BusinessDelegate.html`

Model-View-Controller

The Model-View-Controller architecture compartmentalizes data (model) from the presentation (view) and data from the business logic (controller). This pattern is the hardest on the exam. The idea is closely related to the recent move from two-tier to three-tier architectures. This arrangement allows multiple views to share the same enterprise data model. It is a clear functional separation of roles and a formalization of the data-business-presentation movement that dominated three-tier architectures over the last decade.

Benefits and Gotchas

- Clients access a controller that accesses the model, instead of clients accessing the model directly.
- Another layer must be built, which adds work.
- It is easier to break a project into pieces because the controller API is what both the client developers and the model developers are targeting.
- It is easier to make incremental updates.

- Reusability is possible because the presentation is easy to modify without disturbing underlying data and logic.
- Multiple views of the same data exist.
- The software is easier to maintain due to separation of data from views.

Purpose

Different views of the same data are a common need. Conversely, the same client needs to access different models. This pattern carefully manages communication between the client and model data and functionality. It must allow changing the client or changing the model with minimal impact on the system. This pattern attempts to minimize the impact of changing any of the parts—namely, the model, view, or controller. This separation of concerns is a key advantage of using this pattern.

Solution

Although the primary purpose of MVC is to build UIs, it can be used to establish an analogous notification protocol between nonvisual objects. The `Observer/Observable` objects in java.util were designed with pattern in mind. You should use the Model-View-Controller architecture to decouple presentation from core data access functionality. Also, this pattern enables you to control the communication between them so that multiple views can see the same enterprise data model, or multiple data models can present to the same view. For example, Java uses MVC for JFC/Swing.

Reference

Sun's Model-View-Controller page: `http://java.sun.com/blueprints/patterns/j2ee_patterns/model_view_controller/index.html`

The Front Controller pattern is on the exam even though it is not mentioned in the objectives. Conversely, you probably won't see questions about the Business Delegate pattern even though it is in the objectives. You'll need to know both, however, because Sun isn't likely to remove the Front Controller pattern questions; it just might add questions for the Business Delegate pattern.

Front Controller

This pattern is used as a presentation controller that allows the supporting resources to change without breaking the presentation layer. This pattern presents one entry point to a Web site or service, providing a centralized entry point that controls and manages Web request handling. When the user accesses resources directly without going through a centralized mechanism, the resource may have moved. The Front Controller pattern fixes this problem.

Benefits and Gotchas

- Consistent presentation is offered to the user community.
- It is better to have a central controller allocate shared resources than to have individual resources fend for themselves independently.
- The location of resources may change.
- This controller must delegate the request to the proper resource and view.
- This pattern adds only a little more work to building a Web site at first.
- Multiple resources share common needs, such as security (authentication and authorization).
- This pattern makes the API more stable from the presentation tier's perspective.
- This pattern will now handle any exceptions, whether from the business tier itself or from the plumbing between it and the requester.
- This pattern isolates the presentation and the business tiers from each other by adding a mediator between the two, making it is easier to manage changes on either side.

Solution

Sun recommends using a controller as the initial point of contact for handling a request. This architecture uses the controller to manage the handling of the request, including invoking security services such as authentication and authorization, delegating business processing, managing the choice of an appropriate view, handling errors, and managing the selection of content-creation strategies.

Simplified Web sites expose all resources directly. As a site grows, there comes a time when it is better to decouple the navigation from the resources. There needs to be a controller that manages the requests and decides which resource best satisfies the request. Some of the known uses are Servlet Front Strategy, Command and Controller Strategy, and the Logical Resource Mapping Strategy.

References

- Sun's Front Controller pattern page: `java.sun.com/blueprints/corej2eepatterns/Patterns/FrontController.html`
- An example program that uses the Front Controller pattern: `java.sun.com/blueprints/code/jps11/src/com/sun/j2ee/blueprints/petstore/control/web/MainServlet.java.html`

Practice Questions

Question 1

Which pattern is noted for multiple views to share the same enterprise data?

❍ A. Business Delegate

❍ B. Data Access Object

❍ C. Model-View-Controller

❍ D. Value Object

Answer C is correct. The Model-View-Controller architecture compartmentalizes the data (model) from the presentation (view) and the data from the business logic (controller). The idea is closely related to the industry shift from two-tier to three-tier architectures. This arrangement allows multiple views to share the same enterprise data model.

Question 2

JDBC is a good example of what pattern?

❍ A. Business Delegate

❍ B. Data Access Object

❍ C. Model-View-Controller

❍ D. Value Object

Answer B is correct. JDBC is exactly this pattern. Although JDBC doesn't handle everything, it does handle most relational types. You would probably write a higher-level object to handle files and other types, but then use JDBC to handle RDBMS functionality.

Question 3

Which pattern isolates the presentation tier from the business tier by adding a mediator between the two?

❍ A. Business Delegate

❍ B. Data Access Object

❍ C. Model-View-Controller

❍ D. Value Object

Answer A is correct. The Business Delegate pattern isolates the presentation and business tiers from each other by adding a mediator between the two, making it easier to manage changes on either side.

Question 4

Which pattern interjects a controller between the presentation and the data?

- ❍ A. Business Delegate
- ❍ B. Data Access Object
- ❍ C. Model-View-Controller
- ❍ D. Value Object

Answer C is correct. Different views of the same data are a common need. Conversely, the same client needs to access different models. This pattern carefully manages communication between the client and model data and functionality. It does this by interjecting a controller between the presentation and the data.

Question 5

Which pattern reduces network traffic as one of its primary goals?

- ❍ A. Business Delegate
- ❍ B. Data Access Object
- ❍ C. Model-View-Controller
- ❍ D. Value Object

Answer D is correct. The Value Object model reduces the network overhead by minimizing the number of network calls to get data from the business tier.

Question 6

Which pattern is noted for cache, improving performance and presenting a consistent API to another tier?

- ❍ A. Business Delegate
- ❍ B. Data Access Object
- ❍ C. Model-View-Controller
- ❍ D. Value Object

Answer A is correct. Use a Business Delegate pattern to reduce coupling between presentation-tier clients and business services. The Business Delegate pattern hides the underlying implementation details of the business service, such as lookup and access details of the EJB architecture. This delegate is responsible for reliably transporting messages between the two, often employing some type of a cache.

Question 7

Which pattern has as one of its chief benefits the migration of remote calls to local ones?

- ❍ A. Business Delegate
- ❍ B. Data Access Object
- ❍ C. Model-View-Controller
- ❍ D. Value Object

Answer D is correct. The Value Object pattern is used to collect remote data into an object that is sent to the client so that the client can make local getter calls.

Need to Know More?

Sun's Design Patterns page—`http://java.sun.com/blueprints/patterns/j2ee_patterns/index.html`

Sun Java Center J2EETM Pattern article—`http://developer.java.sun.com/developer/technicalArticles/J2EE/patterns/`

J2EE Patterns Catalog—`http://developer.java.sun.com/developer/restricted/patterns/J2EEPatternsAtAGlance.html`

Hillside Group Patterns Home Page—`http://hillside.net/patterns/`

Portland Pattern Repository—`http://c2.com/ppr`

Java Guru: Patterns FAQ Home Page—`www.jguru.com/faq/Patterns`

Sample Test

Question 1

Which design pattern is used to decouple presentation from core data access functionality?

- ❍ A. Business Delegate
- ❍ B. Data Access Object
- ❍ C. Model-View-Controller
- ❍ D. Value Object

Question 2

Which design pattern is used to minimize coupling between presentation-tier clients and the application service API?

- ❍ A. Business Delegate
- ❍ B. Data Access Object
- ❍ C. Model-View-Controller
- ❍ D. Value Object

Question 3

Which design pattern provides a layer that has a uniform API to access disparate information sources?

- ❍ A. Business Delegate
- ❍ B. Data Access Object
- ❍ C. Model-View-Controller
- ❍ D. Value Object

Question 4

How would you define a custom tag in a tag library?

❍ A.

```
<tag>
     <name>whatColorIsIt</name>
     <tagclass>examples.ColorTagHandler</tagclass>
     <info>echos text</info>
     <attribute-name>
           color
     </attribute-name>
</tag>
```

❍ B.

```
<taglib>
     <name>whatColorIsIt</name>
     <tagclass>examples.ColorTagHandler</tagclass>
     <info>echos text</info>
</taglib>
```

❍ C.

```
<taglib>
     <name>whatColorIsIt</name>
     <tagclass>examples.ColorTagHandler</tagclass>
     <info>echos text</info>
     <attribute>
           <name>color</name>
           <required>true</required>
           <rtexprvalue>false</rtexprvalue>
     </attribute>
</taglib>
```

❍ D.

```
<tag>
     <name>whatColorIsIt</name>
     <tagclass>examples.ColorTagHandler</tagclass>
     <info>echos text</info>
     <attribute>
           <name>color</name>
           <required>true</required>
           <rtexprvalue>false</rtexprvalue>
     </attribute>
</tag>
```

Question 5

Read the following code snippet.

```
<taglib>
    <taglib-uri>
            http://www.yourcompany.com/yourTagLibrary
    </taglib-uri>
    <taglib-location>
       /WEB-INF/yourTagLibrary.tld
    </taglib-location>
</taglib>
```

What statement applies to this code snippet?

❍ A. The **tablib** element of the deployment descriptor is required if you use a **taglib** directive in a JSP page that references a TLD by name (indirectly) rather than by location (directly).

❍ B. This tag goes into the WEB-INF/myApplication/web.xml file.

❍ C. This definition is incorrect because the **taglib-uri** should have been **uri**.

❍ D. This definition is incorrect because the **taglib** should have been **tag**.

Question 6

How would you retrieve servlet-initialization parameters?

❍ A.

```
String value =
     getServletConfig().getInitParameter("paramName");
```

❍ B.

```
String value =
     getServletConfig().getInitParameter(paramIndex);
```

❍ C.

```
String value =
     getServletConfig().getParameter("paramName");
```

❍ D.

```
String value =
     getServletConfig().getParameter(paramIndex);
```

Question 7

How do you declare initialization parameters for the servlet in the deployment descriptor?

❍ A.

```
<web-app>
  <servlet>
    <servletname>servletName</servletname>
    <servletclass>com.myCo.MyServlet</servletclass>
    <initparam>
      <paramname>color</paramname>
      <paramvalue>blue</paramvalue>
    </initparam>
  </servlet>
</web-app>
```

❍ B.

```
<web-app>
  <servlet>
    <servlet-name>servletName</servlet-name>
    <servlet-class>com.myCo.MyServlet</servlet-class>
    <init-param>
      <name>color</name>
      <value>blue</value>
    </init-param>
  </servlet>
</web-app>
```

❍ C.

```
<web-app>
  <servlet>
    <name>servletName</name>
    <class>com.myCo.MyServlet</class>
    <init-param>
      <param-name>color</param-name>
      <param-value>blue</param-value>
    </init-param>
  </servlet>
</web-app>
```

❍ D.

```
<web-app>
  <servlet>
    <servlet-name>servletName</servlet-name>
    <servlet-class>com.myCo.MyServlet</servlet-class>
    <init-param>
      <param-name>color</param-name>
      <param-value>blue</param-value>
    </init-param>
  </servlet>
</web-app>
```

Question 8

What method is called by the servlet container to process a GET request?

❍ A.

```
public String doGet(HttpServletRequest req,
                    HttpServletResponse resp)
       throws IOException { //code }
```

❍ B.

```
public void doGet(HttpServletRequest req,
                    HttpServletResponse resp)
       throws IOException { //code }
```

❍ C.

```
public String doGet(HttpServletRequest req,
                    HttpServletResponse resp)
       throws ServletException { //code }
```

❍ D.

```
public void doGet(ServletRequest req,
                    ServletResponse resp)
       throws ServletException { //code }
```

Question 9

What method is called by the servlet container just before this servlet is put into service?

❍ A. **public void init() throws IOException { //code }**

❍ B. **public void start() throws IOException { //code }**

❍ C. **public void service() throws ServletException { //code }**

❍ D. **public void init() throws ServletException { //code }**

Question 10

What method is called by the servlet container just after the servlet is removed from service?

❍ A. **public void destroy() { // code... }**

❍ B. **public void destroy() throws ServletException { // code... }**

❍ C. **public void finalize() throws ServletException { // code... }**

❍ D. **public void finalize() { // code... }**

Question 11

How would you add an entry to the log file from a servlet assuming that e is an initialized **Exception** object?

❍ A. **getServletConfig().log("An exception occurred", e);**

❍ B. **getServletConfig().logger(e);**

❍ C. **getServletContext().log(e);**

❍ D. **getServletContext().log("An exception occurred", e);**

Question 12

Assuming that the servlet method for handling HTTP **GET** requests is **doGet(HttpServletRequest req, HttpServletResponse res)**, how do you get a request parameter in that servlet?

❍ A. **String value = req.getInitParameter("name");**

❍ B. **String value = res.getParameter("name");**

❍ C. **String value = req.getParameter("name");**

❍ D. **String value = req.getInitParameter(10);**

Question 13

Assuming that the servlet method for handling HTTP **GET** requests is **doGet(HttpServletRequest req, HttpServletResponse resp)**, which two statements are true regarding the following code snippet? (Choose two.)

```
Enumeration enum = req.getParameterNames();
```

- ❑ A. This is how you retrieve the names of all request parameters.
- ❑ B. This is how you would then get the name of the next request parameter:
  ```
  name = (String)enum.nextElement();
  ```
- ❑ C. The code snippet in the question will not work. The return type is a String array, not an Enumeration object.
- ❑ D. This would have worked had the code been:
  ```
  String[] names = req.getParameterNames();
  ```

Question 14

What is the deployment descriptor element that maps a servlet name to the full path (do not include the brackets)?

____

Question 15

Which two of the following statements are true regarding declaring a servlet instance in a deployment descriptor? (Choose two.)

- ❑ A. The servlet element specifies the fully qualified class name of the servlet.
- ❑ B. The tags are nested within **<web-app> </web-app>** tags.
- ❑ C. The tags do not define parameters.
- ❑ D. The tags are **<servlet-instance></servlet-instance>**.

Question 16

How do you perform a server-side include whose content gets translated within the JSP page?

- ❍ A. **include** action
- ❍ B. **include** directive
- ❍ C. **include** scriptlet
- ❍ D. **include** expression

Question 17

Which two of the following methods are used to access object attributes within the session scope? (Choose two.)

- ❑ A. **getNames**
- ❑ B. **getSessionAttributes**
- ❑ C. **getAttribute**
- ❑ D. **getAttributeNames**

Question 18

How would you include dynamic content in a JSP page that doesn't get translated within the context of the current page?

- ❍ A. **<%@ page import="footer.html" %>**
- ❍ B. **include** directive
- ❍ C. **<%@include file="footer.html" %>**
- ❍ D. **jsp:include**

Question 19

Which two of the following pairs of JSP life-cycle events are in the correct chronological order so that the second term occurs after the first, but not necessarily immediately so? (Choose two.)

- ❑ A. **jspInit**, **jspService**
- ❑ B. Create instance, call **_jspService**
- ❑ C. Directive includes, translate page
- ❑ D. Call **jspInit**, call **jspDestroy**

Question 20

What is the interface used to access values and resources and to set object attributes within the session scope?

❍ A. **HttpSession**

❍ B. **RequestSession**

❍ C. **HttpRequestSession**

❍ D. **Session**

Question 21

Which two of the following are valid attributes of the JSP **page** directive? (Choose two.)

❑ A. **extends="package.class"**

❑ B. **errorPage="true"**

❑ C. **buffer="false"**

❑ D. **import="package.class"**

Question 22

How many servlet mappings in a deployment descriptor may be defined for one Web app?

❍ A. Unlimited.

❍ B. Servlet mappings don't go into the deployment descriptor.

❍ C. Zero.

❍ D. One.

Question 23

What method accesses attributes within the request scope?

❍ A. **getAttributes**

❍ B. **getNames**

❍ C. **getAttributeNames**

❍ D. **getNamedAttribute**

Question 24

What is the filename of the deployment descriptor file?

____

Question 25

What is an example of an expression?

- ❍ A. **<%= count %>**
- ❍ B. **<% String count=4; %>**
- ❍ C. **<% out.print("hello"); %>**
- ❍ D. **<%! String count=4; %>**

Question 26

Which one of the following is the most likely trigger to cause a browser to use the HTTP **HEAD** method?

- ❍ A. Client sends updated information to server.
- ❍ B. Server sends HTTP **HEAD** to client.
- ❍ C. Server requests HTTP **HEAD** of client.
- ❍ D. Client checks resource modification date/time.

Question 27

Which one of the following is not an attribute of the **jsp:useBean** tag?

- ❍ A. **scope**
- ❍ B. **name**
- ❍ C. **type**
- ❍ D. **class**

Question 28

Type the name of the method for deleting an attribute from a session object. (Do not include parentheses or parameters.)

____

Question 29

Which two statements are true regarding a distributable? (Choose two.)

- ❑ A. A given **ServletContext** instance may exist on different JVMs.
- ❑ B. Servlet context-init parameters are not likely to be shared across different JVMs.
- ❑ C. A different **ServletContext** instance may exist on different JVMs.
- ❑ D. Servlet context-init parameters are likely to be shared across different JVMs.

Question 30

How could you reference a session in a servlet?

- ❍ A. **Session mySession = Context.getSession();**
- ❍ B. **Session mySession = pageContext.getHttpSession();**
- ❍ C. **HttpSession mySession = pageContext.getHttpSession();**
- ❍ D. **HttpSession mySession = pageContext.getSession();**

Question 31

Which two of the following methods are used to access resources within the context scope? (Choose two.)

- ❑ A. **getSession**
- ❑ B. **getNamedDispatcher**
- ❑ C. **getDispatcher**
- ❑ D. **getRequestDispatcher**

Question 32

Which two of the following methods are used to access values and resources and to set object attributes within the session scope? (Choose two.)

- ❑ A. **setAttribute**
- ❑ B. **removeAttributeName**
- ❑ C. **deleteAttribute**
- ❑ D. **removeAttribute**

Question 33

Read the following code snippet.

```
<form method="POST" action="j_security_check">
        <input type="text" name="j_username">
        <input type="password" name="j_password">
</form>
```

Which two statements are true regarding this code snippet? (Choose two.)

- ❑ A. This can be used for BASIC security.
- ❑ B. This can be used for FORM security.
- ❑ C. The input field names are predefined.
- ❑ D. This can be used for POST security.

Question 34

What interface and method name should be used to acquire a binary stream for the response?

- ❍ A. **ServletResponse.getOutputStream**
- ❍ B. **ServletResponse.getStream**
- ❍ C. **ServletResponse.getWriterStream**
- ❍ D. **ServletResponse.getWriter**

Question 35

How do you append text to the output stream in a JSP page?

- ❍ A. **JspWriter.out.println("welcome to the customer page!");**
- ❍ B. **outputStream.print("hello");**
- ❍ C. **out.add("outputStream");**
- ❍ D. **out.println("outputStream");**

Question 36

Which two of the following pairs are equivalents? (Choose two.)

❑ A.

```
<% yourCode %>
<jsp:scriptlet>

yourCode
</jsp:scriptlet>
```

❑ B.

```
ServletContext.useBean("beanName",id,scope, class);

<jsp:useBean id="customer" scope="page" class=
➥"session.Customer" />
```

❑ C.

```
<%@ taglib uri="URIForLibrary" prefix="tagPrefix" %>

<jsp:taglib uri="URIForLibrary" prefix="tagPrefix" />
```

❑ D.

```
<%@ page att="val" %>

<jsp:directive.page att="val"/>
```

Question 37

How can you set several attributes of a Bean at the same time?

- ❍ A. You can't. They must be done individually.
- ❍ B. You do this with the deployment descriptor.
- ❍ C. You use the **jsp:setProperty** action with the **property** attribute set to the wildcard *.
- ❍ D. You use the **jsp:useBean** and list the attributes in this tag together.

Question 38

What interface and method name should be used to retrieve HTTP request header information?

- ❍ A. **ServletRequest.getNames**
- ❍ B. **HttpServletRequest.getHeaderNames**
- ❍ C. **HttpServletRequest.getHeaders**
- ❍ D. **ServletRequest.getHeadNames**

Question 39

Read the following listing.

```
1.  <html>
2.    <body>
3.
4.      <% x = x - 15; %>
5.      New customers: <%= x %>
6.    </body>
7.  </html>
```

What should be inserted on line 3 to allow successful compilation and produce an output of **New** customers: 20?

- ❍ A. **<%! int x = 35 %>**
- ❍ B. **<%@ int x = 35; %>**
- ❍ C. **<% int x = 35 ; %>**
- ❍ D. **int x = 35;**

Question 40

Read the following code snippet.

```
<%= myBean.getColor() %>
```

What option will produce the same result?

❍ A. **<jsp:getProperty name=myBean property=color />**

❍ B. **<jsp:getProperty "myBean.getColor" />**

❍ C. **<jsp:getProperty bean1.getColor/>**

❍ D. **<jsp:getProperty name="myBean" property="color" />**

Question 41

How do you set the scope of a Bean in a JSP page?

❍ A. Set the **scope** attribute of the **jsp:useBean** action.

❍ B. Set it in the deployment descriptor.

❍ C. Set it with the response object.

❍ D. Set it by assigning it to the given object, such as **session** or **application**.

Question 42

Which interface and method name should be used to retrieve the names of all HTML form parameters from the request?

❍ A. **ServletRequest.getParameterNames**

❍ B. **ServletRequest.getParameters**

❍ C. **Request.getParameters**

❍ D. **Request.getParameterValues**

Question 43

What method retrieves the value of an initialization parameter if you provide the name of the parameter to the **ServletContext** object?

____

Question 44

Given a JSP tag type **<%="Que" %>**, identify the equivalent type of JSP action.

- ❍ A. **<jsp:text>**
- ❍ B. **<jsp:declaration>**
- ❍ C. **<jsp:expression>**
- ❍ D. **<jsp:scriptlet>**

Question 45

What is a tag handler?

- ❍ A. An XML file that defines the properties and location of the tag-handler class file
- ❍ B. A tag used in a JSP page that declares a handle for referencing a JavaBean
- ❍ C. An element of the deployment descriptor
- ❍ D. A custom tag class

Question 46

How would you import classes into a JSP page?

- ❍ A. **<% java.util.Calendar cal = new java.util.Calendar(); %>**
- ❍ B. **jsp:import**
- ❍ C. **<%@ import "java.util.Calendar" %>**
- ❍ D. **<%@ page import="java.util.*, java.lang.*" %>**

Question 47

Which two of the following are best associated with the HTTP **HEAD** method? (Choose two.)

- ❑ A. It has a body.
- ❑ B. It has no body.
- ❑ C. It is a modified **POST**.
- ❑ D. It is a modified **GET**.

Question 48

Read the following code snippet.

```
<web-app>
   <error-page>
      <error-code>404</ error-code>
      <location>/404.html</location>
   </error-page>
</web-app>
```

Which two statements are true regarding this code snippet? (Choose two.)

- ❑ A. This tells the container which page to return if a servlet throws an exception.
- ❑ B. This tells the container which page to return if a JSP page throws an exception.
- ❑ C. This is in the web.xml file.
- ❑ D. This tells the container the default page to return when it can't find a requested resource.

Question 49

How do you declare a taglib for use in a JSP page?

- ❍ A. Deployment descriptor
- ❍ B. **taglib** directive
- ❍ C. **jsp:tag-lib**
- ❍ D. TLD

Question 50

How would you implement the method(s) in a tag handler to handle a simple tag such as **<yourLibrary:whatColorIsIt size="medium"/>**?

❍ A.

```
public SimpleTag extends TagSupport {
  private String size = "small";
  public int doStartTag() throws JspException {
    try {
      pageContext.getOut().print("Hello.");
    } catch (Exception ex) {
      throw new JspTagException("SimpleTag: " +
        ex.getMessage());
    }
    return SKIP_BODY;
  }
  public int doEndTag() {
    return EVAL_PAGE;
  }
  public void setSize(String s)
  {
     this.size = s;
  }
}
```

❍ B.

```
public SimpleTag extends Tag {
  public void setSize(String s)
  {
     this.size = s;
  }
  public int doStartTag() throws JspException {
    try {
      pageContext.getOut().print("Hello.");
    } catch (Exception ex) {
      throw new JspTagException("SimpleTag: " +
        ex.getMessage());
    }
    return SKIP_BODY;
  }
}
```

❍ C.

```
public SimpleTag implements TagSupport {
  public int doStartTag() throws JspException {
      out.print("Hello.");
    return SKIP_BODY;
  }
  public void setSize(String s)
  {
     this.size = s;
  }
  public int doEndTag() {
    return EVAL_PAGE;
  }
}
```

❍ D.

```
public SimpleTag implements TagSupport {
  public int doStartTag() throws JspException {
    try {
      pageContext.getOut().print("Hello.");
    } catch (Exception ex) {
      throw new JspTagException("SimpleTag: " +
        ex.getMessage());
    }
    return SKIP_BODY;
  }
  public void setSize(String s)
  {
     this.size = s;
  }
  public int doEndTag() {
    return EVAL_PAGE;
  }
}
```

Question 51

What is the base class for tag handlers that don't process the body of a custom tag?

❍ A. **TagSupport**

❍ B. **Tag**

❍ C. **BodyTag**

❍ D. **BodyTagSupport**

Question 52

What method is used for iterations when processing a custom tag?

❍ A. **doAfterBody**

❍ B. **doEndTag**

❍ C. **doTagIteration**

❍ D. **doNextBody**

Question 53

What is the base interface for tag handlers that want to repeatedly process a tag's body a set number of times?

❍ A. **TagSupport**

❍ B. **IterationTag**

❍ C. **BodyTag**

❍ D. **BodyTagSupport**

Question 54

Which two of the following use correct syntax? (Choose two.)

❑ A.

```
<% if (Calendar.getInstance().get(Calendar.AM_PM)
➥==Calendar.AM) {
%>
Good Morning
<%
} else {
%>
Good Afternoon
<%
}
%>
```

❑ B.

```
<jsp:for iterator="i" count="10">
<p>Iterations: <%= i %><br />
</jsp:for>
```

❑ C.

```
<% for ( int i=0; i < 10; i++) {
%>
<p>Iterations: <%= i %><br />
<%
}
%>
```

❑ D.

```
<jsp:if condition="<%=myBoolean%>
This is true
</jsp:if>
```

Question 55

Which two of the following are implicit objects available to your JSP page? (Choose two).

❑ A. **JspWriter**

❑ B. **HttpSession**

❑ C. **out**

❑ D. **page**

Question 56

Read the following code snippet:

```
<web-app>
   <error-page>
      <exception-type>javax.servlet.
ServletException</exception-type>
      <location>/servlet/ErrorDisplay</location>
   </error-page>
</web-app>
```

Which two statements are true regarding this code snippet? (Choose two.)

❑ A. This tells the container which page to return if a servlet throws an exception.

❑ B. This tells the container which page to return if a JSP page throws an exception.

❑ C. This is in the servlet.xml file.

❑ D. This tells the container the default page to return when it can't find a requested resource.

Question 57

Which two of the following are the ways you write a message and the Throwable's stack trace to a servlet log? (Choose two.)

❑ A. **HttpServlet.log(String msg, Throwable t)**

❑ B. **GenericServlet.log(String msg, Throwable t)**

❑ C. **HttpResponse.log(String msg, Throwable t)**

❍ D. **HttpSession.log(String msg, Throwable t)**

Question 58

How do you return an HTTP error that causes the server to generate and send an appropriate server-specific page? (Do not include parentheses or parameters.)

____

Question 59

What is the Web app deployment descriptor element name for the servlet context-init parameters?

- ❍ A. **<init-param>**
- ❍ B. **<context-init>**
- ❍ C. **<context-init-param>**
- ❍ D. **<context-param>**

Question 60

Which is the most likely trigger that might cause a browser to use the HTTP **POST** method?

- ❍ A. Using the refresh HTML **HEAD META** tag.
- ❍ B. Submitting an HTML form with the **method** attribute set to **post**.
- ❍ C. The user types a URL in the address bar and hits Enter.
- ❍ D. The user clicks the Back button.

Answer Key

This chapter is an answer key to the multiple-choice exam in Chapter 12, "Sample Test."

1. C
2. A
3. B
4. D
5. A
6. A
7. D
8. B
9. D
10. A
11. D
12. C
13. A, B
14. `servlet-mapping`
15. A, B
16. B
17. C, D
18. D
19. B, D
20. A
21. A, D
22. A
23. C
24. web.xml
25. A
26. D
27. B

28. `removeAttribute`
29. B, C
30. D
31. B, D
32. A, D
33. B, C
34. A
35. D
36. A, D
37. C
38. B
39. C
40. D
41. A
42. A
43. `getInitParameter`
44. C
45. D
46. D
47. B, D
48. C, D
49. B
50. A
51. A
52. A
53. B
54. A, C
55. C, D
56. A, B

57. A, B

58. `sendError`

59. D

60. B

Question 1

Answer C is correct. You would use the Model-View-Controller architecture to decouple presentation from core data access functionality. Also, this pattern enables you to control the communication between them so that multiple views can see the same enterprise data model or so that multiple data models can present to the same view. Swing user interfaces usually implement the Model-View-Controller design pattern, where Sun uses the model as the underlying logical representation, the view as the visual representation, and the controller as the part that handles user input. When a model changes (when the user modifies text in a text field), it notifies all views that depend (listen) on it. This enables you to present a single set of data in a list, a table, or simple text presentations. As you update the data model, the model notifies the view. In this architecture, the controller determines what action to take when the user alters the model (typing text into field). So, the model is the underlying data model (sometimes encapsulated as a separate object), the view(s) is the UI component, and the controller, effectively, is the event-handling code that syncs the model to the view(s).

Question 2

Answer A is correct. The industry trend for large systems is to minimize coupling between presentation-tier clients and the business service API. This isolates the two so that a change in either side can be managed by the middle layer. Sun recommends using a Business Delegate pattern to reduce coupling between presentation-tier clients and business services. The Business Delegate pattern hides the underlying implementation details of the business service, such as lookup and access details of the EJB architecture.

Question 3

Answer B is correct. Various parts of an application require access to persistent stores such as databases and files. The APIs are inconsistent between types of stores and even between vendors of the same type of storage. There needs to be a layer with a uniform API for accessing these disparate data sources. This pattern is very useful in any application that requires access to several data source types, or even an application that accesses only one but that might switch in the future. Use this pattern to design a Data Access Object that abstracts the access API to various data sources. JDBC is an example of this pattern.

Question 4

Answer D is correct. You define a custom tag in a tag library so that the container can map XML tags to underlying class methods in a tag library descriptor (TLD) file. This file defines the XML tags that you can use in JSP to access the associated Java class. Your container (for example, Tomcat) uses the TLD to convert the XML in your JSP page into Java code. TLD files themselves are written in XML notation.

Question 5

Answer A is correct. The syntax shown is correct. The `tablib` element of the deployment descriptor is required if you use a `taglib` directive in a JSP page that references a TLD by name (indirectly) rather than by location (directly).

Question 6

Answer A is correct. The servlet container supports the capability to store startup and configuration information for a servlet. After the container instantiates the servlet, it makes this information available to the servlet instance. Option A correctly demonstrates how you would retrieve a servlet-initialization parameter. Option B is wrong because it is expecting a numeric index. Options C and D have incorrect syntax.

Question 7

Answer D is correct. It correctly declares an initialization parameter for the servlet in the deployment descriptor. The initialization parameters for the servlet are specified in the deployment descriptor (the web.xml file). The other options have incorrect syntax.

Question 8

Answer B is correct. The `doGet` method is called by the servlet container to process a `GET` request. Option B is the only correctly written example of this method.

Question 9

Answer D is correct. The `init` method is called by the servlet container just before this servlet is put into service. Option D is the only correctly written example of this method.

Question 10

Answer A is correct. The `destroy` method is called by the servlet container just after the servlet is removed from service. Option B has an incorrect signature. Options C and D name `finalize`, a method not called directly in your servlet code. `finalize()` is a method not usually overridden in servlets.

Question 11

Answer D is correct. The servlet container provides a simple logging facility for a servlet to log text messages and exceptions. You get the servlet context through the `getServletContext` method, and you use the context object's `log` method. You can either pass a String alone or pass a String and an exception object.

Question 12

Answer C is correct. Assuming that the servlet method for handling HTTP `GET` requests is `doGet(HttpServletRequest req, HttpServletResponse resp)`, you get a request parameter in that servlet by calling the `getParameter` method of the request object. Option C is the only correctly written call to this method.

Question 13

Answers A and B are correct. The `getParameterNames` method of the request object returns an Enumeration of String objects, with each String containing the name of a request parameter or an empty Enumeration if the request has no parameters. You can then walk through the Enumeration with the `nextElement` method to grab the actual name as a String. The other options don't apply to getting request parameters.

Question 14

`servlet-mapping` is the correct answer. When a request is received by the container, it must determine which servlet should handle it. Using the deployment descriptor, you can map certain paths (aliases) to a specific servlet. You define this mapping with the `servlet-mapping` element. The alias is appended after the context root in an HTTP request URL.

Question 15

Answers A and B are correct. You'll need to match the name with a description of purpose or functionality for the servlet instance deployment descriptor element. Regarding declaring a servlet instance in a deployment descriptor, you specify the fully qualified class name of the servlet, and you can provide servlet-initialization parameters that are retrievable within the servlet.

Question 16

Answer B is correct. The `include` directive includes text that is translated along with the JSP page. For example, `<%@include file="companyHeader.html" %>` is the `include` directive that inserts the text of the companyHeader.html file and translates it in place as if it had been typed into the original JSP code at the point where the `include` directive is placed. `jsp:include action` retrieves the output of the resource during execution, not at the time of translation.

Question 17

Answers C and D are correct. The exam will ask you to identify the interfaces and methods to access values and resources, and to set object attributes within the session scope. The `HttpSession.getAttribute(java.lang.String name)` method returns the object bound with the specified name in this session, or `null` if no object is bound under the name. Similarly, `HttpSession.getAttributeNames()` returns an Enumeration of String objects containing the names of all the objects bound to this session.

Question 18

Answer D is correct. The `jsp:include` is an `include` action that includes static or dynamic content in a JSP page that doesn't get translated because the material is included at the time of the execution.

Question 19

Answers B and D are correct. You need to understand each step of the cycle and know the order of the steps. The following are the elements of the JSP page life cycle in the correct sequence: translate page, compile JSP page, load class, create instance, call `jspInit`, call `_jspService`, and call `jspDestroy`.

Question 20

Answer A is correct. You need to be able to identify the interface and methods to access values and resources, and to set object attributes within the session scope. The `HttpSession` interface provides a way to identify a user across more than one page request or visit to a Web site, and to store information about that user. The servlet container uses this interface to create a session between an HTTP client and an HTTP server. The session persists for a specified time period, across more than one connection or page request from the user. A session usually corresponds to one user, who may visit a site many times. The server can maintain a session in many ways, such as using cookies or rewriting URLs. This interface allows servlets to view and manipulate information about a session, such as the session identifier, creation time, and last accessed time. It also allows servlets to bind objects to sessions, enabling user information to persist across multiple user connections.

Question 21

Answers A and D are correct. The following are attributes of the JSP `page` directive: `language="java"`, `extends="package.class"`, `import="{package.class ¦ package.*}, ..."`, `session="true¦false"`, `buffer="none¦8kb¦sizekb"`, `autoFlush="true¦false"`, `isThreadSafe="true¦false"`, `info="text"`, and `errorPage="relativeURL"`. Be careful: The buffer takes an Nkb value, not a Boolean.

Question 22

Answer A is correct. To demonstrate that you understand the structure and deployment of modern servlet Web applications, the exam will ask you to match the name with a description of purpose or functionality for the URL to a named servlet-mapping deployment descriptor element. Essentially, an unlimited number of servlet mappings in a deployment descriptor may be defined for one Web app.

Question 23

Answer C is correct. The exam expects you to identify the interface and method for accessing values and resources, and to set object attributes within the request scope. The `ServletRequest.getAttributeNames()` method returns an Enumeration containing the names of the attributes available to this request. This method returns an empty Enumeration if the request has no attributes available to it.

Question 24

web.xml is the correct answer. web.xml is the deployment descriptor file used by the container to configure an application. Each application has its own.

Question 25

Answer A is correct. Option A is an example of an expression. Expressions are a shortcut for appending text to the output stream. The syntax is this:

```
<%="some text" %>
```

Notice that you do not use the semicolon terminator in an expression.

Question 26

Answer D is correct. For the HTTP `HEAD` method, you'll be expected to identify triggers that might cause a browser to use this method, and identify benefits or functionality of this method. A browser or application will sometimes send a request to a server just to check the status or get information (for example, "Can you handle fileupload?") from the server. The `HEAD` method returns the same header lines that a `GET` method would return; however, no body or content is returned. This is often accomplished by calling `doGet()`, setting the headers but not setting any output, and then returning the response (without any body) to the requester. The primary benefit of this method is message size. The `HEAD` method receives and returns very small messages. Therefore, it is fast and lightweight on both ends.

Question 27

Answer B is the correct answer. The attributes for the `jsp:useBean` tag are: (1) `id`, the case-sensitive name used to identify the object instance in the specified scope. This name doubles as the scripting variable name declared and initialized with that object reference. (2) `scope`, the scope within which the reference is available. The default value is `page`. The options are `page`, `request`, `session`, and `application`. (3) `class`, the fully qualified name of the class. If the `class` and `beanName` attributes are not specified, the object must be present in the given scope. The class must not be abstract (or an interface) and must have a public, no-argument constructor, but the implicit `no args` constructor will suffice. (4) `beanName`, the name of a Bean, as expected by the `instantiate()` method of the `java.beans.Beans` class. This name can be set dynamically by an expression as a value. (5) `type`, which, if specified, defines the type of the variable defined. The type is required to be the class itself, a superclass of the class, or an interface implemented by the class specified. If unspecified, the value is the same as the value of the `class` attribute.

Question 28

`removeAttribute` is the correct answer. This is the name of the method for deleting an attribute from a session object. The `HttpSession` object automatically is created for a request that remains alive for subsequent requests by the same client until the session times out or another event kills that session. The session stores state between page views. Remember that the session is on by default; if you don't want it on, use `"session=false"` in the JSP `page` directive.

Question 29

Answers B and C are correct. The exam expects you to identify the uses, interfaces (or classes), and methods to achieve the feature of servlet context-initialization parameters. Deploying a distributable Web application is not easy. For one thing, servlet context-init parameters are not likely to be shared across different JVMs. Also, a different `ServletContext` instance may exist on different JVMs.

Question 30

Answer D is correct. This is how you reference a session in a servlet. The `PageContext` encapsulates the complete state of a single request execution of a single JSP page or servlet.

Question 31

Answers B and D are correct. You should be able to identify the interfaces and methods used to access values and resources, and to set object attributes within the context scope. The `getNamedDispatcher(java.lang.String name)` method returns a `RequestDispatcher` object that acts as a wrapper for the named servlet. Servlets (and JSP pages also) may be given names via server administration or via a Web application deployment descriptor. A servlet instance can determine its name using `ServletConfig.getServletName()`. Similarly, the `RequestDispatcher getRequestDispatcher(java.lang.String path)` returns a `RequestDispatcher` object that acts as a wrapper for the resource located at the given path. A `RequestDispatcher` object can be used to forward a request to the resource or to include the resource in a response. The resource can be dynamic or static. The pathname must begin with a `/` and is interpreted as relative to the current context root. Use `getContext` to obtain a `RequestDispatcher` for resources in foreign contexts. This method returns `null` if the `ServletContext` cannot return a `RequestDispatcher`.

Question 32

Answers A and D are correct. You must identify the interfaces and methods to access values and resources, and to set object attributes within the session scope. The `HttpSession.removeAttribute` method removes the object bound with the specified name from this session. If the session does not have an object bound with the specified name, this method does nothing. After this method executes, and if the object implements HttpSessionBindingListener, the container calls HttpSessionBindingListener.valueUnbound. The container then notifies any HttpSessionAttributeListeners in the Web application. Going the other way, the HttpSession.setAttribute method binds an object to this session, using the name specified. If an object of the same name is already bound to the session, the object is replaced. After this method executes, and if the new object implements HttpSessionBindingListener, the container calls HttpSessionBindingListener.valueBound. The container then notifies any HttpSessionAttributeListeners in the Web application.

Question 33

Answers B and C are correct. This is similar to BASIC, except that a form is used with predefined fields. These fields must be named j_username and j_password, respectively, and the form method and action must be named POST and j_security_check, respectively.

Question 34

Answer A is correct. You should be able to identify the interface and method name that should be used to acquire a binary stream for the response. To send binary data in a MIME body response, use the ServletOutputStream returned by getOutputStream(). To send character data, use the PrintWriter object returned by getWriter(). To mix binary and text data—for example, to create a multipart response—use a ServletOutputStream.

Question 35

Answer D is correct. Option A is wrong because you will generate an error if you instantiate a JSPWriter as out because the translator does that already. Options B and C have incorrect syntax.

Question 36

Answers A and D are correct. Options A and D are accurate pairs in which the top line of code shown is scriptlet and the bottom is the XML equivalent. Notice that options B and C are wrong because there is no scriptlet for either `useBean` or `taglib` actions.

Question 37

Answer C is correct. There are three ways to assign values to JavaBean properties using the `jsp:setProperty` element: with the `value` attribute, with the `param` attribute using a named parameter, and with the `param` attribute using the wildcard. You can set the property directly with the `value` attribute of the `setPropery` action. You can set several attributes simultaneously like this:

```
<jsp:setProperty name="addressBean" property="*"/>
```

You'll notice that the property is set to the wildcard star. That tells the container to match as many request parameters with JavaBean properties as possible. If the request parameter is named `color`, the container will assign its value to the JavaBean property of the same name through the `setColor` method in the JavaBean. If several request parameter names have matching JavaBean property names, only one tag is needed to transfer all the form field values to the corresponding JavaBean properties.

Question 38

Answer B is correct. For the exam, you need to identify the interface and method name that should be used to retrieve HTTP request header information. The `getHeaderNames` method returns an Enumeration of all the header names that this request contains. From this Enumeration you can retrieve the individual values like this:

```
Enumeration e = request.getHeaderNames();
while (e.hasMoreElements())
{
    String headerName = (String)e.nextElement();
    String headerValue = request.getHeader
(headerName);
    out.println(headerName);
    out.println(headerValue);
}
```

Question 39

Answer C is correct. Option C shows the correct syntax for declaring the integer `n` with a value of `35`, which will result in the value `25` in the output. All other options have incorrect syntax for the JSP page.

Question 40

Answer D is correct. You use the `useBean`, `getProperty`, and `setProperty` standard tags in XML to instantiate a Bean and to get and set the Bean's properties. A `<jsp:getProperty>` action places the value of a Bean instance property into the implicit `out` object. The String representation is sent to the HTTP response stream. Unlike a scriptlet, which can get a value and assign it to a variable, the `getProperty` action converts the Bean property value to a String and immediately adds that String to the output stream.

Question 41

Answer A is correct. You use a tag such as `<jsp:useBean id="address" class="que.scwcd.AddressBean" scope="page" />` to declare a Bean and set its scope.

Question 42

Answer A is correct. You need to know the interface and method name that should be used to retrieve HTML form parameters from the request. The interface and method used to retrieve the names of all HTML form parameters from the request is `ServletRequest.getParameterNames`, which returns an Enumeration of all the form parameter names that this request contains.

Question 43

`getInitParameter` is the correct answer. `getInitParameter` is the method name that retrieves the value of an initialization parameter if you provide the name of the parameter to the `ServletContext` object. These parameters are set in the deployment descriptor.

Question 44

Answer C is correct. The tag type is an expression, and the equivalent XML-based tag is shown in option C. They both append text to the output stream.

Question 45

Answer D is correct. A tag handler is a special JavaBean that is the compiled class referenced by the JSP page through custom tags. It has access to the same objects that your JSP page has. The JSP page passes in attributes of the custom tag and the body between opening and closing custom tags. The output from the tag handler replaces the tag in the JSP page.

Question 46

Answer D is correct. This shows the correct way to import classes. Although the syntax is correct in option A, this creates an instance and is not considered importing a class.

Question 47

Answers B and D are correct. You need to know about the HTTP `HEAD` method. For example, you must identify triggers that might cause a browser to use this method, and you must identify benefits or functionality of this method. A browser or application will sometimes send a request to a server just to check the status or get information (for example, "Can you handle fileupload?") from the server. The `HEAD` method returns the same header lines that a `GET` method would return; however, no body or content is returned. This is often accomplished by calling `doGet()`, setting the headers but not setting any output, and then returning the response (without any body) to the requester. The primary benefit of this method is message size. The `HEAD` method receives and returns very small messages. Therefore, it is fast and lightweight on both ends.

Question 48

Answers C and D are correct. This code snippet goes in the Web deployment descriptor (web.xml). This tells the container the default page to return when it can't find a requested resource.

Question 49

Answer B is correct. You declare your tag library in your JSP page using a `taglib` directive (`jsp:taglib`). This declaration maps a prefix (this is how you reference your tag library) to a URI that the container resolves to a TLD, directly if a path to the TLD file is given or indirectly if a name is declared. In the latter case, the container looks in the deployment descriptor to match this name to an actual TLD file location.

Question 50

Answer A is correct. This shows you how to write a class handler to process the tag in question. The other options all have incorrect syntax. A tag handler must implement either the `Tag` or the `BodyTag` interfaces or must extend `TagSupport` or `BodyTagSupport` classes. Interfaces can be used to make an existing Java object a tag handler. For most cases, you will extend the `TagSupport` class or the `BodyTagSupport` class. These classes and interfaces are contained in the javax.servlet.jsp.tagext package.

Question 51

Answer A is correct. `TagSupport` is the base class for new tag handlers. Your tag handlers that don't mess with the body of a custom tag extend this class. The `TagSupport` class implements the `Tag` and `IterationTag` interfaces and adds additional convenience methods, including getter methods for the properties in `Tag`. It has the methods `doAfterBody`, `doEndTag`, `doStartTag`, `getParent`, and `release`.

Question 52

Answer A is correct. The `doAfterBody` method is used for iterations (`IterationTag`). It is called after every body evaluation to control whether the body will be re-evaluated. If this method returns `EVAL_BODY_AGAIN`, the body is re-evaluated. If it returns `SKIP_BODY`, the body is skipped and `doEndTag` is invoked next.

Question 53

Answer B is correct. The `IterationTag` interface extends `Tag` by defining one additional method that controls the reevaluation of its body. It has the field `EVAL_BODY_AGAIN` and the method `doAfterBody`.

Question 54

Answers A and C are correct. These are examples of correctly written conditional and iteration scriptlets. The other options have invalid syntax.

Question 55

Answers C and D are correct. Options A and B are the types of implicit objects `out` and `session`, respectively. The `out` object is of type `JspWriter` and is used to write to the client. The `page` object is an instance of the given page's implementation class processing the current request, which is equivalent to using the `this` keyword in a servlet.

Question 56

Answers A and B are correct. This is how you configure the deployment descriptor to handle specific exceptions. The `exception-type` element defines which exception, and the `location` element tells the container where to get the contents for the returned error message. Notice that this defines a specific exception type, and the location may be dynamic (such as `jsp` or `servlet`). The container is specified so that servlets must catch all exceptions except those that subclass `ServletException`, `IOException`, and `RuntimeException`.

Question 57

Answers A and B are correct. You write a message and the Throwable's stack trace to a servlet log with the `log` method of the `GenericServlet` interface, like this: `GenericServlet.log(String msg, Throwable t)`. The `log` method is also defined for `ServletContext`. Notice that `HttpServer` (choice A) has the `log` method because `HttpServer` inherits it from the `GenericServlet` abstract class.

Question 58

`sendError` is the correct answer. You use this method to return an HTTP error that causes the server to generate and send an appropriate server-specific page. The `sendError` method causes the server to generate and send an appropriate server-specific page describing the error. You can override the default message by using the `error-page` element in the deployment descriptor (web.xml).

Question 59

Answer D is correct. You need to know how to identify the uses for and the interfaces (or classes) and methods to achieve the feature of servlet context-initialization parameters. In the deployment descriptor, the `context-param` element declares the Web application's servlet context-initialization parameters. The syntax is `<!ELEMENT context-param (param-name, param-value, description?)>`.

Question 60

Answer B is correct. This question helps you identify triggers that might cause a browser to use this method, and identify benefits or functionality of this method. The `POST` method is triggered by the browser when the HTML form's action is set to `POST`. This method is more sophisticated than a `GET` request. Normally, a Web form has fields whose names and value are sent to the server in key-value pairs. The `POST` method is designed for posting long messages (for example, to a bulletin board, newsgroup, or mailing list); providing a block of data, such as the result of submitting a form; and submitting long data fields to a database (such as a SQL insert of a lengthy string).

Servlet API Snapshot

This appendix helps you prepare for the exam by describing the servlet API. Whereas the chapters explained the various portions of the API in detail, this appendix gives you a simple listing of the classes, methods, and fields as a reference.

Many methods are not described here, such as the `ServletContext` `getMinorVersion()` and `getServerInfo()` methods. These methods, while useful, are unlikely to be on the exam, so they are ignored here. Of course, you can look at the complete API at any time. The complete Java Servlet 2.3 Specification is at `http://jcp.org/aboutJava/communityprocess/first/jsr053/index.html`.

This appendix describes the javax.servlet package, mostly taken from the content that is generated from the javadocs, which define the actual Java classes and interfaces. You don't have to know the entire API. However, every class and method on the exam is here, along with a few more for completeness. Among all the classes and interfaces, the `Servlet` interface is the central abstraction of the servlet API. The specification ensures that all servlets implement this interface. This is usually done by extending a class that implements the `Servlet` interface. Although two classes in the servlet API implement the `Servlet` interface, `GenericServlet` and `HttpServlet`, we will focus only on `HttpServlet`; it's the `HttpServlet` class methods that will appear on the exam.

The Servlet 2.3 API defines the interfaces, classes, methods, fields, and constants that you will use to build servlets. The Web Component Developer Exam is filled with questions on this API. Therefore, it is helpful to have an appendix that simply filters the most important parts of the Servlet 2.3 API.

The Java 2 Web Component Developer Exam covers version 2.3 of the Servlet API and version 1.2 of JavaServer Pages.

Overview of the Servlet API

The Servlet 2.3 API consists of two packages: javax.servlet and javax.servlet.http. Although the exam also covers JSP 1.2, in this appendix we will focus only on these two servlet packages. The base functionality is defined in the javax.servlet package whose classes and interfaces outline a generic, protocol-independent implementation. This means that you can use it for non-Web applications, too. Of course, the exam targets the Web, so the HTTP protocol is the only one discussed in the book. The `javax.servlet.http` interface defines classes and interfaces that are specific to the Hypertext Transfer Protocol (HTTP).

Request/response filtering was introduced with version 2.3 of the Servlet API. Filter questions are not covered by the exam, so they are not discussed in the book.

Understanding the javax.servlet Package Interfaces, Classes, and Exceptions

The following sections describe the interfaces, classes, and exceptions of the javax.servlet package.

Interfaces

The following subsections describe the interfaces of the javax.servlet package.

RequestDispatcher

The `RequestDispatcher` interface defines the `forward()` and `include()` methods for use as request wrappers. It enables requests to be processed and then forwarded to other elements of a Web application. It also allows the results of other application elements to be included in the response. A `RequestDispatcher` object is created with the path or name of the resource to be dispatched.

Servlet

The `Servlet` interface defines methods that are implemented by all servlets. A default implementation of these methods is provided by `GenericServlet`, an abstract class that is often extended in the javax.servlet package.

The following methods are used to control the servlet life cycle:

- `void init(ServletConfig config)`—Invoked by the servlet container to put the servlet in service
- `void service(ServletRequest req, ServletResponse res)`—Invoked by the servlet container to enable a servlet to respond to a request

- `void destroy()`—Invoked by the servlet container to remove the servlet from service

These methods provide access to servlet configuration information:

- `ServletConfig getServletConfig()`—Returns the `ServletConfig` object that is associated with the servlet
- `String getServletInfo()`—Returns the servlet's information string

ServletConfig

The `ServletConfig` interface defines methods for accessing servlet configuration information. Configuration information is passed as a series of name/value pairs.

Methods also provide access to the servlet's name and `ServletContext` object:

- `String getInitParameter(String name)`—Returns the value of the specified parameter
- `Enumeration getInitParameterNames()`—Returns an `Enumeration` of the names of the servlet's initialization parameters
- `ServletContext getServletContext()`—Returns the `ServletContext` object corresponding to the servlet

ServletContext

The `ServletContext` interface defines methods for accessing application-scope attributes. It is limited to a single JVM and, therefore, should not be used when clustering is in effect. The `ServletContext` methods provide access to objects that are placed in application scope:

- `Object getAttribute(String name)`—Returns the object corresponding to the named attribute.
- `Enumeration getAttributeNames()`—Returns an `Enumeration` of the defined attribute names.
- `void removeAttribute(String name)`—Removes the attribute from the servlet context.
- `void setAttribute(String name, Object object)`—Sets the object associated with the specified attribute name.
- `String getInitParameter(String name)`—Returns the value of the named initialization parameter.

- `Enumeration getInitParameterNames()`—Returns an `Enumeration` of the initialization parameter names.
- `ServletContext getContext(String url)`—Returns the `ServletContext` object that corresponds to the specified URL. The URL must be on the same server.
- `RequestDispatcher getNamedDispatcher(String name)`—Returns a `RequestDispatcher` object that acts as a wrapper for the named servlet.
- `RequestDispatcher getRequestDispatcher(String path)`—Returns a `RequestDispatcher` object that acts as a wrapper for the resource located at the specified path.
- `void log(String msg)`—Writes the message to the servlet log file.
- `void log(String message, Throwable throwable)`—Writes the message to the servlet log file along with a stack trace for the `Throwable` object.

ServletContextAttributeListener

The `ServletContextAttributeListener` interface defines methods for handling the `ServletContextAttributeEvent`. These methods are as follows:

- `void attributeAdded(ServletContextAttributeEvent scab)`
- `void attributeRemoved(ServletContextAttributeEvent scab)`
- `void attributeReplaced(ServletContextAttributeEvent scab)`

ServletContextListener

The `ServletContextListener` interface defines methods for handling the `ServletContextEvent`. This listener is passed the `ServletContextEvent` object, which holds the information indicating the creation or destruction of a `ServletContext`. The `contextDestroyed()` method handles the destruction of a `ServletContext`. Lastly, the `contextInitialized()` method handles the creation of a `ServletContext` object.

ServletRequest

The `ServletRequest` interface provides a protocol-independent definition of the methods used to access the information contained in a client request of a servlet. These methods provide access to nearly all of the information contained in the original request.

A `ServletRequest` object is created by the servlet container and is made available to a servlet via its `service()` method. `ServletRequest` is extended by `javax.servlet.http.HttpServletRequest`.

`ServletRequest` defines several methods for accessing request data:

- `Object getAttribute(String name)`—Returns the object associated with the attribute name
- `Enumeration getAttributeNames()`—Returns an `Enumeration` of the request's attributes
- `void removeAttribute(String name)`—Removes an attribute from this request
- `void setAttribute(String name, Object o)`—Sets the value of an attribute of this request
- `String getParameter(String name)`—Returns the value of the specified request parameter
- `Enumeration getParameterNames()`—Returns an `Enumeration` of the names of the parameters of this request
- `String[] getParameterValues(String name)`—Returns an array of the values of the specified request parameter
- `RequestDispatcher getRequestDispatcher(String path)`—Returns a `RequestDispatcher` object that acts as a wrapper for the resource located at the specified path

ServletResponse

The `ServletResponse` interface encapsulates a response sent from the servlet to the client. A `ServletResponse` object is automatically created by the servlet container and passed to a servlet via its `service` method. `ServletResponse` defines several methods for configuring, assembling, and sending response information:

- `void setContentType(String type)`—Sets the content type of the response being sent to the client
- `java.io.PrintWriter getWriter()`—Returns a `PrintWriter` object for writing character data to the client
- `void flushBuffer()`—Forces any content in the buffer to be written to the client

SingleThreadModel

The `SingleThreadModel` interface is implemented by servlets that are required to handle a single request at a time. This interface is intended to make sure that a single servlet thread is executed at a given point in time, providing thread safety. This interface defines no methods.

Classes

The following subsections describe the classes of the `javax.servlet` package.

GenericServlet

The `GenericServlet` class defines a basic implementation of the `Servlet` interface in a protocol-independent manner. It also implements the `ServletConfig` and `java.io.Serializable` interfaces. It is extended by `javax.servlet.http.HttpServlet`.

ServletContextAttributeEvent

The `ServletContextAttributeEvent` is generated as the result of changes to the attributes of the servlet context. The `getName()` method returns the name of the attribute that was changed. The `getValue()` method returns the value of the changed attribute.

ServletContextEvent

The `ServletContextEvent` class is the parent class of `ServletContextAttributeEvent`. It provides notifications about changes to the servlet context of a Web application. The `getServletContext()` method provides access to the affected `ServletContext` object.

ServletRequestWrapper

The `ServletRequestWrapper` class provides an implementation of the `ServletRequest` interface that can be extended and tailored to modify the way that a request is processed. A `ServletRequest` object is provided as an argument to the `ServletRequestWrapper` constructor. The methods of `ServletRequestWrapper` can be overridden to provide the wrapped effect. `ServletRequestWrapper` is extended by `HttpServletRequestWrapper`.

ServletResponseWrapper

The `ServletResponseWrapper` class provides an implementation of the `ServletResponse` interface that can be extended and tailored to modify the way that a response is processed. A `ServletResponse` object is provided as an argument to the `ServletResponseWrapper` constructor. The methods of `ServletResponseWrapper` can be overridden to provide the wrapped effect. `ServletResponseWrapper` is extended by `HttpServletResponseWrapper`.

Exceptions

The following subsection describes the lone exception of the javax.servlet package.

ServletException

The `ServletException` exception extends `java.lang.Exception` to provide a base class for defining servlet-related extensions. The `getRootCause()` method provides access to the exception (if any) that results in the throwing of `ServletException`.

The javax.servlet.http Package

The javax.servlet.http package defines eight interfaces and seven classes. These interfaces and classes are summarized here.

Interfaces

The following subsections describe the interfaces of the javax.servlet.http package.

HttpServletRequest

The `HttpServletRequest` interface extends `javax.servlet.ServletRequest` to support HTTP. An `HttpServletRequest` object is automatically created by the servlet container and is provided as an argument to HttpServlet's `doXXX()` methods.

`HttpServletRequest` provides numerous HTTP-specific methods for accessing the client's request. Some important methods are listed here:

- `String getHeader(String name)`—Returns the value of the specified request header.
- `Enumeration getHeaderNames()`—Returns an `Enumeration` of all the header names that are associated with the request.
- `Enumeration getHeaders(String name)`—Returns an `Enumeration` of all the values of the specified request header.
- `int getIntHeader(String name)`—Returns the value of the specified request header as an `int`.
- `String getMethod()`—Returns the name of the HTTP method associated with the request.

- `HttpSession getSession()`—Returns the current session associated with this request or, if the request does not have a session, creates one.
- `HttpSession getSession(boolean create)`—Returns the current `HttpSession` associated with this request, or, if there is no current session and `create` is `true`, returns a new session. Otherwise, `null` is returned.

HttpServletResponse

The `HttpServletResponse` interface extends `javax.servlet.ServletResponse` to support HTTP. An `HttpServletResponse` object is automatically created by the servlet container and is provided as an argument to `HttpServlet`'s `doXXX()` methods.

`HttpServletResponse` also defines a number of response error code constants. It provides numerous methods for manipulating the response sent to the client.

The methods marked with a preceding star are most likely to be on the exam, but the others have some likelihood of appearing as well. The following are the `HttpServletResponse` methods:

- `void addCookie(Cookie cookie)`—Adds the specified cookie to the response.
- `void addHeader(String name, String value)`—Adds a response header with the given name and value.
- `void addIntHeader(String name, int value)`—Adds a response header with the given name and integer value.
- `boolean containsHeader(String name)`—Returns a Boolean indicating whether the named response header has already been set.
- `*String encodeRedirectURL(String url)`—Encodes the specified URL for use in the `sendRedirect()` method. It appends the session ID in it.
- `*String encodeURL(String url)`—Encodes the specified URL by including the session ID in it.
- `*void sendError(int sc)`—Sends an error response to the client using the specified status.
- `*void sendError(int sc, String msg)`—Sends an error response to the client using the specified status code and descriptive message.
- `*void sendRedirect(String location)`—Sends a temporary redirect response to the client.

- `void setHeader(String name, String value)`—Sets a response header with the given name and value.
- `void setIntHeader(String name, int value)`—Sets a response header with the given name and integer value.
- `*void setStatus(int sc)`—Sets the status code for this response.

HttpSession

The `HttpSession` interface defines methods that provide access to persistent session-state information. These methods are used to get and set attributes in the session scope (`getAttribute()` and `setAttribute()`). Methods are also provided to get access to the session creation time, last access time, maximum timeout interval, and session ID. The `invalidate()` method is used to terminate an HTTP session.

HttpSessionActivationListener

The `HttpSessionActivationListener` interface defines methods for handling the `HttpSessionActivationEvent`. These methods are `sessionDidActivate()` and `sessionWillPassivate()`.

HttpSessionAttributeListener

The `HttpSessionAttributeListener` interface defines methods for handling the `HttpSessionAttributeEvent`. These methods are `attributeAdded()`, `attributeRemoved()`, and `attributeReplaced()`.

HttpSessionBindingListener

The `HttpSessionBindingListener` interface defines methods for objects that listen for `HttpSessionBindingEvent` events. The `valueBound()` method is invoked when an object is bound to an `HttpSession`. The `valueUnbound()` method is invoked when an object is unbound from an `HttpSession`.

HttpSessionListener

The `HttpSessionListener` interface defines methods for handling `HttpSessionEvent`. The `sessionCreated()` method is used to handle the creation of a new `HttpSession` object. The `sessionDestroyed()` method handles the destruction of an `HttpSession` object.

Classes

The following sections describe the classes of the javax.servlet.http package.

Cookie

The `Cookie` class encapsulates HTTP cookies. It enables cookies to be retrieved or set. Cookies are retrieved via `HttpServletRequest.getCookies()`. Cookies are set via `HttpServletResponse.addCookie()`. Both version 0 (Netscape) and version 1 (RFC 2109) cookies are supported. Created cookies are version 0, by default. The `Cookie` class implements the `Cloneable` interface.

HttpServlet

The `HttpServlet` class is an abstract class that extends `javax.servlet.GenericServlet` to provide support for HTTP. It is extended to create custom servlets. It supports the HTTP `GET`, `POST`, `PUT`, `DELETE`, `OPTIONS`, and `TRACE` requests via protected methods of the form `doGet()`, `doPost()`, `doPut()`, `doDelete()`, `doOptions()`, and `doTrace()`. These methods take an `HttpServletRequest` object and an `HttpServletResponse` object as their parameters.

These protected `doXXX()` methods are overridden to handle specific request types. Remember that the `service` method dispatches to the appropriate `doXXX()` method.

HttpServletRequestWrapper

The `HttpServletRequestWrapper` class provides the capability to wrap and modify incoming `HttpServletRequest` objects. It extends `ServletRequestWrapper` and implements `HttpServletRequest`.

The request to be wrapped is passed to this class's constructor. Because this class implements the methods of `HttpServletRequest`, all the request methods can then be invoked on the wrapped object. These methods can be overridden to produce the new wrapped results.

HttpServletResponseWrapper

The `HttpServletResponseWrapper` class provides the capability to wrap and modify outgoing `HttpServletResponse` objects. It extends `ServletResponseWrapper` and implements `HttpServletResponse`.

The response to be wrapped is passed to this class's constructor. Because this class implements the methods of `HttpServletReponse`, all the response methods can then be invoked on the wrapped object. These methods can be overridden to produce the new wrapped results.

HttpSessionBindingEvent

The `HttpSessionBindingEvent` class extends `HttpSessionEvent` (which extends `java.util.EventObject`) to define an event that is sent to an `HttpSessionBindingListener` when an object is bound or unbound from the current `HttpSession`.

The `String getName()` method returns the attribute name of the object.

The `HttpSession getSession()` method returns the associated `HttpSession` object.

HttpSessionEvent

The `HttpSessionEvent` class is the parent class of `HttpSessionBindingEvent`. It is used to provide notifications of changes to sessions within a Web application. It defines one method, `getSession()`, that returns the `HttpSession` object of the affected session.

Summary

In this appendix, you reviewed the details of the Servlet API. You learned the purpose of the classes and interfaces of the Servlet API and covered important methods of these classes and interfaces. This is something you can refer to periodically. Also, you should scan this the night before the exam.

JSP Syntax Snapshot

This appendix helps you prepare for the exam by providing you with a syntax reference to the main features of JSP, the subject of Chapter 8, "JavaServer Pages (JSP)." Sometimes it is useful to have a quick reference. This appendix provides you with a simple listing of the syntax elements with brief examples.

This appendix comes largely from Sun's specification and documentation (see `http://java.sun.com/products/jsp/syntax.pdf`). I've tried to make it more readable by keeping the most essential information and tossing out the rest.

The Java 2 Web Component Developer Exam covers JavaServer Pages version 1.2.

Syntax Rules

You should keep a few general syntax rules in mind:

- All tags are case sensitive.
- A pair of single quotes is equivalent to a pair of double quotes. This is generally true in HTML tags as well. Note that single quotes must be matched with single quotes, and doubles must be matched with doubles.
- Outside of quotes, spaces don't count, but inside they do. Also, spaces are not allowed between an equals sign and an attribute value. This is consistent with current XML/HTML tagging practices, in that spaces are supposed to be used only to separate attribute-value pairs from each other and from the name of the tag.
- JSP tags and their XML equivalents cannot be mixed (well) within a page. You don't throw JSP inside an XML tag. Likewise, you must be very careful if you try to use an XML tag inside, say, a scriptlet.
- A page in one syntax can include or forward to a page in the other syntax.
- How do you quote JSP? You would do this in an online JSP tutorial, for example. You have to escape some of the syntax so the engine knows to pass it through as text and not interpret it. Notice that without the JSP beginning tag, the engine treats it as text, so you can have as much Java code pass through as text as you'd like. You might do this if your Web page is a Java tutorial. You can tell the container "Ignore this Java—I want it to

print on the page" by simply escaping part of the start tag. Here are some examples: `<\%`, `%\>`, `\'`, `\"`. Note that, overall, it is best to place text that you want to pass through between the `jsp:text` elements.

Format Conventions

These are the formatting conventions used in this appendix, the same ones used by Sun:

- code = fixed
- **bold** = default
- *italics* = user-defined
- ¦ = or
- [ ] = optional
- { } = required choice
- ... = list of items
- + = can repeat

Syntax Explanations and Examples

The main elements of JSP syntax are presented in the following sections.

HTML or Output Comment

These are plain HTML comments that are passed through to the client. The client doesn't process these. There is nothing special about them; the servlet container ignores them, passing them through as text. Notice that you can use a scriptlet to insert text in the comment before it is sent off to the client. For example, you can datestamp a comment.

JSP Syntax

```
<!-- comment [ <%= expression %> ]-->
```

XML Syntax

None.

Example

```
<%@ page language="java" %>
<html>
        <head>
           <title>Hidden Comment</title>
        </head>
        <body>
           <h1>Hidden Comment</h1>
           <!--
              Any text between these delimiters
              is passed through by the processor and is
              included in the response
              including this: <%="scriplet"%>.
           -->
        </body>
</html>
```

This produces:

```
<html>
        <head>
           <title>Hidden Comment</title>
        </head>
        <body>
           <h1>Hidden Comment</h1>
           <!--
              Any text between these delimiters
              are passed through by the processor and are
              included in the response
              including this: scriplet.
           -->
        </body>
</html>
```

Hidden Comment

The text within a hidden comment (`<%-- --%>`) is ignored by the JSP container. Unlike HTML comments, within which you can embed scriptlets, scriptlets do not have a hidden comment. The JSP container does not process anything within the `<%--` and `--%>` characters. A hidden comment is not inserted into the response.

JSP Syntax

```
<%-- comment --%>
```

XML Syntax

None.

Example

```
<%@ page language="java" %>
<html>
        <head>
           <title>Hidden Comment</title>
        </head>
        <body>
           <h1>Hidden Comment</h1>
           <%--
              Any text between these delimiters
              is ignored by the processor is are not
              included in the response
           --%>
        </body>
</html>
```

The previous JSP page produces the following HTML:

```
<html>
        <head>
           <title>Hidden Comment</title>
        </head>
        <body>
           <h1>Hidden Comment</h1>
        </body>
</html>
```

Declaration

A declaration declares variables or methods that you can use afterward in the JSP page. The declaration must precede these variables' use in the JSP page. Code placed in the declaration is translated to be class level and outside the `service` method, whereas code in an expression or scriptlet is included *in* the `service` method. You can place numerous declarations between the delimiters. The following rules apply:

- Terminate the declaration with a semicolon. This is the same for scriptlets but the opposite of an expression.
- You don't have to declare variables or methods that are already declared in imported packages.
- Because a static include file is treated as original JSP source, declarations in these must precede use. Conversely, declared variables are accessible from include files if the `include` directive comes after the declaration. Be careful with this: It is easy to get spaghetti code because the references to variables in the included code have to come after a declaration for those variables. Conversely, when you use includes, be mindful of what is declared in the include file. The scope of a declaration does not include dynamic resources included with `<jsp:include>`.

JSP Syntax

```
<%! declaration; [ declaration; ]+ ... %>
```

XML Syntax

```
<jsp:declaration>
   declaration; [ declaration; ]+ ...
</jsp:declaration>
```

Example

```
<%! String firstName = new String("Patricia"); %>
<%! int customerCount = 84; %>
```

Expression

A JSP expression can be any valid Java expression. The container evaluates it, converts the result to a `String`, and appends this `String` to the output stream. The only surprise with this element is that you do not use a semicolon to terminate the statement. If you remove the equals sign from the opening delimiter, then you have a scriptlet and must use a semicolon even though it is the same Java expression. Notice that any code you place in `<%= %>` is translated to be inside `out.println()` statements in the generated servlet.

JSP Syntax

```
<%= expression %>
```

XML Syntax

```
<jsp:expression>
   expression
</jsp:expression>
```

Example

```
<%@ page language="java" %>
<% String message ="This expression is simply a String." %>
<html>
        <head>
           <title>Hidden Comment</title>
        </head>
        <body>
           <h1>Expression </h1>
           <%=message%>
        </body>
</html>
```

Scriptlet

This contains a code fragment, containing valid Java statements and local variable declarations. These statements and declarations are translated to be placed in a method (the `_jspService` method).

JSP Syntax

```
<% code fragment %>
```

XML Syntax

```
<jsp:scriptlet>
   code fragment
</jsp:scriptlet>
```

Example

```
<jsp:root
    xmlns:jsp="http://java.sun.com/JSP/Page"
    version="1.2">
<jsp:directive.page import="java.util.Date" />
<jsp:scriptlet>
    Date date = new Date();
    String message = getDate(date);
</jsp:scriptlet>
<jsp:text>
     <html>
        <head>
           <title>Expression in XML Syntax</title>
        </head>
        <body>
           <h1 align="center">
                <jsp:expression>message</jsp:expression>
           </h1>
        </body>
     </html>
</jsp:text>
<jsp:declaration>
    String getDate(Date date)
    {
        String message = "The date is: " + date;
        return message;
    }
</jsp:declaration>
</jsp:root>
```

That produces this:

```
<html>
      <head>
        <title >Expression in XML Syntax</title>
      </head>
      <body>
        <h1 align="center">The date is: Fri Jun 21 09:47:22 PDT 2002
```

```
        </h1>
      </body>
</html>
```

include Directive

An `include` directive inserts all the text in the named file into the JSP page at the point of the tag. Notice that it is as if this text is part of the JSP, so it is processed along with the rest of the JSP. This is called a static process. In other words, the container copies the text in the file referenced and does not process it in any way before being inserted into the JSP page. The included file can be any text, including pieces of JSP, HTML, XML, or plain text. After this text is included, it is parsed as if it had been in the original JSP page. Be aware that the includes are processed before translation.

JSP Syntax

```
<%@ include file="relativeURL" %>
```

XML Syntax

```
<jsp:directive.include file="relativeURL" />
```

Example

```
<jsp:root
    xmlns:jsp="http://java.sun.com/JSP/Page"
    version="1.2">
<jsp:text>
     <html>
        <head>
           <title>Example Include</title>
        </head>
        <body>
           <h1 align="center">
                <jsp:directive.include file="message.txt" />
           </h1>
        </body>
     </html>
</jsp:text>
</jsp:root>
```

message.txt contains:

```
This text was included from another file.
```

The output is (minor tweaks to spacing for printing):

```
<html>
        <head>
              <title >Example Include</title>
        </head>
        <body>
```

```
            <h1 align="center">This text was included
                                    from another file.
            </h1>
        </body>
</html>
```

page Directive

This tag is the most powerful one of the bunch. It defines attributes that apply to an entire JSP page. See Chapter 8 for a complete explanation with examples.

Notice that you can use the page directive more than once. However, you can use each attribute only once; imports are the only exception. Also, you can place the page directive anywhere on the page. I strongly recommend grouping these tags together, normally at the top or bottom of the file.

JSP Syntax

```
<%@ page
   [ language="java" ]
   [ extends="package.class" ]
   [ import="{package.class ¦ package.*}, ..." ]
   [ session="true¦false" ]
   [ buffer="none¦8kb¦sizekb" ]
   [ autoFlush="true¦false" ]
   [ isThreadSafe="true¦false" ]
   [ info="text" ]
   [ errorPage="relativeURL" ]
   [ contentType="mimeType [ ; charset=characterSet ]" ¦
     "text/html ; charset=ISO-8859-1" ]
   [ isErrorPage="true¦false" ]
   [ pageEncoding="characterSet ¦ ISO-8859-1" ]
%>
```

XML Syntax

```
<jsp:directive.page pageDirectiveAttrList />
```

Example

```
<%@ page import="java.util.*" %>
```

or

```
<jsp:directive.page import="java.util.*"/>
```

taglib Directive

The taglib directive tells the container that you will use custom tags. It names the tag library and specifies the tag prefix to use when referencing tags from the library. You can use many `taglib` directives in a single page, but the prefix defined for each must be unique.

JSP Syntax

```
<%@ taglib uri="URIForLibrary" prefix="tagPrefix" %>
```

XML Syntax

No direct equivalent, but you can specify a tag library in <jsp:root>.

Example

```
<%@ taglib uri="/que_taglib_message" prefix="message" %>
<%@ page language="java" %>
<html>
        <head>
           <title>Tag Library</title>
        </head>
        <body>
           <h1>Tag Library</h1>
           <message:insert definition="appendix" parameter="syntax"/>
        </body>
</html>
```

<jsp:text>

A `jsp:text` element allows you to add text that you want sent to the client unaltered within the XML tags. The text that you place in here is appended literally to the output stream.

JSP Syntax

None. There is no direct syntax. Anything that is not JSP syntax is "text."

XML Syntax

```
<jsp:text>
   your text
</jsp:text>
```

Example

```
        <jsp:root
            xmlns:jsp="http://java.sun.com/JSP/Page"
            version="1.2">
        <jsp:text>
             <html>
                <head>
                   <title>jsp:text Example</title>
                </head>
                <body>
```

```
            <h1 align="center">
                This is a jsp:text example.
            </h1>
        </body>
    </html>
</jsp:text>
</jsp:root>
```

<jsp:include>

The `<jsp:include>` element allows you to include text in a JSP page. There are two kinds: One is static (text is simply inserted as if it were part of the original JSP page), and the other is dynamic (text is processed first and then only the result is inserted into the JSP page). If it is dynamic, you can use a `<jsp:param>` clause to pass the name and value of a parameter to the resource.

JSP Syntax

```
<jsp:include page="{relativeURL ¦ <%= expression %>}"
   flush="true¦ false" />
```

or

```
<jsp:include page="{relativeURL ¦ <%= expression %>}"
   flush="true¦false" >
   <jsp:param name="parameterName"
      value="{parameterValue ¦ <%= expression %>}" />+
</jsp:include>
```

XML Syntax

```
<jsp:include page="{relativeURL ¦ %= expression %}"
   [ flush="true ¦ false" ] />
```

or

```
<jsp:include page="{relativeURL ¦ %= expression %}"
[ flush="true ¦ false" ] >
   [ <jsp:param name="parameterName"
      value="{parameterValue ¦ %= expression %}" /> ] +
</jsp:include> }
```

Example

```
<jsp:include page="company_logo.html" />
<jsp:include page="salesTax.jsp">
   <jsp:param name="state" value="CA" />
   <jsp:param name="amount" value="359.92" />
</jsp:include>
```

<jsp:plugin>

This tag tells the browser to load an applet or bean. You have to specify both the applet/bean and the plug-in. If the client can't find the plug-in, the browser should display a dialog box to initiate the download of the plug-in software.

JSP Syntax

```
<jsp:plugin
   type="bean¦applet"
   code="classFileName"
   codebase="classFileDirectoryName"
   [ name="instanceName" ]
   [ archive="URIToArchive, ..." ]
   [ align="bottom¦top¦middle¦left¦right" ]
   [ height="{displayPixels ¦  <%= expression %>}"]
   [ width="{displayPixels ¦  <%= expression %>}"]
   [ hspace="leftRightPixels" ]
   [ vspace="topBottomPixels" ]
   [ jreversion="JREVersionNumber ¦ 1.2" ]
   [ nspluginurl="URLToPlugin" ]
   [ iepluginurl="URLToPlugin" ] >
   [ <jsp:params>
      [ <jsp:param name="parameterName"
         value="{parameterValue ¦ <%= expression %>}" /> ]+
   </jsp:params> ]
   [ <jsp:fallback> text message if plugin download fails </jsp:fallback> ]
</jsp:plugin>
```

XML Syntax

```
<jsp:plugin
   type="bean¦applet"  code="classFileName"
   codebase="classFileDirectoryName"
   [ name="instanceName" ]  [ archive="URIToArchive, ..." ]
   [ align="bottom¦top¦middle¦left¦right" ]
   [ height="{displayPixels ¦ %= expression %}" ]
   [ width="{displayPixels ¦ %= expression %}"]
   [ hspace="leftRightPixels" ] [ vspace="topBottomPixels"]
   [ jreversion="JREVersionNumber ¦ 1.2" ]
   [ nspluginurl="URLToPlugin" ]
   [ iepluginurl="URLToPlugin" ]  >
   [ <jsp:params>
      [ <jsp:param name="parameterName"
         value="{parameterValue ¦ %= expression %}" /> ]+
   </jsp:params> ]
   [ <jsp:fallback>  text message if plugin download fails
   </jsp:fallback>  ]
</jsp:plugin>
```

Example

```
<jsp:plugin type="applet" code="houseViewer.class" codebase="/html">
   <jsp:params>
      <jsp:param name="property_listing" value="A33IN" />
```

```
   </jsp:params>
   <jsp:fallback>
      <p>Unable to load applet</p>
   </jsp:fallback>
</jsp:plugin>
```

<jsp:useBean>

The `<jsp:useBean>` element locates or instantiates a JavaBeans component. If it does not exist, the container will attempt to instantiate it from a class or serialized template. You can access a JavaBeans component, but not an enterprise bean directly. However, you can call a JavaBean that, in turn, calls an EJB.

JSP Syntax

None

XML Syntax

```
<jsp:useBean id="beanInstanceName"
   scope="page|request|session|application"
{
   class="package.class" [ type="package.class" ]|
   beanName="{package.class | <%= expression %>}"
      type="package.class" |
   type="package.class"
}
{ /> | > other elements </jsp:useBean> }
```

Example

```
<jsp:useBean id="houseLotBean" scope="session" class="session.Realestate" />
<jsp:setProperty name="houseLotBean" property="id" value="33245" />
```

<jsp:setProperty>

This element sets the value of one or more properties in a bean, using the bean's setter methods. Of course, the `<jsp:useBean>` tag must be declared first. The most frequent mistake with this tag is not matching the value of name in `<jsp:setProperty>` with the value of `id` in `<jsp:useBean>`. Another common one is miskeying the name of the form parameter whose value you're trying to set to a property of the bean.

JSP Syntax

None

XML Syntax

```
<jsp:setProperty name="beanInstanceName"
{
   property="*" ¦
   property="propertyName" [ param="parameterName" ] ¦
   property="propertyName" value="{stringLiteral ¦ <%= expression %>}"
}
/>
```

Example

```
<jsp:setProperty name="houseLotBean" property="id" value="33245" />
```

Another example takes the values of all form fields coming in from a form and assigns them to bean properties that have the same names as these form fields:

```
<jsp:setProperty name="request" property="*" />
```

<jsp:forward>

This element forwards the request object (which has all the client request information) from one JSP page to another resource. The target can be an HTML file, another JSP page, or a servlet, as long as it is in the same application context as the forwarding JSP page. Note that the lines in the source JSP page after the `<jsp:forward>` element are not processed.

The biggest problem you'll have with this one is trying to forward after some output has been sent to the client. This happens if you are not buffering output (page directive buffer = `none`). If you forward in this situation, you will cause an `IllegalStateException`.

JSP Syntax

None

XML Syntax

```
<jsp:forward page="{relativeURL ¦ <%= expression %>}" />
```

or

```
<jsp:forward page="{relativeURL ¦ <%= expression %>}" >
   <jsp:param name="parameterName"
      value="{parameterValue ¦ <%= expression %>}" /> +
</jsp:forward>
```

Example

```
<jsp:forward page="page_moved_page.htm" />
```

<jsp:getProperty>

This tag is how you retrieve a value from a bean using its getter method.

JSP Syntax

None

XML Syntax

```
<jsp:getProperty name="beanInstanceName" property="propertyName" />
```

Example

```
<jsp:useBean id="tax" scope="page" class="state.Tax" />
Current tax rate is:<jsp:getProperty name="tax" property="taxRate" />
```

Summary

In this appendix, you reviewed the basic syntax of the JSP specification. The list is short, with quick examples, but it is nice to have a concise reference at times. You can refer to Chapter 8 for more details. Also, you should refer to the specification for the last word.

Suggested Readings and Resources

1. Jakarta has a more extensive syntax card that you can grab with Tomcat, at `http://jakarta.apache.org/tomcat/index.html`.
2. Sun's nice JSP syntax card is at `http://java.sun.com/products/jsp/tags/10/tags.html`.
3. The Java Servlet 2.3 API is at `http://java.sun.com/products/servlet/2.3/javadoc/index.html`.
4. The most current version of the JSP specification is at `http://java.sun.com/products/jsp/download.html#specs`.

Resources

This appendix helps you prepare for the exam by providing references to information about Java in general and servlets and JSP in particular. Although the chapters provided many references, too, this appendix gives you a simple listing of my favorites.

References

The amount of reference information available is staggering, but only a little of it is presented in a way that is easy to digest. So, most of my references here were chosen based on reliability and quality of presentation. It is difficult to filter through so much material.

Among the search engines, I like Google the best overall; it's also tops for Java. Sun has partnered with Google. If you go to `http://java.sun.com/search/`, you'll find a Google-powered search, but it returns only Sun references. Consider this your short but best list. However, if you go to Google directly and search the keyword Java, you'll get "can't miss" results. You can go to `http://directory.google.com/Top/Computers/Programming/Languages/Java/?tc=1` as well to get Google's Java directory. Also refer to `http://groups.google.com`, which enables you to search more than 20,000 discussion forums. This is a great resource to help you troubleshoot Java code.

I also use the Yahoo! directory (`http://dir.yahoo.com/Computers_and_Internet/Programming_and_Development/Languages/Java/`) and Lycos engine (`dir.lycos.com/Computers/Programming/Languages/Java/`). These are strong in scope, but their ranking mechanisms are amateurish. Google is better than both, in my opinion.

When you leave the big search engines, you can use the more focused lists. This tier of references includes Java developer sites such as jGuru (`www.jguru.com`) and Java Skyline (`www.javaskyline.com`). These have meaningful descriptions, opinions, and bias that do help you cut to the chase. There are a slew of them, but my favorites are the two I just mentioned.

Then there are bookstore sites such as Amazon (`www.amazon.com`) and Bookpool (`www.bookpool.com`). Review books here before you buy because there are plenty of reader comments. I haven't been surprised by flaming posters, either.

Then again, you might read one of the useless comments such as, "Alain Trottier is a jerk because when we worked together...." Why do they bother to tell us about their career problem in a book review? It has been a pleasant surprise to read the large number of helpful book reviews, of course.

These are nice to see when they write something like, "This book is great but I hate this one aspect" or "This book has good explanations but is full of code errors" or "This book steered me wrong on three exam objectives." Although I have to be careful not to judge the book by one unhappy customer, I do find the facts (found two code errors on page 39) they provide insightful at times.

The following references are what I use most often. They are a moving target, so the book Web site (`www.inforobo.com/scwcd/examcram`) is more current.

Resource names are like a good API (they don't change), but the URLs are like the implementations (they change often). Visit this book's Web site to get the most current addresses for these resources.

Reference List

The primary set of references that I use is small but effective. Table C.1 presents Sun references.

You have to start with Sun. Download these specs and docs because you will use them far more than anything else.

Table C.1 Links to Sun

Name	Description	Chapter
Sun's Java home page	This is your top Java link. Check this weekly to see what new and cool things Sun says are happening to Java.	**http://java.sun.com/**
J2SE 1.4	J2SE is the foundation, so you need this to learn about servlets and JSP.	J2SE 1.4.0 product page (**http://java.sun.com/j2se/1.4/index.html**) Java 2 SDK, Standard Edition, version 1.4 "Summary of New Features and Enhancements" (**http://java.sun.com/j2se/1.4/docs/relnotes/features.html**)

(continued)

Table C.1 Links to Sun *(continued)*

Name	Description	Chapter
		Technical article: "Project Merlin: Front and Center, A Technical Overview of the J2SE" (**http://java.sun.com/features/2001/06/golden.j2se.html**)
J2EE 1.3	J2EE is a collection of APIs built on top of J2SE. These APIs include servlets, JSP, and EJB components.	J2EE information (**http://java.sun.com/j2ee/**) J2EE tutorial (**http://java.sun.com/j2ee/tutorial/**) J2EE downloads (**http://java.sun.com/j2ee/download.html**)
JSP 1.2	JavaServer Pages is very similar to Microsoft Active Server Pages. It's a way to place Java code in an otherwise normal HTML page. A few of the advantages of using JSPs are that they are easier to code than servlets, have XML capabilities, are automatically converted into servlets, and have access to server-side Java objects to return dynamic content to a client. Note the elegant job that JSP does of separating code into presentation (JSP) and business (JavaBeans). Unlike ASP with COM, JSP with JavaBeans is 100% platform independent.	JavaServer Pages technology (**http://java.sun.com/products/jsp/**) JSR 152 (JSP 1.3) (**http://jcp.org/jsr/detail/152.jsp**) JavaServer page—Tomcat@Jakarta (**http://java.sun.com/products/jsp/tomcat/**) JSP implementations and specifications (**http://java.sun.com/products/jsp/download.html**) JavaServer Pages tag libraries (JSTL) (**http://java.sun.com/products/jsp/taglibraries.html**) Technical article: "Web Application Development with JSP and XML Part III: Developing JSP Custom Tags" (**http://developer.java.sun.com/developer/technicalArticles/xml/WebAppDev3/**)

(continued)

Table C.1 Links to Sun *(continued)*

Name	Description	Chapter
Java Servlets 2.3	Java Servlet technology is regular Java, except that you extend certain classes so the Web server can pass requests to and receive responses from the servlet. This is Sun's version of the CGI.	Java Servlet product page (**http://java.sun.com/products/servlet/index.html**) JSR 154 (Servlet 2.4) (**http://jcp.org/jsr/detail/154.jsp**) Java Servlet downloads and specification (**http://java.sun.com/products/servlet/download.html**)
Java Web Service Developer Pack (Java WSDP)	The Java Web Services Developer Pack (Java WSDP) is an all-in-one download containing key technologies to simplify building Web services using the Java 2 Platform. The technologies comprising the Java Web Services Developers Pack include these: JAXM 1.0.1 EA2 JAXP 1.2 EA2 (with XML Schema support) JAXR 1.0 EA2 JAX-RPC 1.0 EA2 JavaServer Pages Standard Tag Library (JSTL) 1.0 Beta 1 Ant Build Tool 1.4.1 Java WSDP Registry Server 1.0 EA2 Web Application Deployment Tool Apache Tomcat 4.1–dev Container	Java technology and Web services (**http://java.sun.com/webservices/index.html**) Java Web Services tutorial (**http://java.sun.com/webservices/tutorial.html**) Java Web services download (**http://java.sun.com/webservices/download.html**) Technical article: "Java Web Services Developer Pack Part 1: Registration and the JAXR API" (**http://developer.java.sun.com/developer/technicalArticles/WebServices/WSPack/**) Technical article: "Deploying Web Services on Java 2, Enterprise Edition (J2EE)" (**http://developer.java.sun.com/developer/technicalArticles/WebServices/wsj2ee/**)

(continued)

Table C.1 Links to Sun *(continued)*

Name	Description	Chapter
Extensible Markup Language (XML)	XML is a universal syntax for describing and structuring data independently from the application logic. XML can be used to define unlimited languages for specific industries and applications.	World Wide Web Consortium (W3C) (**www.w3.org/**) XML.ORG (**www.xml.org**) O'Reilly's XML.COM (**www.xml.com**) Java technology and XML (**http://java.sun.com/xml/**) Java XML Pack (**http://java.sun.com/xml/javaxmlpack.html**) Java technology and XML downloads and specifications (**http://java.sun.com/xml/download.html**) XML FAQ (**http://java.sun.com/xml/faq.html**)
The Java API for XML Processing (JAXP)	JAXP is how Java processes XML using the Document Object Model (DOM), the Simple API for XML (SAX), and the XML Stylesheet Language for Transformations (XSLT). JAXP enables applications to parse and transform XML documents independently of a particular XML processing implementation. Notice that JAXP is built into J2SE 1.4.	JAXP documentation (**http://java.sun.com/xml/jaxp/docs.html**) JAXP downloads and specifications (**http://java.sun.com/xml/downloads/jaxp.html**) JAXP FAQ (**http://java.sun.com/xml/jaxp/faq.html**)
Java Developer Connection	This is Sun's developer network. Membership is free for some tech support, forums, training, early access, newsgroups, and bug reporting. Basically, it's almost an insiders' group.	**http://java.sun.com/jdc**
Java History	This is how it all started.	**http://java.sun.com/features/1998/05/birthday.html**

(continued)

Table C.1 Links to Sun *(continued)*

Name	Description	Chapter
Certification	The home page for the SCWCD exam.	**http://suned.sun.com/US/certification/java/java_web.html**

Table C.2 runs down vendors dedicated to Java.

Table C.2 Vendor Links Dedicated to Java

Name	Description	Chapter
Microsoft's Java home page	This is the home page for Microsoft Technologies for Java. Some very smart people there have useful things to say about Java.	**www.microsoft.com/java/default.htm**
Oracle	Oracle is pushing Java hard and has many downloads and products for Java.	**http://otn.oracle.com/tech/java/content.html**
IBM	Big Blue is serious about Java. I especially love the AlphaWorks free samples.	**www-106.ibm.com/developerworks/java/** IBM's awesome AlphaWorks (**www.alphaworks.ibm.com**)
BEA	Wow! This is the company most dedicated to Java on the planet. Unlike its bigger partners, BEA doesn't spend resources on non-Java products.	**http://dev2dev.bea.com:80/index.jsp**

Table C.3 lists magazines that devote their contents to Java.

Table C.3 Glossy Magazines Dedicated to Java

Name	Description	Chapter
Sys-Con	These guys are my favorite when it comes to Java and related publications—they pack each issue. I even like the ads in the industry-leading *Java Developers Journal*.	**www.sys-con.com**
JavaPro	Closer to earth, Fawcett (publisher) keeps the newbie in mind.	**www.fawcette.com/javapro/**
Java Report	This has less information than the *Java Developers Journal*, but you might like it.	**www.adtmag.com/java/index.asp**

Table C.4 covers Web sites dedicated to Java.

Table C.4 Web Sites Dedicated to Java

Name	Description	Chapter
jGuru	Java Guru is fun and has the best lists of Q&As and FAQs.	**www.jguru.com**
Gamelan	This one has been around for a long time, so it has lots of articles—but it's not organized well.	**http://softwaredev.earthweb.com/java**
dev[x]	JavaZone has articles and a solid code repository (click Sourcebank).	**www.devx.com/java/**
Java Skyline	You don't see this on many lists, but this site has a stellar collection of links.	**www.javaskyline.com**
JSPinsider	This is a nice resource for JSP.	**www.jspinsider.com/index.view**
Servlets.com	Jason Hunter is a Java star and author. His site is all servlets and looks like it was built by a one-man army. What he does for O'Reilly is very good.	**www.servlets.com/index.tea**
JavaLobby	Rick Ross is on a crusade with moxie. I wonder what Microsoft did to incur such wrath?	**www.javalobby.org/**
Serverside.com	Here you'll find articles and lots of chat.	**www.theserverside.com**
JavaRanch	This is a potluck of Java goodies.	**www.javaranch.com/books.jsp**
Jars	You'll find lots of code with ratings here.	**www.jars.com/**
Java Boutique	This site includes many articles and links, but it has zany colors.	**http://java.internet.com/**
JavaPrepare	This nice little site focuses on Java certification. It lists mock exams, too.	**www.javaprepare.com/scwd**
CityJava	This is the world's biggest Java User Group (JUG).	**www.cityjava.org/**

You can find many books on Java. Don't buy all of them: Get this list of books and read nothing else for the next year or two. If you take my advice, you will easily surpass the geek in the next cubicle who buys or scans 50 books a year.

- *Java in a Nutshell* and *Java Examples in a Nutshell: A Tutorial Companion to Java in a Nutshell*, both by David Flanagan. This is another wonderful Nutshell from O'Reilly.
- *Thinking in Java*, by Bruce Eckel (Prentice Hall). Here's someone who actually thinks about what we are trying to do. This book has won many

awards and is mentioned often in the literature. Eckel's book is becoming a classic.

- *Core Servlets and JavaServer Pages*, by Marty Hall (O'Reilly).
- There are several nods here for Sun's outstanding Core Series (Prentice Hall), including:

  Core Java 2, Volume 1 and 2, by Cay S. Horstmann and Gary Cornell

  Advanced JavaServer Pages, by David Geary

  Core J2EE Patterns: Best Practices and Design Strategies, by Deepak Alur, John Crupi, and Dan Malks
- The Gang of Four, or just GoF, told us that programming is a form of building, so software has patterns, too. Check out the book *Design Patterns*, by Erich Gamma, Richard Helm, Ralph Johnson, and John Vlissides (Addison-Wesley).
- *Design Patterns Explained: A New Perspective on Object-Oriented Design*, by Alan Shalloway and James R. Trott (Addison-Wesley). This is a gentle explanation of the GoF.
- *Java Servlet Programming*, by Jason Hunter and William Crawford (O'Reilly). It's a very strong title.
- *Java How to Program, Fourth Edition*. Harvey M. Deitel and Paul J. Deitel (Prentice Hall). These guys are machines that pump out excellent college type textbooks. I love their Java book—it is packed with exercises and examples, all explained carefully and very thoroughly.

Summary

In this appendix, you were presented with several references. These are my favorites and don't represent anyone's opinion. I recommend that you click through them all in one evening; you'll get a good sense of the best of what is out there. Then bookmark the few you really like.

I'm sure I missed your favorite, so please email me with it. Go to the book Web site (`www.inforobo.com/scwcd/examcram`) for my contact information.

What's on the CD-ROM

This appendix is a brief rundown of what you'll find on the CD-ROM that comes with this book. For a more detailed description of the *PrepLogic Practice Tests, Preview Edition* exam simulation software, see Appendix E, "Using *PrepLogic, Preview Edition* Software." In addition to the *PrepLogic Practice Tests, Preview Edition*, the CD-ROM includes the electronic version of the book in Portable Document Format (PDF), several utility and application programs, and a complete listing of test objectives and where they are covered in the book. Finally, a pointer list to online pointers and references are added to this CD. You will need a computer with Internet access and a relatively recent browser installed to use this feature.

PrepLogic Practice Tests, Preview Edition

PrepLogic is a leading provider of certification training tools. Trusted by certification students worldwide, we believe PrepLogic is the best practice exam software available. In addition to providing a means of evaluating your knowledge of the Exam Cram material, *PrepLogic Practice Tests, Preview Edition* features several innovations that help you to improve your mastery of the subject matter.

For example, the practice tests allow you to check your score by exam area or domain to determine which topics you need to study more. Another feature allows you to obtain immediate feedback on your responses in the form of explanations for the correct and incorrect answers.

PrepLogic Practice Tests, Preview Edition exhibits most of the full functionality of the *Premium Edition* but offers only a fraction of the total questions. To get the complete set of practice questions and exam functionality, visit `PrepLogic.com` and order the *Premium Edition* for this and other challenging exam titles.

Again, for a more detailed description of the *PrepLogic Practice Tests, Preview Edition* features, see Appendix E.

Exclusive Electronic Version of Text

The CD-ROM also contains the electronic version of this book in Portable Document Format (PDF). The electronic version comes complete with all figures as they appear in the book. You will find that the search capabilities of the reader comes in handy for study and review purposes.

Easy Access to Online Pointers and References

The Suggested Reading section at the end of each chapter in this Exam Cram contains numerous pointers to Web sites, newsgroups, mailing lists, and other online resources. To make this material as easy to use as possible, we include all this information in an HTML document entitled "Online Pointers" on the CD. Open this document in your favorite Web browser to find links you can follow through any Internet connection to access these resources directly.

Using the *PrepLogic Practice Tests, Preview Edition* Software

This Exam Cram includes a special version of PrepLogic Practice Tests—a revolutionary test engine designed to give you the best in certification exam preparation. PrepLogic offers sample and practice exams for many of today's most in-demand and challenging technical certifications. This special *Preview Edition* is included with this book as a tool to use in assessing your knowledge of the Exam Cram material, while also providing you with the experience of taking an electronic exam.

This appendix describes in detail what *PrepLogic Practice Tests, Preview Edition* is, how it works, and what it can do to help you prepare for the exam. Note that although the *Preview Edition* includes all the test simulation functions of the complete, retail version, it contains only a single practice test. The *Premium Edition*, available at `PrepLogic.com`, contains the complete set of challenging practice exams designed to optimize your learning experience.

Exam Simulation

One of the main functions of *PrepLogic Practice Tests, Preview Edition* is exam simulation. To prepare you to take the actual vendor certification exam, PrepLogic is designed to offer the most effective exam simulation available.

Question Quality

The questions provided in the *PrepLogic Practice Tests, Preview Edition* are written to the highest standards of technical accuracy. The questions tap the content of the Exam Cram chapters and help you to review and assess your knowledge before you take the actual exam.

Interface Design

The *PrepLogic Practice Tests, Preview Edition* exam simulation interface provides you with the experience of taking an electronic exam. This enables you to effectively prepare yourself for taking the actual exam by making the test experience a familiar one. Using this test simulation can help to eliminate the sense of surprise or anxiety you might experience in the testing center because you will already be acquainted with computerized testing.

Effective Learning Environment

The *PrepLogic Practice Tests, Preview Edition* interface provides a learning environment that not only tests you through the computer, but also teaches the material you need to know to pass the certification exam. Each question comes with a detailed explanation of the correct answer and often provides reasons the other options are incorrect. This information helps to reinforce the knowledge you already have and also provides practical information you can use on the job.

Software Requirements

PrepLogic Practice Tests requires a computer with the following:

- Microsoft Windows 98, Windows Me, Windows NT 4.0, Windows 2000, or Windows XP
- A 166 MHz or faster processor is recommended
- A minimum of 32MB of RAM
- As with any Windows application, the more memory, the better your performance
- 10MB of hard drive space

Installing *PrepLogic Practice Tests, Preview Edition*

Install *PrepLogic Practice Tests, Preview Edition* by running the setup program on the *PrepLogic Practice Tests, Preview Edition* CD. Follow these instructions to install the software on your computer.

1. Insert the CD into your CD-ROM drive. The Autorun feature of Windows should launch the software. If you have Autorun disabled, click the Start button and select Run. Go to the root directory of the CD and select setup.exe. Click Open, and then click OK.
2. The Installation Wizard copies the *PrepLogic Practice Tests, Preview Edition* files to your hard drive; adds *PrepLogic Practice Tests, Preview Edition* to your Desktop and Program menu; and installs test engine components to the appropriate system folders.

Removing *PrepLogic Practice Tests, Preview Edition* from Your Computer

If you elect to remove the *PrepLogic Practice Tests,, Preview Edition* product from your computer, an uninstall process has been included to ensure that it is removed from your system safely and completely. Follow these instructions to remove PrepLogic Practice Tests, Preview Edition from your computer:

1. Select Start, Settings, Control Panel.
2. Double-click the Add/Remove Programs icon.
3. You are presented with a list of software currently installed on your computer. Select the appropriate *PrepLogic Practice Tests, Preview Edition* title you wish to remove. Click the Add/Remove button. The software is then removed from you computer.

Using *PrepLogic Practice Tests, Preview Edition*

PrepLogic is designed to be user friendly and intuitive. Because the software has a smooth learning curve, your time is maximized, as you will start practicing almost immediately. *PrepLogic Practice Tests, Preview Edition* has two major modes of study: Practice Test and Flash Review.

Using Practice Test mode, you can develop your test-taking abilities, as well as your knowledge through the use of the Show Answer option. While you are taking the test, you can reveal the answers along with a detailed explanation of why the given answers are right or wrong. This gives you the ability to better understand the material presented.

Flash Review is designed to reinforce exam topics rather than quiz you. In this mode, you will be shown a series of questions, but no answer choices. Instead, you will be given a button that reveals the correct answer to the question and a full explanation for that answer.

Starting a Practice Test Mode Session

Practice Test mode enables you to control the exam experience in ways that actual certification exams do not allow:

- **Enable Show Answer Button**—Activates the Show Answer button, allowing you to view the correct answer(s) and a full explanation for each question during the exam. When not enabled, you must wait until after your exam has been graded to view the correct answer(s) and explanation(s).

- **Enable Item Review Button**—Activates the Item Review button, allowing you to view your answer choices, marked questions, and facilitating navigation between questions.
- **Randomize Choices**—Randomize answer choices from one exam session to the next; makes memorizing question choices more difficult, therefore keeping questions fresh and challenging longer.

To begin studying in Practice Test mode, click the Practice Test radio button from the main exam customization screen. This will enable the options detailed above.

To your left, you are presented with the options of selecting the pre-configured Practice Test or creating your own Custom Test. The pre-configured test has a fixed time limit and number of questions. Custom Tests allow you to configure the time limit and the number of questions in your exam.

The *Preview Edition* included with this book includes a single pre-configured Practice Test. Get the compete set of challenging PrepLogic Practice Tests at `PrepLogic.com` and make certain you're ready for the big exam.

Click the Begin Exam button to begin your exam.

Starting a Flash Review Mode Session

Flash Review mode provides you with an easy way to reinforce topics covered in the practice questions. To begin studying in Flash Review mode, click the Flash Review radio button from the main exam customization screen. Select either the pre-configured Practice Test or create your own Custom Test.

Click the Best Exam button to begin your Flash Review of the exam questions.

Standard *PrepLogic Practice Tests, Preview Edition* Options

The following list describes the function of each of the buttons you see. Depending on the options, some of the buttons will be grayed out and inaccessible or missing completely. Buttons that are accessible are active. The buttons are as follows:

- **Exhibit**—This button is visible if an exhibit is provided to support the question. An exhibit is an image that provides supplemental information necessary to answer the question.
- **Item Review**—This button leaves the question window and opens the Item Review screen. From this screen you will see all questions, your answers, and your marked items. You will also see correct answers listed here when appropriate.
- **Show Answer**—This option displays the correct answer with an explanation of why it is correct. If you select this option, the current question is not scored.
- **Mark Item**—Check this box to tag a question you need to review further. You can view and navigate your Marked Items by clicking the Item Review button (if enabled). When grading your exam, you will be notified if you have marked items remaining.
- **Previous Item**—This option allows you to view the previous question.
- **Next Item**—This option allows you to view the next question.
- **Grade Exam**—When you have completed your exam, click this button to end your exam and view your detailed score report. If you have unanswered or marked items remaining you will be asked if you would like to continue taking your exam or view your exam report.

Time Remaining

If the test is timed, the time remaining is displayed on the upper right corner of the application screen. It counts down the minutes and seconds remaining to complete the test. If you run out of time, you will be asked if you want to continue taking the test or if you want to end your exam.

Your Examination Score Report

The Examination Score Report screen appears when the Practice Test mode ends—as the result of time expiration, completion of all questions, or your decision to terminate early.

This screen provides you with a graphical display of your test score with a breakdown of scores by topic domain. The graphical display at the top of the screen compares your overall score with the PrepLogic Exam Competency Score.

The PrepLogic Exam Competency Score reflects the level of subject competency required to pass this vendor's exam. While this score does not directly translate to a passing score, consistently matching or exceeding this score does suggest you possess the knowledge to pass the actual vendor exam.

Review Your Exam

From Your Score Report screen, you can review the exam that you just completed by clicking on the View Items button. Navigate through the items viewing the questions, your answers, the correct answers, and the explanations for those answers. You can return to your score report by clicking the View Items button.

Get More Exams

Each *PrepLogic Practice Tests, Preview Edition* that accompanies your Exam Cram contains a single PrepLogic Practice Test. Certification students worldwide trust PrepLogic Practice Tests to help them pass their IT certification exams the first time. Purchase the *Premium Edition* of PrepLogic Practice Tests and get the entire set of all new challenging Practice Tests for this exam. PrepLogic Practice Tests—Because You Want to Pass the First Time.

Contacting PrepLogic

If you would like to contact PrepLogic for any reason, including information about our extensive line of certification practice tests, we invite you to do so. Please contact us online at `http://www.preplogic.com`.

Customer Service

If you have a damaged product and need a replacement or refund, please call the following phone number:

800-858-7674

Product Suggestions and Comments

We value your input! Please email your suggestions and comments to the following address:

`feedback@preplogic.com`

License Agreement

YOU MUST AGREE TO THE TERMS AND CONDITIONS OUTLINED IN THE END USER LICENSE AGREEMENT ("EULA") PRESENTED TO YOU DURING THE INSTALLATION PROCESS. IF YOU DO NOT AGREE TO THESE TERMS DO NOT INSTALL THE SOFTWARE.

Glossary

Apache Jakarta Tomcat

An add-on for the popular Apache Web server that provides a servlet container for executing servlets and JSPs. Tomcat is the reference implementation for Sun's servlet technology.

application session

Session that encapsulates parameters that are visible to a single user for all servlets in this application (as opposed to application parameters, which are visible to all users).

authentication, authorization

Authentication is the process of confirming the identity of a user and admitting that user to one or more roles based on identity. Authorization is the process of granting access to specific resources to a specific user or role.

bean properties

Properties of the bean that are exposed via `get/set` method pairs. These properties can be accessed via the `jsp:getProperty` tag and mutated via the `jsp:setProperty` tag.

bean scope and attributes

An instance of a bean can persist for the duration of a single page, a complete request, an entire session (all pages for one user), or an application (all pages for all users). Attributes are the publicly accessible properties of the bean.

Business Delegate

Pattern that reduces the dependency between tiers. It is an attempt to make tiers interchangeable so that one tier can access the services of any other.

certification exam voucher

A document that you must purchase from Sun and bring with you the day of the SCWCD test so that you can be seated.

context parameters

Application-wide parameters passed to the servlet from the context in which it is running.

custom tags

XML tags embedded within JSP that execute sever-side tag handlers. The tag handler contains the code that will be executed; the custom tag serves as an XML-based interface for executing this code. Custom tags run inside their own variable spaces, separate from the JSPs that call them.

Data Access Object

The pattern that provides the connection between the business logic tier and the resource (usually database or file) tier. The Data Access Object represents a general interface to the resources layer: It handles all calls to it. JDBC is an example of this.

design patterns

According to Sun, "A design pattern describes a proven solution to a recurring design problem, placing particular emphasis on the context and forces surrounding the problem, and the consequences and impact of the solution."

development environment

A software program that provides programming, debugging, and code-management features for developing software. Popular Java development tools include VisualAge, JBuiler, Forte, and Visual Café.

directive

Indicated with `<%@ %>`. A directive provides information that the servlet container will need to properly translate, compile, and execute the JSP. Page directives enable you to set properties for the current page, taglib directives enable you to import tag libraries for use in your JSP, and include directives include text from another file.

doEndTag()

This method is called after the container completes the `doStartTag()` method. Notice that the body of your custom tag might or might not have been evaluated, depending on the return value of `doStartTag()`. It can return either the `EVAL_PAGE` or `SKIP_PAGE` fields.

doStartTag()

This method is called when the container first starts to process a custom tag. Note that when this method is invoked, the body has not yet been evaluated. It can return either the `EVAL_BODY_INCLUDE` or `SKIP_BODY` fields.

error codes

Three-digit codes returned to the client when an error is received.

exception

An error generated by Java code that can be caught and gracefully recovered from. This differs from an error in that an error usually halts the application suddenly terminating it.

expression

Indicated with `<%= %>`. An expression evaluates the Java expression within the tag and returns output as part of the servlet's output stream.

get/set method pairs

Methods internal to a JavaBean that allow a private variable (property) to be accessed or mutated, respectively.

implicit object

Objects that are automatically instantiated and made available to your JSP code, such as request, response, and session objects.

ISP

Internet service provider, an organization that provides dial-up or broadband Internet connectivity to individuals or organizations.

JavaBean

A Java class that has no argument constructor, is serializable, and has `get/set` methods for setting properties. In JSP applications, JavaBeans contain the business logic of the application and are accessed from JSP pages via the `jsp:useBean`, `jsp:getProperty`, and `jsp:setProperty` tags.

JavaBeans Development Kit (BDK)

Free software from Sun Microsystems that facilitates the development, testing, and deployment of JavaBeans.

JFC/Swing architecture

The Java Foundation Classes (JFC) are components that implement a wide array of user interface improvements over the traditional Abstract Windowing Toolkit (AWT). The Swing components, part of the AWT, are pure Java components that do not require native peers, as the AWT components did. In addition, the Swing components support Model-View-Controller architecture, wherein the components serve as views populated from a data model.

JSP

JavaServer Pages, an easy-to-use source code language for writing Java servlets that enables you to more elegantly blend HTML and Java. The JSP code is automatically translated by the container into servlets. JSPs combine HTML or XML with regions of Java programming code.

JSP container

The framework that translates the JSP to a servlet, compiles the servlet, executes the resulting servlet, and destroys the resulting servlet when appropriate.

JSP page life cycle

The life cycle of a JSP page from translation through destruction. For a list of the process steps in the life cycle, examine Table 8.1 in Chapter 8, "JavaServer Pages (JSP)."

listeners

Interfaces that allow an object to monitor changes to the attribute lists of sessions within a given Web application.

logging

Recording errors or other information to a file for later review.

Model-View-Controller

Architecture that compartmentalizes the data (model) from the presentation (view) from the business logic (controller). This pattern is the hardest on the exam. The idea is closely related to the recent move from two-tier to three-tier architectures. This arrangement allows multiple views to share the same enterprise data model. Java Swing is an example of this.

nested tags

XML elements that are nested inside other XML elements. JSP custom tags can be written to permit nesting of other XML elements, even additional JSP custom tags, within a custom tag.

practice/mock exam

A sample exam that simulates the real certification exam. To properly take a sample exam, you should recreate the testing environment as best you can, completing the questions in the standard time frame (SCWCD is 90 minutes), without external aids. Note that the practice/mock exam might be substantially easier than the actual certification exam with which your students will be confronted.

Prometric Testing Center

A facility approved by Sylvan Prometric to securely administer certification exams. You must take the SCWCD exam at a Prometric Testing Center.

redirection

Redirecting the browser from one URL to another.

scriptlet

Indicated with `<% %>`. Scriptlets contain code that will be executed within the servlet's `service` method.

security constraint

Read/write/modify permissions set on a per-user or per-role basis for a specific resource.

sendError()

The method of `HttpServletResponse` used to notify the client of a servlet error.

servlet

A Java program that runs on a server and implements the Servlet 2.3 API.

servlet and JSP specifications

The official standards for Java servlets and JSP, as published by Sun. You can obtain copies of these specifications at java.sun.com or jcp.org. As of this writing, the latest specifications are Servlet 2.3 and JSP 1.2.

servlet container

A Web server extension that runs Java servlets and JavaServer Pages.

servlet forwarding and includes

Servlet forwarding is the use of the RequestDispatcher to route the `HttpServletRequest` and `HttpServletResponse` objects to another servlet or JSP for processing. Control does not return to the servlet initiating the forward. Servlet including is the use of the RequestDispatcher to route copies of the `HttpServletRequest` and `HttpServletResponse` objects to another servlet for processing. Control returns to the servlet initiating the include.

servlet hosting

A service that enables you to run your Java servlets and JSPs on another organization's server. One example of a servlet host is EZPublishing (`www.ezpublishing.com`). See `www.javahosts.net/allhosts.php` for a list of servlet-hosting companies.

servlet life cycle

The process whereby a servlet is created, processes requests for some duration of time, and is destroyed. `init()` is called when the servlet is created. `service()` is called to process each individual request. `destroy()` is called when the servlet is shutdown.

session

The session object enables you to store variables across multiple servlets/pages for a given user.

session attribute

A value stored in the session object for later retrieval. Session attributes are scoped to a single user across all pages and servlets in the application.

session events

Events that affect a session. The key session events are `sessionDidActivate()`, `sessionWillPassivate()`, `attributeAdded()`, `attributeRemoved()`, and `attributeReplaced()`.

session ID

An ID number that uniquely identifies each session.
It is generated by the servlet container.

session timeout

When the session is concluded after a specified period of inactivity. At this point, all session variables are cleared automatically.

setStatus()

The method of `HttpServletResponse` used to return a status code to the client.

single-thread model
A model in which only one thread can execute a given servlet at a given time. Although this eliminates issues of concurrency, it can also greatly impair application performance.

status codes
Three-digit codes that indicate to the client whether the server received and processed the request successfully. The codes identify a wide variety of success, warning, and error conditions.

study plan
A set of steps that you will follow to successfully study for the exam. To be successful, a study plan must have a due date attached to each step, and the person executing the plan must meet each due date.

tag attributes and bodies
Attributes are named pieces of information stored within the opening tag of a custom tag, whereas bodies are information stored between the open and close tags of a custom tag. For example, in `<dbtags:select type="SQL">* FROM clients</dbtags:select>`, `type="SQL"` is an attribute and `* FROM clients` is part of the tag body.

tag library
Reusable Java components that are accessible from within your JSPs via XML tags.

tag library descriptor
Defines the custom tags that you can use in JSP to access the associated Java class. Your container (for example, Tomcat) uses the TLD to convert the XML in your JSP page into Java code.

taglib directive
The taglib directive makes a tag library available for use in a JSP by specifying the location of the tag library descriptor and the namespace prefix to use when referring to the tag.

thread safety
Because multiple threads can execute a single servlet simultaneously, it is important that the servlet's code be thread safe. That is, no problems should arise if the same block of code is executed simultaneously by two or more threads. Blocks of code that are not inherently thread safe should be synchronized to prevent parallel execution.

value objects
This pattern is an object that encapsulates a set of remote values locally so that attempts to get the values of those attributes are local calls. This reduces network traffic.

Web application
A Web application is made up of all the servlets, HTML pages, JSPs, classes, and other resources that act as a single application on a Web server.

Web archive file

The single file into which the application's files are combined. The Web archive file ends in .war and is based on the Zip format.

WebApp deployment descriptor

web.xml, the XML file that specifies the configuration of the application. The Web reads this file upon startup, so changes to it won't be seen by the application until it is recycled again.

XML (Extensible Markup Language)

An SGML-based language developed by the World Wide Web Consortium to facilitate data interchange among applications. The JSP JavaBean tags are XML tags and thus conform to XML syntax rules (such as case sensitivity and the requirement that all open tags have a corresponding close tag at the proper location).

Index

Symbols

A

B

C

E

H

I

J

K - L

M

Q - R

S

T

U

V

W

X-Y-Z